JN111541

重要ニュースの論説で
語彙・読解力を磨く

ジャパンタイムズ

社説集
2022

The Japan Times
Editorials
2022

ジャパンタイムズ出版 編

英文解説 北村一真

the japan times 出版

▶ 「本物」の英語世界に飛び込むために

北村一真

はじめに

　少し自分の経験を語ることをお許しいただきたい。まだ大学生になったばかりの頃だったと思うが、英語が多少わかるようになって、次々に新しい英文に挑戦したいと思っていた時期があった。当時、最も手軽に初見の英文を手に入れる方法は、鉄道駅の売店やコンビニエンス・ストアで購入できる「ジャパンタイムズ」などの英字新聞だった。へえ「社説」は英語で "editorial" と言うのか、などと無邪気な発見に心を弾ませながら、初めて同紙の社説を英語で読み切った時の喜びは今も覚えている。その後、年間の社説を集めた『ジャパンタイムズ社説集』なる本が毎年刊行されていることを知り、そちらにも手を出すようになっていった。

　当時はあくまで自分で好きなようにやっていただけで、十分に生かし切れていたとは言えない。しかし、振り返ってみれば、社説集を用いた英語学習は学生時代の自分に足りないものを補ってくれる要素を大いに含んでいたと思う。語学学習では中級からさらに一歩先に進むために、どこかの段階で学習者用に作られた教材を離れて、「本物」の世界に飛び込んでいかなければならない時がやってくる。この社説集のような存在はまさにそのための架け橋やヒントを提供してくれる。ここでは、自分自身の経験も参考にしながら、それぞれに得意不得意のある中級レベル以上の英語学習者がどのように本書を活かすことができるかを述べてみたい。

●本書の特徴：『ジャパンタイムズ社説集』とはどういう本か

　まずは、本書『ジャパンタイムズ社説集』の特徴から説明しておこう。本書は数十年以上にわたって刊行されている伝統的なシリーズの最新版であり、2022年にジャパンタイムズ紙に掲載された社説(editorial)のうち、新型コロナウイルスやウクライナ戦争、安倍元首相暗殺事件など、特に注目度の高いトピックに関するものを選定して掲載したものだ。すべての英文記事に語注と日本語訳が付いていて、かつ、この2022年版からは重要箇所の構文や表現の解説も追加されているため、英語を読む訓練をしながら過去1年間の時事問題や話題のニュースを振り返ることができる構成になっている。

●想定される英語レベルと目的

　どのような教材についても言えることだが、この社説集を英語学習に使用する場合も、適したレベルや目的、また、有効な活用法というものが存在する。それぞれを確認してみよう。最初に、使用する際の使用者のレベルと目的についてだ。英字新聞の社説と聞くと難解な内容について堅苦しい文章で書かれたものを想像する人もいるかもしれないが、過度に警戒する必要はない。むしろ、社説は扱っている事件の詳細な最新情報を提供するというよりは、その事件の大局を一歩下がったところから論じていることが多いため、当該のニュースを常日頃から事細かに追いかけていない人でも読みやすいという側面がある。

　一方で、本格的な英字新聞の文章には違いないため、一定の英語の読解力が使用の際の前提になることは理解しておく必要がある。具体的に言うと、大学入試レベルの英語のリーディングが得意だった（得意な）人、資格試験ならTOEIC 700点以上で、実用英語検定の準1級以上の取得を考えている人向けだと言える。特にこの段階にある人は、基本的な英語の知識はあるものの、自信を持って洋書や新聞、雑誌そのものを読んだり、英語のニュースを視聴したりするにはまだ経験値が足りていないことが多く、自分の読みが正しいかをある程度確認しながら、一定レベルの英文を読む訓練を積んでいくことが必要になる。本書はかなりの分量の英文を語注や和訳とともに掲載しているため、その目的に十分適っていると言える。しかも、過去1年間で話題になった時事問題を扱った英文なので、少し難しいと感じても背景知識を活用しながら読み進めることも可能だ。

　また、本書は、語彙力増強という観点からも有益だ。時事英文やニュース、小説やエッセイなどの娯楽作品をストレスなく楽しむためには1万〜1万5000語レベルの語彙力が必要と言われている。しかし、日本の高校や大学で英語がかなり得意だったという人でもこのレベルの語彙力にはなかなか到達してはいない。多くの英語学習者にとって、実践的な英語力を獲得するためには語彙力増強が1つの大きな課題となるということだ。もちろん、難単語にフォーカスを当てた単語帳なども一定数存在しているが、単語と意味が並んでいるだけのリスト的な単語帳で覚えるのは苦痛だという声もよく耳にする。本書の社説の英文には上で述べたような1万語以上のレベルの単語が数多く登場するため、実際の記事の中で文脈や使い方を確認しながら、上級英単語の知識を増やしていけるという強みがある。ドリル形式ではなく、英文を読みながら単語を習得したいというタイプの人にとっては最適と言える。

さらに、もう少し上級レベルの読者であれば、本書を受信ではなく発信の観点から使用することもできる。掲載されている社説をほとんど問題なく読める人でも、日本語訳を見てそれを英語で表現できるかと言われればかなり難しいと感じるのではないだろうか。そういう人にとって、本書の英文は日常的にニュースになっている事柄、話題を呼んでいる事柄を英語で表現するとどうなるのかについての情報の宝庫だと言える。作文力やスピーキングでの表現力を鍛えたい人にとっても有益な素材となるだろう。実用英語検定の二次試験では社会問題などについて論じることも求められるため、その対策としても有効だ。

●具体的な活用法

さて、ここまで、本書について、どのようなレベルの人がどういう目的で使用するのに適しているかを述べてきたが、ここからは本書のより具体的な活用法について3段階に分けて説明していくとしよう。

精読の訓練に 中級

①じっくり読む ➡ ②理解があやしい箇所を訳す ➡ ③本の訳と比較

まず、ある程度英語は得意だが、英字新聞の社説をしっかり読むとなると自信がないところもあると感じる人は、じっくりと時間をかけて細かく読んでいくことをおススメする。その際、構造や表現をすんなりと理解できなかった箇所は日本語に訳してみて、注釈や解説などをヒントにしながら和訳と比較してみるとよい。中級の段階で伸び悩む人に多いのが、何となく英文の大まかな意味はわかるものの、標準レベルの文法や語彙の知識に意外な抜けがあって、正確な理解が問われる場面で十分な力を発揮できないというタイプだ。こういう人が一歩先に進むためには、知識の抜けを1つ1つ見つけ出して潰していく必要がある。本書の英文には特別奇を衒ったような表現はほとんど登場しないが、文章を読んでいく際に頻繁に用いられる文法や語彙がフル活用されているため、その目的に適っている。

語彙力強化と速読、リスニング対策 中級〜上級

①語注を使って意識的に単語・表現を覚える ⬌ ②音声に合わせて速読する

難しい単語を確認しながらゆっくりと読めば英文の意味がきっちりとわかるとい

う人には、語彙とスピードに特化した訓練をおススメしたい。まずは語彙のほうから説明しよう。ここまでにも述べたように、基礎力を身につけている人にとって一歩先を目指す上で1つの大きな課題となるのが語彙力だ。本書で語注が付いている単語や表現は難しく思えても、そのほとんどが時事英文、フィクション、ノンフィクション、娯楽作品などで頻繁に用いられるものなので、ただ英文を読むだけで終わりにせず、これらの語を意識的に覚えていくことで英語の受信能力を確実に上げることができる。結果として身についた語彙力は当然ながら、資格試験で高得点を狙ったり、レベルの高い級に挑戦したりする際にも役立つだろう。

　一方、スピードのほうについてはアプリやPCで聞くことのできる音声と合わせて活用するのが有効な方法だ。本書の英文記事はすべてに音声が付いており、2パラグラフにつき1分程度のスピードで英文を読み上げている。これと同じスピードで理解することを1つの基準にして速読の練習をしてみよう。英語を正しく読むことはできるが、音声になるとまったく聞き取れないという話を聞くことがあるが、こういう人の場合、読むスピードが十分な速度に達していないことがリスニングに対応できない要因の1つになっている。実際、英語メディアのニュースなどは新聞記事とさほど変わらない難度の英語を遅くても1分間に150語以上のスピードで話しているため、これらを聞き取って理解するには、そのレベルの英語を同じスピードで読む力が必要となるのだ。音声スピードに合わせて本書の記事を読むのはそのための訓練として最適である。

　もちろん、リスニングの方がむしろやりやすいという人は、英文を読む前に先に音声を聞くことから始めてもよい。リスニングを得意とする中級者に見られるパターンとして、シンプルな会話や短い文であれば聞き取って理解できるが、1文が長くなると苦戦するというケースがある。本書の場合、元が新聞の記事であるから、日常的な会話のやりとりよりはるかに息の長い1文も出てくる。これを使ってリスニングの練習をすることで、ニュースやスピーチ、レクチャーなどで出てくる硬めの表現に慣れると同時に、聞き取れなかった場合、どこに原因があるのかを英文を確認しながら分析することも可能になるだろう。何となく意味を理解できるということにとどまらず、ディクテーションなどを通じて音声を正確に聞き取って再現できるというレベルを目指せばリスニング力も読解力も大きく向上するはずだし、また、次に見る表現力にも結び付くはずだ。

発信への応用 上級

①英文を読んで理解する ➡ ②音声をお手本にして音読
➡ ③特に印象に残った箇所を暗唱&発話

　最後に、本書の記事を読んだり、音声を聞いたりして理解する分にはさほど困らないが、発信力をより高めたいという、上級レベルの人に適した学習法として、音読と暗唱にも触れておこう。音読については以下のような手順を踏むことがおススメだ。まず記事の英文を読んで理解する。念のため和訳で意味を確認してもよい。意味が十分に理解できたら、音声を聞き、リズムや区切り方を手本にして自分でも発音をしてみる。お手本と一致しないところについては、できるだけ近づけられるよう繰り返し音読するのが望ましい。これだけでも効果はあるが、さらに力をつけるために有効なのが暗唱である。記事のうち、特に印象に残ったもの、興味深いと思ったものをいくつか選び、何も見ずにスラスラと発話できるようになるまで覚えこむというやり方だ。覚えるとは言っても、棒読みで単語を並べられるだけではダメだ。お手本に従って音読している時と同様に発音できるようになることを目指すのがポイントである。時間と労力を要する訓練法には違いないが、意味を頭に思い浮かべた際に口をついて該当する英文が出てくるくらいまでにこの練習をやり込めば、反射的にアウトプットできる英語表現のレパートリーが大幅に増えることになる。作文は言うまでもなく、即座に意味を持ったカタマリで英語を発することが求められるスピーキングでのスキル向上も期待できるだろう。

終わりに

　以上、本書を英語学習に活用する際の適したレベルや目的、また、それぞれの目的に合わせた本書の使い方について述べてきたが、これらはあくまで例に過ぎず、この中からどれか1つを必ず選んで実行しなければならないというわけではもちろんない。それぞれの好みに合わせて自分なりの活用法を考案してもよいし、上に挙げたものを適宜組み合わせて工夫してもよい。ただし、どのような学習法であれ、一定期間、少なくとも半年くらいは継続しなければ効果は出ないと考えてほしい。これなら続けられる、というやり方を見極めて取り組むことが重要である。本書が読者の皆さんの英語学習に少しでも貢献できれば解説執筆者としてもこれに勝る喜びはない。

目次

「本物」の英語世界に飛び込むために（北村一真）.........................iii
音声のご利用方法.........................xii

■ 巻頭特集　ウクライナ侵攻

① **Unite to protect Ukraine and the global order**
.........................02　**Tracks 002-008**
世界はウクライナと国際秩序を守るために団結せよ　>>2022年1月29日

② **Hold Russian soldiers and their leaders accountable for war crimes**.........................10　**Tracks 009-018**
ロシア兵とその指導者に戦争犯罪の責任を負わせよ　>>2022年4月9日

③ **Learning the wrong nuclear lessons from the Ukraine war**.........................18　**Tracks 019-026**
ウクライナ戦争から誤った核の教訓を学ぶ　>>2022年4月30日

④ **The United Nations finds itself at a tipping point**
.........................28　**Tracks 027-034**
岐路に立つ国連　>>2022年9月24日

英文解説.........................36
訳.........................40

■ 第1章　国際

① **An aging China poses new challenges**
.........................54　**Tracks 035-042**
中国の高齢化がもたらす新たな課題　>>2022年1月22日

② **Ukraine crisis pushes the world's hungry over the brink**.........................62　**Tracks 043-049**
ウクライナ危機が世界の飢餓を崖っぷちに追い込む　>>2022年6月11日

③ **Execution of Myanmar democracy activists reveals junta's true colors**.........................70　**Tracks 050-056**
ミャンマーの民主化運動家の処刑により露呈する軍事政権の本質　>>2022年7月30日

④ **Revered and reviled, Mikhail Gorbachev remade the world** 80 **Tracks 057-065**

称賛と非難をともに浴びたミハイル・ゴルバチョフ氏は世界を作り変えた　>>2022年9月3日

⑤ **Queen Elizabeth II: The end of an era for Britain and the world** 90 **Tracks 066-074**

エリザベス2世逝去：英国そして世界にとっての一時代の終焉　>>2022年9月17日

⑥ **Time for Japan and China to get their relationship right** 100 **Tracks 075-083**

日本と中国は関係を正すべき時を迎えている　>>2022年10月1日

英文解説 110
訳 117

▌ 第2章　国内政治・外交

① **Japan needs a real economic security strategy** 136 **Tracks 084-090**

日本には真の経済安全保障戦略が必要　>>2022年1月8日

② **Time for Japan to embrace realism in dealings with Russia** 144 **Tracks 091-099**

日本はロシアとの対応で現実主義を受け入れるべき時だ　>>2022年3月26日

③ **Biden's visit takes the Japan-U.S. partnership to new heights** 154 **Tracks 100-107**

バイデン大統領訪日で日米パートナーシップはさらなる高みへ　>>2022年5月28日

④ **Kishida's next moves will determine fate of Abe legacy** 162 **Tracks 108-116**

岸田首相の次の手立てが安倍元首相のレガシーの命運を決める　>>2022年7月17日

英文解説 172
訳 177

■ 第3章　経済・財政

① **Tokyo Stock Exchange might not be ready for 'prime' time just yet**.................190　**Tracks 117-125**
東証は「プライム」の機がまだ熟していないかもしれない　>>2022年1月15日

② **A weaker yen is no longer the asset of the past**
....198　**Tracks 126-132**
円安はもはやかつてのような資産ではない　>>2022年4月23日

英文解説..206
訳...208

■ 第4章　社会・文化

① **Government clarity needed as Japan eyes border reopening for tourism**.................216　**Tracks 133-141**
訪日観光再開に向けて政府は明確な意思疎通を　>>2022年5月21日

② **Japan's disappointing ruling on same-sex marriage**
....226　**Tracks 142-148**
大阪地裁、同性婚に関し残念な判決　>>2022年6月25日

③ **A despicable attack on Shinzo Abe — and a nation**
....236　**Tracks 149-154**
安倍晋三氏、および国家に対する卑劣な攻撃　>>2022年7月9日

④ **An ice skating superstar steps down**.........242　**Tracks 155-160**
フィギュアスケート界のスーパースター、競技会引退　>>2022年7月23日

英文解説..250
訳...254

カバーデザイン／山之口正和＋沢田幸平(OKIKATA)
本文デザイン／ハーモナイズデザイン(松森 雅孝、柳沢 由美子)
写真提供／AP(p. 1)、新華社／共同通信イメージズ(p. 53)、AP(p. 99)、
ロイター＝共同(p. 135)、共同通信社(p. 189, 215)
ナレーター／クリス・コプロウスキー、ジェニファー・オカノ

● 監修・英文解説者紹介

北爪 隆 きたづめ・たかし

1962年生まれ。東京外国語大学英米語学科卒業。
フリーランスエディター。
ジャパンタイムズ報道部長、整理部長、編集局長、論説委員長、執行役員などを歴任。

北村 一真 きたむら・かずま

杏林大学准教授。慶應義塾大学大学院後期博士課程単位取得満期退学。学生時代に関西の大学受験塾、隆盛ゼミナールで難関大対策講座を担当。著書に『英文解体新書』『英文解体新書2』(研究社)、『英語の読み方』(中公新書)、『知識と文脈で深める上級英単語ロゴフィリア』(共著・アスク)など。

● 翻訳・語注執筆者紹介(50音順)

宇都宮 まどか うつのみや・まどか

1968年生まれ。州立カリフォルニア大学バークレー校政治学科卒業。ジャパンタイムズ「週刊ST」、「Japan Times Weekly」主任を経て、翻訳者、英語学習アドバイザー。
訳書に『英語で読むからよくわかる チューデイ先生のなるほど英語レッスン超基本編』(ジャパンタイムズ出版)。

桑田 健 くわた・たけし

1965年生まれ。東京外国語大学英米語学科卒業。
訳書に『マギの聖骨』『ウイルスの暗躍』などの「シグマフォース・シリーズ」、『セドナの幻日』(以上、竹書房)、『地球 驚異の自然現象』(河出書房)、『ビッグデータベースボール』『アストロボール』『プロジェクト・ネメシス』『プロジェクト・マイゴ』(以上、KADOKAWA)、『セックス・イン・ザ・シー』(講談社)、『サッカーはなぜ11人対11人で戦うのか』(扶桑社)などがある。

小川 貴宏 こかわ・たかひろ

1962年生まれ。東京外国語大学英米語学科卒業。
同大学修士課程(ゲルマン系言語専攻)修了。英国Exeter Universityで応用言語学修士号を取得。防衛大学校准教授を経て、現在、成蹊大学教授。
著書に『Sound Right! 14のグループで覚える英語の発音』、翻訳・解説執筆に『英語で見る! 聴く! BBCドキュメンタリー&ドラマ BOOK 1』(以上、ジャパンタイムズ出版)がある。

音声のご利用方法

本書に掲載されているすべての英文記事の読み上げ音声をお聞きいただくことができます。

※「2020年上半期」版より、付属CDのご提供を終了いたしました。

スマートフォン 📱

1. ジャパンタイムズ出版の音声アプリ「OTO Navi」をインストール

2. OTO Naviで本書を検索
3. OTO Naviで音声をダウンロードし、再生

3秒早送り・早戻し、繰り返し再生などの便利機能つき。学習にお役立てください。

パソコン 💻

1. ブラウザからジャパンタイムズ出版のサイト「BOOK CLUB」にアクセス

https://bookclub.japantimes.co.jp/book/b617141.html

2. 「ダウンロード」ボタンをクリック
3. 音声をダウンロードし、iTunesなどに取り込んで再生

※音声はzipファイルを展開(解凍)してご利用ください。

巻頭特集

ウクライナ侵攻

4月5日、国連安全保障理事会で、ロシアの戦争犯罪を糾弾するウクライナのゼレンスキー大統領

Unite to protect Ukraine and the global order

世界はウクライナと国際秩序を守るために団結せよ

January 29, 2022 ●Tracks 002-008 / 解説 p. 36、訳 p. 40

Track 002

1 The West is facing its biggest crisis with Russia since the end of the Cold War, three decades ago.

2 Having massed over 100,000 troops on its border with Ukraine, the prospect of a large-scale land war on the European continent is very real. Moscow has presented an extensive list of demands to Washington and other Western capitals, but the bottom line for Russian President Vladimir Putin is simple: Russia is entitled to a sphere of influence in which its concerns override those of all other states. In his mind, only such an arrangement will provide the security and status that Putin believes his country deserves.

Track 003

3 Those demands are unreasonable. All countries deserve security but not at the expense of the sovereign rights of others. Putin wants nothing less than a rewriting of the rules of international order. He must be resisted.

4 Angered by the steady expansion of Western influence eastward toward Russia's borders, Putin has labored to create a buffer zone. If those governments resist him, he undermines them. In the case of Ukraine, the Kyiv government's growing alignment with the West prompted him to reclaim Crimea in 2014 and foment unrest in and the possible partition of the eastern part of that country.

▼ **About This Editorial** ▼

2月24日、ロシアはウクライナへの侵攻を開始したが、1月の時点でロシアはウクライナとの国境に大量の兵員を配置し、世界、特に西側諸国は紛争の勃発を強く懸念していた。その背景にはプーチンのNATO拡大への憂慮と自国の勢力圏復活への野望があった。国家間の対等性という世界秩序が破壊されようとしている。

1
- □ [タイトル]order 秩序
- □ the West 西側諸国→旧ソ連・ロシアを中心とした旧共産主義(「東側」)諸国に

対して西欧や米国などを指す東西冷戦 (the Cold War)時代の名残の概念

2
- □ mass 集結させる
- □ troops 軍隊、兵員
- □ prospect 見通し、発生の可能性
- □ large-scale 大規模な
- □ land war 地上戦、陸上戦
- □ Moscow モスクワ→ロシア政府。ある国の首都名はその国の政府を表す
- □ extensive 多項目にわたる
- □ Washington 米国政府

- □ capital 首都、(それぞれの国の)政府
- □ bottom line 核心、最も大事な点
- □ be entitled to ... …を手にする権利がある
- □ sphere (力が及ぶ)範囲、勢力圏
- □ concern 関心事、利害
- □ override …に優先する
- □ arrangement 取り決め、合意
- □ deserve …にふさわしい

3
- □ unreasonable 不条理な、不当な
- □ at the expense of ... …を犠牲にして
- □ sovereign right 主権

- □ nothing less than ... まさに…にほかならないもの
- □ rewriting 書き換え
- □ resist …に抵抗する

4
- □ anger …に怒りを抱かせる、怒らせる
- □ eastward 東方への
- □ labor to *do* 努めて〜しようとする
- □ buffer zone 緩衝地帯
- □ undermine 転覆させる、潰そうとする
- □ Kyiv キーウ→ウクライナの首都

- □ alignment 提携、協力関係
- □ reclaim (手放したものを)取り戻す
- □ foment あおる、画策する
- □ unrest 社会不安、暴動
- □ partition 分離(独立)

Track 004

5   Like his fellow nationalists, Putin believes that Ukraine is not a real state but is an integral part of the Russian motherland. According to that logic, any demand by it, or another similarly situated county — i.e., a former Soviet republic — for autonomy from Russia must be the product of foreign subversion. Indeed, there is a pervasive belief among Russians that those countries are part of a plot to encircle, isolate and ultimately strangle their country.

6   In December, Russia presented two draft treaties to the United States and the North Atlantic Treaty Organization (NATO) that called for legally binding limits on the deployment of troops, missile systems, aircraft and warships in areas where they could be considered a threat to the other side. The proposals not only demanded a halt to any future NATO expansion to Central and Eastern Europe, but rollback to its borders in the 1990s. The proposals would even deny those countries the right to buy weapons from the West to defend themselves.

Track 005

7   The U.S. and its allies promptly rejected those demands while offering to negotiate on other issues, such as nuclear arms control and limits on military exercises. Russian officials equally quickly rejected that counteroffer, demanding a focus on their "main issue," which is, Russian Foreign Minister Sergei Lavrov emphasized, NATO's "further expansion to the east and the deployment of strike weapons" that could threaten Russia. Putin's spokesperson was blunt, saying, "There is not much cause for optimism."

5
- □ his fellow ... 彼と同類の…
- □ nationalist 国家（至上）主義者
- □ integral 不可分の、不可欠な
- □ motherland 祖国、本国、本土
- □ demand by A for B AがBを要求すること
- □ similarly situated 同じような立場・状況にある
- □ former Soviet republic 旧ソ連を構成する共和国→ソ連は形式上、数々の共和国からなる連邦制だった
- □ autonomy 自治、自律
- □ subversion 破壊［転覆、反乱］行為
- □ pervasive 蔓延した、広く行き渡った
- □ plot 陰謀
- □ encircle 取り巻く
- □ strangle …の息の根を止める、潰す

6
- □ draft 草案段階の
- □ treaty 条約、協定
- □ the North Atlantic Treaty Organization 北大西洋条約機構
- □ call for ... …を求める
- □ legally binding 法的拘束力を持つ
- □ limit on ... …に制限をかけること
- □ deployment （軍事的）展開
- □ the other side もう一方→ロシア
- □ not only A but B Aに加えてBも
- □ halt 停止
- □ rollback 復元、以前に戻すこと
- □ 1990s →1988〜1991年にソビエト連邦構成国が相次いで主権宣言を出し、1991年ソ連が崩壊。「独立国家共同体」が発足するも後に有名無実化した
- □ deny A B AにBを与えない

7
- □ ally 同盟国
- □ nuclear arms control 核兵器の制限、核軍縮
- □ military exercises 軍事演習
- □ official 関係者、当局者
- □ equally 同様に
- □ counteroffer 逆提案、提案返し
- □ focus on ... …に議論を絞ること
- □ Foreign Minister 外務大臣、外相
- □ emphasize 強調する
- □ strike weapon 攻撃用武器→「防衛のための武器」に対して
- □ spokesperson 広報官、代弁者 →Lavrov 外相のこと
- □ blunt ぶっきらぼうな
- □ cause 原因、理由
- □ optimism 楽観論

8   Intelligence officials reportedly believe Putin has not made a decision on how to proceed and will likely wait a few weeks before doing so. Weighing heavily on his thinking are the upcoming Beijing Winter Olympic Games. Any military move would overshadow that event, angering Putin's chief diplomatic ally and partner, Chinese President Xi Jinping.

Track 006

9   In the interim, the priority is forging a united front among Western nations that ensures that Russia will pay a price if it chooses conflict. Russia, Putin and other key officials must be punished for disturbing the peace, destabilizing Europe and challenging the global order. Ukraine should be provided the means to defend itself; claims that such weapons threaten Russia are nonsense. Sanctions should be prepared to hurt the individuals behind the decision to fight, as well as key segments of the Russian economy. There should be no doubt about consequences if Moscow chooses war.

10   Putin is betting that neither consensus nor concerted action is possible. He apparently believes that the trans-Atlantic alliance is divided and that there is no substantive commitment to the sovereignty of Central and Eastern European states if Western European interests can be threatened if they try to protect their neighbors. Putin is convinced that he has leverage, particularly when it comes to the energy that his country supplies to the region.

8
- ☐ intelligence 諜報→ここは西側関係者
- ☐ reportedly 伝えられるところでは
- ☐ proceed 先に進む、行動を起こす
- ☐ weigh (heavily) on ... …に (重く) の しかかる、…に (大きく) 影響する
- ☐ upcoming 近々開催される
- ☐ overshadow …に悪影響を及ぼす、 …の盛り上がりをそぐ
- ☐ diplomatic 外交上の、外交面での
- ☐ Chinese President 中国国家主席
- ☐ Xi Jinping 習近平

9
- ☐ in the interim 当面
- ☐ priority 優先事項
- ☐ forge 作る、組む
- ☐ united front 統一戦線、共同戦線
- ☐ pay a price 代償を払う、痛い目を見る
- ☐ conflict 紛争、 (軍事) 衝突
- ☐ disturb 乱す、妨害する
- ☐ destabilize 不安定化させる
- ☐ means 手段
- ☐ claim 主張
- ☐ sanction 制裁 (措置)
- ☐ hurt →ここの目的語は individuals と key segments
- ☐ segment 分野、部門
- ☐ there should be no doubt about ... …について疑問の余地がないように するべきだ
- ☐ consequence (生じる) 結果

10
- ☐ bet that ... …に違いないと考える
- ☐ consensus 意見の一致
- ☐ concerted 歩調を合わせた
- ☐ apparently どうやら…のようだ
- ☐ trans-Atlantic 大西洋を挟んだ
- ☐ alliance 同盟→ここでは NATO のこと
- ☐ divided 意見が分かれた、分裂した
- ☐ substantive 実質的な、具体的な
- ☐ commitment 関与、介入
- ☐ sovereignty 主権
- ☐ interests 利害、利益
- ☐ neighbors →中・東欧諸国を指す
- ☐ leverage 影響力、相手を従わせる力
- ☐ when it comes to ... …関連なら
- ☐ energy →天然ガスなど
- ☐ the region →ここでは西ヨーロッパを 指す

Track 007

11   Japan has been fairly quiet about the brewing conflict. In their videoconference last week, Prime Minister Fumio Kishida and U.S. President Joe Biden said they would work closely together to deter Russian aggression against Ukraine, and Kishida pledged close coordination with the U.S., other partners and the international community on taking strong action in response to any attack. Also last week, Japanese and French foreign and defense ministers in their two-plus-two meeting reaffirmed their full respect for the sovereignty and territorial integrity of Ukraine.

12   In truth, there is relatively little Japan can do in or about Ukraine, apart from showing diplomatic support and making clear Western resolve and unity. But Japanese engagement parallels its invitation to European nations to participate in Indo-Pacific security and must be pursued.

Track 008

13   The outcome of this crisis will affect Japan, like all countries. Putin aims to rewrite the most basic rule of international politics: the equality of nations. In his world, some countries are more equal than others and their demands and concerns outweigh all others. Acquiescence to his demands would not only transform the balance of power in Europe, but it would set a precedent that China would claim as well.

14   In that world, Japan would be less sovereign, independent and free than it is today. That is unacceptable.

(880 words)

11
- □ quiet 沈黙した、態度を表明しない
- □ brewing 生じつつある
- □ videoconference ビデオ(リモート)会議
- □ work closely together 緊密に連携する
- □ deter 抑止する、防ぐ
- □ aggression 侵略(行為)
- □ close coordination 緊密な協調
- □ partner 友好国、同盟国
- □ international community 国際社会
- □ in response to ... …に対して
- □ foreign and defense ministers 外務大臣と防衛[国防]大臣
- □ two-plus-two 2プラス2(ツープラスツー)の→主に安全保障分野での外務・防衛トップの会合の通称
- □ reaffirm 再確認する、再是認する
- □ integrity 一体性、保全、不可侵

12
- □ there is little ... …はほとんどない
- □ apart from ... …を除けば
- □ make clear ... …を明確に示す
- □ resolve 決意
- □ unity 団結、結束
- □ engagement 関わりを持つこと
- □ parallel …に匹敵する
- □ Indo-Pacific インド太平洋(インド洋・西太平洋)地域の
- □ pursue 推し進める

13
- □ rewrite 書き換える
- □ the equality of nations 国家間の対等性
- □ outweigh …より重要である
- □ acquiescence 屈服、黙認すること
- □ transform 変容させる
- □ balance of power 力関係
- □ set a precedent 前例を作る
- □ claim 主張する→中国の場合、対台湾で覇権を主張する可能性がある

14
- □ sovereign 主権がある、主権が認められる

Hold Russian soldiers and their leaders accountable for war crimes

ロシア兵とその指導者に戦争犯罪の責任を負わせよ

April 9, 2022 ●Tracks 009-018 / 解説 P. 37、訳 p. 43

Track 009

1 The images are gruesome, horrifying and unmistakable.

2 War crimes are being committed during the Russian invasion of Ukraine and judging from the amount of evidence, its appearance throughout the country and Russia's past practice, brutality and illegality appear to be a deliberate policy.

Track 010

3 The government of Japan has rightly identified these acts as war crimes, condemned them and demanded justice. It will not be easy, but the quest for accountability must be deliberate and unyielding. The perpetrators must be found and punished.

4 As Russian troops have withdrawn from areas under their control, evidence of horrific brutality is mounting. At the end of his speech to the United Nations Security Council earlier this week, Ukrainian President Volodymyr Zelenskyy played a short video that showed corpses of Ukrainian civilians in towns across the country. The government of Ukraine claims that at least 300 civilians were tortured and killed by Russian troops in the town of Bucha, part of a much larger campaign of violence.

Track 011

5 The pictures turn the stomach. There are individuals with hands tied behind their backs and single bullet wounds to the back of the head, or shots through the eyes. Bodies have been mutilated and burned. There are mass graves. There are multiple reports of rape and torture.

▼ About This Editorial ▼

ロシア軍が撤退した後のウクライナの町では、拷問を受けて虐殺されたと思われる民間人の死体が多く発見された。そのおぞましい映像は世界に衝撃を与えるとともに、戦争犯罪に手を染めたロシア軍兵士や指導者を決して許してはならないという機運を大いに高めることにもなった。

1
- [タイトル]hold A accountable for B AにBの責任を負わせる
- gruesome 凄惨な
- unmistakable 紛れもない

2
- invasion 侵攻
- judging from ... …から判断すると
- appearance 出現
- brutality 残虐行為
- illegality 違法行為
- deliberate 計画的な

3
- rightly 当然ながら
- identify A as B AをBと見なす
- condemn 糾弾する
- demand justice 法の裁きを求める
- accountability 説明責任
- unyielding 断固とした
- perpetrator 犯人

4
- troops 軍隊
- withdraw from ... …から撤退する
  →withdrawnはwithdrawの過去分詞形
- horrific 恐ろしい
- mount …が増える
- the United Nations Security Council 国連安全保障理事会
- corpse 死体
- civilian 一般市民
- torture 拷問する
- campaign 軍事作戦

5
- turn the stomach 胃をむかむかさせる、吐き気を催させる(ほどおぞましい)
- individual 人
- with hands tied behind *one's* back 後ろ手に縛られて
- bullet wound 銃創
- mutilate 切断する
- mass grave 集団墓地
- multiple 複数の

11

6   This barbarous violence has been seen elsewhere; Russian forces, for example, were charged with targeting civilians during the Syrian civil war. In a 2020 report, the U.N. Human Rights Council blamed the Russian Air Force for indiscriminate attacks on civilian targets in Syria "amounting to a war crime." Human rights groups have accused Russian troops of war crimes in Georgia and Chechnya as well.

Track 012

7   Chief Cabinet Secretary Hirokazu Matsuno called the acts "a war crime." Prime Minister Fumio Kishida was equally forthright, saying the killing of civilians is "an inhumane act and against international law, and can never be condoned."

8   NATO Secretary-General Jens Stoltenberg said the alliance had reliable evidence of war crimes committed in Bucha and other cities in Ukraine. U.S. Secretary of State Antony Blinken called reports of Russian war crimes "more than credible," adding that "It's a deliberate campaign to kill, to torture, to rape, to commit atrocities. … The evidence is there for the world to see."

Track 013

9   Russia denies the charges. Ambassador to the United Nations Vassily Nebenzia said Russian troops were not targeting civilians. Foreign Minister Sergei Lavrov dismissed the evidence as "fake" and "staged," while other Kremlin officials called the accusations a "monstrous forgery" to discredit Russia.

10   Zelenskyy demanded that the U.N. convene a Nuremberg-style tribunal to investigate and prosecute Russian war crimes, seeking justice against anyone who issued orders to commit such acts or carried them out. The International Criminal Court (ICC), the U.N. tribunal in The Hague, launched an investigation of possible war crimes in March.

6
- □ barbarous 野蛮な、残忍な
- □ elsewhere ほかの場所で→ウクライナ以外の国で、という意味
- □ forces 軍隊
- □ be charged with ... …で告発される
- □ target 標的にする;標的
- □ Syrian シリアの
- □ civil war 内戦
- □ the U.N. Human Rights Council 国連人権理事会
- □ indiscriminate 無差別な
- □ amount to ... …に相当する
- □ accuse A of B AをBで非難する、告発する

7
- □ Chief Cabinet Secretary 官房長官
- □ forthright 率直な、きっぱりとした
- □ inhumane 非人道的な
- □ condone 許す

8
- □ NATO 北大西洋条約機構→North Atlantic Treaty Organizationの略
- □ Secretary-General 事務総長
- □ alliance 同盟→ここではNATOのこと
- □ reliable 信頼できる
- □ Secretary of State 国務長官
- □ more than credible 十分に信用に足る→このmore thanは「非常に、このうえなく」の意味
- □ atrocity 残虐行為
- □ The evidence is there for the world to see. 証拠は世界の誰の目にも明らかだ

9
- □ ambassador 大使
- □ dismiss A as B AをBだとはねつける
- □ staged でっちあげの
- □ Kremlin クレムリン→ここではロシア政府のこと
- □ accusation 非難、告発
- □ monstrous 途方もない
- □ forgery 偽造、捏造
- □ discredit …の信用を失墜させる

10
- □ convene 招集する、開く
- □ Nuremberg ニュルンベルク→第二次世界大戦のドイツの戦争犯罪を裁く国際裁判が開かれたドイツの都市
- □ -style …的な
- □ tribunal 裁判(所)
- □ prosecute 訴追する
- □ issue （命令を）出す
- □ the International Criminal Court 国際刑事裁判所
- □ investigation 調査

Track 014

11 Evidence is being collected by human rights groups, media organizations, independent observers, as well as governments and international institutions like NATO — and private satellite imagery has proven false Moscow's claims that bodies were planted after the withdrawal of its forces. The Group of Seven foreign ministers announced Thursday that their governments would assist the ICC.

12 Indictments are sure to follow. Still, finding the accused and holding them accountable is another matter. Capturing the soldiers responsible for atrocities is often a matter of luck, since casualties are high and troops are frequently rotated. If there is in fact a policy to inflict terror on civilian populations, then there will be even more incentive to move troops to reduce the risk of capture and trial.

Track 015

13 Finding those up the chain of command who issued the orders, individuals just as guilty as those who pulled the trigger, will be harder still. There has to be "knowing" violation of the law of war. A policy that licenses indiscriminate violence is hard to prove; officials can claim ignorance of what happened down the chain of command.

14 Charging those at the very top of the Russian government, such as President Vladimir Putin, Foreign Minister Lavrov or Minister of Defense Sergei Shoigu, is the ultimate challenge. U.S. President Joe Biden has called Putin a "war criminal" who "should be held accountable." Proving his knowledge of war crimes will be extremely difficult; heads of criminal organizations rarely communicate such orders directly. Winks and nods send messages but in a way that ensures deniability.

11
- ☐ media organization 報道機関
- ☐ independent 独立系の
- ☐ observer 観測筋、監視者
- ☐ institution 機関
- ☐ satellite 衛星
- ☐ imagery 画像
- ☐ prove false Moscow's claims that ... …だというロシア政府の主張が虚偽だと証明する→proven は prove の過去分詞形
- ☐ plant (ひそかに)置く
- ☐ withdrawal 撤退
- ☐ the Group of Seven 主要先進7カ国、G7

12
- ☐ indictment 訴追
- ☐ be sure to *do* 〜するのは確実だ
- ☐ the accused 被告人→the＋形容詞／過去分詞で「その性質を持った人々」
- ☐ responsible for ... …の責任を問われるべき
- ☐ a matter of luck 運次第
- ☐ casualty 犠牲者
- ☐ rotate 入れ替える
- ☐ inflict 与える
- ☐ terror テロ行為、恐怖
- ☐ incentive 動機
- ☐ trial 裁判

13
- ☐ those up the chain of command 指揮系統の上にいる人
- ☐ knowing 意図的な
- ☐ violation 違反
- ☐ law of war 戦時国際法
- ☐ license …の権限を与える
- ☐ claim ignorance of ... …を知らないと主張する
- ☐ down the chain of command 指揮系統の下で

14
- ☐ ultimate 究極の
- ☐ extremely 極めて
- ☐ criminal organization 犯罪組織
- ☐ rarely めったに…ない
- ☐ winks and nods send messages 目配せとうなずきで意図を伝える→言葉を使わずになくそれとなく伝えるということ
- ☐ in a way that ... …というやり方で
- ☐ ensure 確かにする
- ☐ deniability 否認できること

Track 016

15 Putin likely can be charged with instigating a "war of aggression" against Ukraine. This is a clear violation of international law according to the U.N. Charter and the statutes of the ICC (although Russia withdrew from the tribunal in 2016).

16 The only way that Putin and those around him face justice will be if they are turned over to a court by other Russians. That is possible only if pressure is intensified and the costs of refusal become too painful.

Track 017

17 Kishida said that Japan will join the U.S. and other advanced economies in another round of sanctions to demonstrate "our resolve to never allow war crimes." Europe is moving closer to ending its imports of energy supplies from Russia, a move that would be a hammer blow to the economy. That breaking point, though, may be long delayed. Putin has cast this as a war of survival for Russia and the sanctions reinforce that claim.

18 Nevertheless, even if the odds of getting justice are long, we must try. Fortunately, there are no statutes of limitations for war crimes. There is reason to hope, too. Leaders such as Slobodan Milosevic, Charles Taylor and Laurent Gbagbo, the former presidents of Serbia, Liberia and Ivory Coast, respectively, all ended up in the dock at the ICC. That means we must act in ways that make clear our commitment to accountability.

Track 018

19 There cannot be business as usual. What has occurred in Ukraine is too plain and too horrific. Failure to act ensures that this violence — this inhumanity — will be repeated.

(974 words)

15
- ☐ instigate 引き起こす
- ☐ war of aggression 侵略戦争
- ☐ the U.N. Charter 国連憲章
- ☐ statute 規定

16
- ☐ face justice 裁き・報いを受ける
- ☐ be turned over to ... …に引き渡される
- ☐ only if ... …の場合にのみ
- ☐ intensify 強化する
- ☐ cost 代償
- ☐ refusal 拒否
- ☐ painful 痛みを伴う

17
- ☐ advanced economy 先進経済国
- ☐ sanction 制裁
- ☐ resolve 決意
- ☐ hammer blow 大きな打撃
- ☐ breaking point 限界点
- ☐ be long delayed 大きく遅れる
- ☐ cast A as B AをBと見なす
- ☐ reinforce 強める

18
- ☐ nevertheless それでもなお
- ☐ odds 見込み
- ☐ long (見込みが)小さい
- ☐ statute of limitations 時効
- ☐ respectively それぞれ
- ☐ end up in ... 結局は…に行き着く
- ☐ dock 被告席
- ☐ make clear ... …をはっきりさせる
- ☐ commitment 取り組み

19
- ☐ business as usual いつも通りのやり方
- ☐ failure to act 行動しないこと
- ☐ inhumanity 非人道的行為

Learning the wrong nuclear lessons from the Ukraine war

ウクライナ戦争から誤った核の教訓を学ぶ

April 30, 2022　　　　●Tracks 019-026 / 解説 p. 38、訳 p. 46

Track 019

1　Among the many disturbing legacies of Russia's invasion of Ukraine, one of the most alarming is its seeming confirmation of the utility of nuclear weapons.

2　The war has given policymakers and publics reason to believe that a nuclear arsenal contributes to national security. If those conclusions go unchallenged, nuclear proliferation is likely to follow. Nothing could be more dangerous.

Track 020

3　The nuclear shadow has clouded the Ukraine conflict. Weeks before the invasion, Russia conducted maneuvers with its nuclear forces which, when combined with the marshaling of its military on the Ukraine border, signaled Moscow's readiness to fight with all its capabilities. Shortly after the invasion began, Russian President Vladimir Putin said that he was putting his country's "deterrent forces" — its nuclear weapons — on "a special regime of alert" and warned that intervention by the West would lead to "consequences you have never seen."

4　Other Russian officials underscored their country's nuclear options. Dmitry Medvedev, deputy chairman of the national security council, reminded the world that Russian doctrine allows nuclear strikes against an enemy that only uses conventional weapons. He added "that we are ready to give a worthy response to any infringement on our country, on its independence."

核兵器の使用も辞さないというロシアの姿勢は世界を不安に陥れた。それが一定の抑止力を示したことには、ロシアのウクライナ侵攻を注視する他国も気づいているだろう。核開発の意欲を持ち、ミサイル発射実験を続ける北朝鮮がそこから何を学んだか、大いに気がかりなところだ。

1
- □ disturbing 不穏な
- □ legacy 遺産
- □ alarming 警戒するべき
- □ seeming 見かけの
- □ confirmation 確認
- □ utility 実用性、有用性、役に立つこと

2
- □ policymaker 政策立案者
- □ arsenal 兵器、備蓄
- □ contribute to ... …に貢献する
- □ go unchallenged 疑問を持たれないまま進む
- □ proliferation 拡散

3
- □ cloud …に暗雲を投げかける
- □ conflict 戦争、紛争
- □ conduct 実施する
- □ maneuvers 大演習
- □ when combined with ... …と組み合わさった時
- □ marshaling 動員
- □ signal 合図する、意思表示する
- □ readiness 準備ができていること
- □ capability 能力、戦力
- □ deterrent (forces) 抑止力
- □ special regime of alert 特別警戒態勢
- □ intervention 介入
- □ consequence 結果

4
- □ underscore 強調する
- □ option 選択肢
- □ deputy 副…
- □ national security council 国家安全保障会議
- □ remind the world that ... 世界に…だと思い出させる
- □ doctrine 政策
- □ strike 攻撃
- □ conventional weapons 通常兵器→大量破壊兵器（核兵器や生物兵器など）以外の兵器
- □ worthy 値する、相応の
- □ infringement 侵害

Track 021

5   Russian Foreign Minister Sergei Lavrov warned that the risks of nuclear war are now "very, very significant and should not be underestimated," while Defense Minister Sergei Shoigu said that nuclear "readiness" was a priority. Since Russia possesses the world's largest stockpile of nuclear weapons — approximately 6,000 warheads — those comments must be taken seriously.

6   The idea that Russia could resort to such weapons — that its independence or sovereignty could be threatened and thus justify their use — is both absurd and chilling. Its arsenal and the leadership's capacity for delusion — evident throughout the course of the war — mean that such warnings cannot be dismissed.

Track 022

7   To some degree, threats have worked. The prospect of escalation beyond the nuclear threshold has restrained the West from deeper intervention in the conflict. If those governments believe that their direct involvement could push Putin to monstrous decisions, then it is hard not to argue that they have been deterred.

8   That is certainly the lesson that will be learned by other governments studying this war. If the West has been deterred, then those countries will likely question the value of U.S. security guarantees. They will wonder if Ukraine's 1994 decision to give up its nuclear weapons — it possessed about one-third of the Soviet arsenal after the USSR collapsed — was a mistake. (It didn't have the launch codes, so the utility of those weapons was questionable.) That logic was reinforced by Svitlana Zalishchuk, foreign policy adviser to Ukraine's deputy prime minister, who agreed that giving up those nuclear weapons was a mistake.

5
- [ ] significant 著しい
- [ ] underestimate 軽視する、見くびる
- [ ] priority 優先事項
- [ ] possess 保有する
- [ ] stockpile 備蓄
- [ ] approximately 約…
- [ ] warhead 弾頭

6
- [ ] resort to ... …(手段)に訴える
- [ ] sovereignty 主権
- [ ] threaten 脅かす
- [ ] justify 正当化する
- [ ] absurd 馬鹿げた
- [ ] chilling ぞっとする
- [ ] delusion 妄想
- [ ] evident 明らかな
- [ ] the course of the war 戦局
- [ ] dismiss (重要でないと)片づける

7
- [ ] to some degree ある程度まで
- [ ] prospect 可能性、見込み
- [ ] escalation 拡大
- [ ] threshold 入口、基準点
- [ ] restrain A from B AがBするのを控えさせる
- [ ] intervention 介入
- [ ] involvement 関与
- [ ] monstrous 恐ろしい
- [ ] deter 抑止する

8
- [ ] study 注視する、精査する
- [ ] question …に疑問を呈する
- [ ] security guarantee 安全保障
- [ ] give up ... …を放棄する
- [ ] USSR ソビエト社会主義共和国連邦
  →Union of Soviet Socialist Republicsの略
- [ ] collapse 崩壊する
- [ ] launch code 発射コード
- [ ] questionable 疑わしい
- [ ] reinforce 強化する
- [ ] foreign policy 外交政策
- [ ] adviser 顧問

Track 023

9 North Korean Leader Kim Jong Un won't learn anything from the Ukraine experience; rather, it will confirm that his — his father's and his grandfather's — pursuit of a nuclear weapon was the right strategy all along. North Korea has been determined to acquire a nuclear arsenal to ensure the survival of its regime. Speaking at a military parade this week, Kim warned that "If any forces try to violate the fundamental interests of our state, our nuclear forces will have to decisively accomplish its unexpected second mission." Moreover, the military "should be fully prepared to … put their unique deterrent in motion at any time."

10 Those remarks were only the most recent signs of Kim's determination to not only acquire, but hone, a nuclear capability. North Korea has conducted 13 missile tests this year — a record — including in March what is thought to have been an ICBM capable of hitting any target in the United States.

Track 024

11 There are also signs that Pyongyang will soon conduct a nuclear test, its first since declaring a self-imposed moratorium in 2017. A test is thought necessary to fulfill the objective Kim laid out in a January 2021 speech of developing "ultramodern tactical nuclear weapons."

9
- ☐ confirm 裏付ける
- ☐ pursuit 追求
- ☐ strategy 戦略
- ☐ all along ずっと
- ☐ be determined to *do* ～すると強く決意する
- ☐ acquire 手に入れる
- ☐ ensure 確かなものにする
- ☐ regime 政権
- ☐ military parade 軍事パレード
- ☐ violate 侵害する
- ☐ interests 利益
- ☐ decisively 断固として
- ☐ accomplish 果たす
- ☐ unexpected second mission →金正恩はこの日の演説で、北朝鮮の核戦力の基本的な使命は「戦争の抑止」だとする一方、他国が北朝鮮の基本的利益を侵害しようとする場合は「想定外の第2の使命を果たす」と述べ、明言は避けたものの「攻撃目的の核戦力の使用」を示唆したものと見られている
- ☐ put ... in motion …を稼働させる

10
- ☐ remarks （演説などでの）発言
- ☐ determination 強い決意
- ☐ hone …に磨きをかける
- ☐ nuclear capability 核能力、核戦力
- ☐ ICBM 大陸間弾道ミサイル →intercontinental ballistic missile の略
- ☐ capable of *doing* ～することが可能な

11
- ☐ self-imposed 自主的な
- ☐ moratorium 一時停止
- ☐ fulfill 実現させる
- ☐ objective 目的
- ☐ lay out ... …を明らかにする
- ☐ ultramodern 超現代的な、最新鋭の
- ☐ tactical nuclear weapon 戦術核兵器

12 The "reassuring" explanation for this is that Kim is frustrated by his inability to move U.S. President Joe Biden and is trying to get him to pay more attention to North Korea. He wants Washington to make Pyongyang a diplomatic priority, restore its status and address its concerns. He has dismissed Biden's policy of demanding genuine steps toward denuclearization as a "petty trick" and has ordered his country to prepare for a "long-term confrontation." The election of a conservative president in South Korea, the loss of a progressive ally in Seoul and Biden's upcoming trip to Asia all reinforce his determination to act.

`Track 025`

13 The more troubling explanation is that Kim is thinking more expansively about nuclear capabilities, perhaps drawing on the Ukraine experience. In this case, the respect that Western governments have shown Russia, with their restrained response, has encouraged the North Korean leadership to focus on nuclear weapons' ability to coerce — to force adversaries to bend to its will — rather than their ability to deter. Kim's presence at an April test of a short-range missile, which some experts think could be the country's "first tactical nuclear weapon delivery system," lends credence to this view.

14 Kim's reasoning — and those who think like him — is wrong on two counts. First, it mistakenly values nuclear weapons. South Korea and Japan, unlike Ukraine, are treaty allies explicitly protected by the U.S. nuclear umbrella. The ability to strike the U.S. means little given the U.S. ability to utterly destroy North Korea — without even using nuclear weapons.

12
- □ reassuring 安心感を与えるような
- □ be frustrated by ... …によっていら立っている
- □ inability できないこと
- □ pay more attention to ... …にもっと注意を払う
- □ diplomatic 外交的な
- □ restore 回復させる
- □ status 地位
- □ address …に対応する
- □ concern 懸念、関心事
- □ denuclearization 非核化
- □ petty 狭量な
- □ long-term 長期的な
- □ confrontation 対立
- □ ally 味方
- □ upcoming 来るべき

13
- □ troubling 不安感を与えるような、厄介な
- □ expansively 広い視野で
- □ draw on ... …を参考にする
- □ restrained 控えめな
- □ encourage ... to *do* …に~するように促す
- □ leadership 指導部
- □ focus on ... …を重視する
- □ coerce 強要する、抑圧する
- □ adversary 敵対国
- □ bend to one's will ～の意のままに屈服させる
- □ presence 出席、同席
- □ short-range 短距離の
- □ lend credence to ... …に信憑性を与える

14
- □ reasoning 論理
- □ count 論点
- □ mistakenly 誤って
- □ value …に価値を認める
- □ treaty ally 条約同盟国
- □ explicitly 明確に
- □ nuclear umbrella 核の傘
- □ strike 攻撃する
- □ given …を考慮すると→このgivenは前置詞としての働き
- □ utterly 徹底的に

Track 026

15 Second, they fail to recognize the cost of acquiring those weapons. The pursuit of a nuclear capability, in defiance of his international commitments and in violation of international law, establishes Kim and his country as outlaws. The ensuing sanctions and marginalization — which Putin and Russia are now beginning to experience — should be proof that nuclear weapons endanger national security more than they ensure it.

(964 words)

15
- □ fail to *do* 〜することができない、〜していない
- □ recognize 認識する
- □ cost 代償
- □ in defiance of ... …に背いて
- □ in violation of ... …に違反して
- □ establish A as B AをBとして確立させる
- □ outlaw 無法者
- □ ensuing それに続く
- □ sanction 制裁
- □ marginalization 疎外化
- □ endanger 危険にさらす

The United Nations finds itself at a tipping point

岐路に立つ国連

September 24, 2022　　　●Tracks 027-034 / 解説 p. 39、訳 p. 49

Track 027

1　If ever there was a time for the United Nations to show its utility, it would be when one member state was invaded by another and the rule-based international order, the cornerstone of the U.N. system, would appear threatened as a result.

2　Instead, the world body has been shaken, incapable of mustering action to protect a member, itself or the order that gives the institution meaning and purpose.

Track 028

3　Prime Minister Fumio Kishida condemned the impotence of the world body and called for structural reform in remarks to the United Nations General Assembly earlier this week. He is not the first Japanese prime minister to make this case, but few have done so at a time of greater peril or urgency.

4　U.N. Secretary-General Antonio Guterres is right to warn that the "United Nations Charter and the ideals it represents are in jeopardy." The "colossal global dysfunction" that he bemoaned in remarks to the annual opening of the General Assembly is the result of more than just the war in Ukraine. It encompasses the inflation that has been triggered and the global food crisis that has followed in its wake. It includes the inability to address climate change despite its intensifying and terrifying impacts. It is vast human migration triggered by man-made and natural causes. It is widening inequality that compounds the consequences of all other challenges.

第77回国連総会が9月13日、米ニューヨークで開幕し、アントニオ・グテーレス事務総長や岸田文雄首相は、機能不全が続く安全保障理事会をはじめとする国連の改革を訴えた。戦争、インフレ、食糧危機や気候変動などの問題を前に、改革の灯は消してはならない。

1
- □ [タイトル]find *oneself* at ... いつの間にか…という状況にある
- □ [タイトル]tipping point 転換点
- □ utility 有用性
- □ invade …に侵攻する
- □ international order 国際秩序
- □ cornerstone 礎
- □ appear …のように見受けられる
- □ threaten 脅かす

2
- □ the world body 国際機関→ここでは国連のこと
- □ incapable of *doing* ～することができない
- □ muster 奮い起こす
- □ institution 機関

3
- □ condemn 非難する
- □ impotence 無力、無策
- □ call for ... …を求める
- □ structural reform 構造改革
- □ remarks (演説などでの)発言
- □ the United Nations General Assembly 国連総会
- □ make a case 主張する
- □ peril 危機
- □ urgency 緊急性

4
- □ U.N. Secretary-General 国連事務総長
- □ the United Nations Charter 国連憲章
- □ ideal 理念、理想
- □ represent 掲げる、象徴する
- □ in jeopardy 危機にさらされて
- □ colossal 巨大な
- □ dysfunction 機能不全
- □ bemoan 嘆く
- □ encompass 含む
- □ trigger 引き起こす
- □ in *one's* wake ～の後で、～に続いて
- □ address …に対処する
- □ intensifying 深刻化する
- □ terrifying 恐ろしい
- □ vast 膨大な
- □ migration 移動、移住
- □ widen 拡大する、広げる
- □ inequality 不平等
- □ compound 悪化させる
- □ consequences 影響
- □ challenge 課題、問題

Track 029

5   None of these problems is unprecedented or unpredicted. We have watched them unfold. We have let them metastasize. Guterres' conclusion is hard to wave away: "The international community is not ready or willing to tackle the big dramatic challenges of our age" even though they "threaten the very future of humanity and the fate of our planet."

6   For Kishida and other reformers, a crucial first step is reform of the U.N. Security Council. That body, charged with providing a bulwark against international disorder, has instead been paralyzed by the power of its five permanent members. Their possession of a veto ensures that no action can be taken that challenges their interests as they define them.

Track 030

7   Thus, today, Russia can and has blocked action that would stop its invasion of a sovereign state. Kishida warned that continued inaction in the face of blatant injustice "tramples on the vision and principles of the U.N. Charter" and "the credibility of the United Nations is at stake." Worse, this wanton violation of international law threatens to unleash other governments who contemplate similar action elsewhere in the world. French President Emmanuel Macron was equally stark in his speech to the world body, warning that the world was close to an era of permanent conflict, "where sovereignty and security will be determined by force, by the size of armies."

8   The stakes have only gotten higher following Russian President Vladimir Putin's remarks this week that his country "would use all the instruments at its disposal to counter a threat against its territorial integrity," a not-so-subtle reference to his readiness to use nuclear weapons if he felt a need to do so. This nuclear blackmail is utterly unacceptable.

5
- □ unprecedented 前代未聞の、前例の ない
- □ unpredicted 予期されてない
- □ watch ... unfold …の展開を見守る
- □ metastasize 広まる、はびこる
- □ conclusion 結び（の言葉）
- □ wave away はねつける
- □ be willing to *do* 進んで〜する
- □ dramatic 劇的な
- □ the very まさにその…、…そのもの
- □ fate 運命

6
- □ reformer 改革論者
- □ crucial 極めて重要な
- □ the U.N. Security Council 国連安 全保障理事会
- □ charge with ... …の責任を負う
- □ bulwark 防波堤
- □ disorder 混乱
- □ paralyze 無力化する
- □ permanent member 常任理事国
- □ possession 有すること
- □ veto 拒否権
- □ ensure 確実にする
- □ challenge …に異議を唱える
- □ define 定義する、考える

7
- □ sovereign state 主権国家
- □ inaction 不作為、無策
- □ in the face of ... …を前に
- □ blatant あからさまな
- □ injustice 不正
- □ trample on ... …を踏みにじる
- □ principle 理念、原理
- □ credibility 信頼性
- □ at stake 危機にひんして、（…が）賭け られて
- □ wanton 理不尽な
- □ unleash 解き放つ
- □ contemplate 考えている
- □ stark 赤裸々な、明確な
- □ conflict 紛争
- □ determine 決定する
- □ force 武力

8
- □ stake 危険の度合い、（物事の）深刻さ、 重大さ
- □ instrument 手段
- □ at *one's* disposal 〜の自由に使える
- □ counter …に対抗する
- □ territorial integrity 領土的一体性
- □ not-so-subtle あからさまな
- □ reference to ... …への言及
- □ readiness 用意があること
- □ nuclear blackmail 核による脅迫
- □ utterly まったく

Track 031

9 It is completely predictable, however, in the aftermath of a failed invasion driven by self-serving readings of history and unhinged dreams of empire. It is enabled by the failure of the Nuclear Non-Proliferation Treaty Review Conference, which convened to no discernible effect last month. Kishida is the only Japanese prime minister to attend that meeting, and he blamed Russia for the inability of the group to even release a joint statement at its conclusion.

10 Nuclear issues are Kishida's passion. That is understandable as his constituency includes Hiroshima where the first atomic bomb was dropped in World War II. In his August speech, he unveiled his "Hiroshima Action Plan," an initiative that would reinforce the nuclear taboo, promote reductions in nuclear arsenals, increase the transparency of stockpiles of weapons and related materials and promote the peaceful use of nuclear energy. Speaking to the General Assembly this week, Kishida pledged to fight for "a world without nuclear weapons," and "ensure that Nagasaki remains the last place to suffer an atomic bombing."

Track 032

11 Calls for U.N. reform typically focus on the Security Council. It has been proposed that its membership be expanded, that new permanent members be added or that the five permanent members be stripped of their veto. The procedural hurdles to any change are high: Revising the Charter needs ratification by a two-thirds majority of members, including all five permanent Security Council members.

12 Ultimately, hopes for reform have foundered for two simple reasons. Those with power refuse to give it up and those that seek more power are stymied by rivals who don't wish to be disadvantaged in their bilateral competition.

9
- ☐ in the aftermath of ... …の結果
- ☐ driven by ... …に駆り立てられた
- ☐ self-serving 自分勝手な
- ☐ reading 解釈
- ☐ unhinged 常軌を逸した
- ☐ empire 帝国
- ☐ enable 可能にする
- ☐ the Nuclear Non-Proliferation Treaty Review Conference 核拡散防止条約再検討会議
- ☐ convene 開かれる
- ☐ to no effect 何の効果・結果もなく
- ☐ discernible 目に見える
- ☐ release 発する
- ☐ joint statement 共同声明

10
- ☐ constituency 選挙区
- ☐ unveil 発表する
- ☐ initiative 取り組み
- ☐ reinforce 強化する
- ☐ reduction 削減
- ☐ nuclear arsenal 核兵器
- ☐ transparency 透明性
- ☐ stockpile 備蓄
- ☐ related material 関連物質
- ☐ pledge 誓う

11
- ☐ calls for ... …の要請
- ☐ typically 通常は
- ☐ focus on ... …に集中する
- ☐ propose 提案する
- ☐ membership 加盟国数
- ☐ be stripped of ... …を剥奪される
- ☐ procedural 手続き上の
- ☐ revise 改正する
- ☐ ratification 批准
- ☐ two-thirds 3分の2

12
- ☐ ultimately 結局のところ
- ☐ founder 完全に失敗する
- ☐ seek 求める
- ☐ stymie 阻む
- ☐ disadvantage …に不利益を与える
- ☐ bilateral 二国間の

13 For many, focus on the Security Council is misplaced. Attention is better put on the myriad institutions of the U.N. system that are working to address specific issues that impact the daily lives of hundreds of millions, if not billions, of people around the world. While they are not immune to the geopolitical pressures — and frequent paralysis — that have captured the Security Council, that ground level work is far more likely to escape them.

14 That there are substantive obstacles to reform doesn't mean that we must give up hope. Those who seek a world of equality, democracy and a world governed by rules must continue to insist on their vision of world order. Even if they don't prevail today, they shape the debate and hold to international scrutiny those who prefer a world in which power determines outcomes. The ruthlessness of their proposed order must be exposed for what it is.

15 It will be frustrating but justice is rarely easy. After all, the United Nations was born in the rubble of World War II, which followed the first world war by less than two decades. It is a grim reminder of the stakes — and the possibilities.

(970 words)

13
- focus on ... …への集中
- misplaced 見当違いの
- myriad 無数の
- specific 具体的な
- A, if not B A、ひょっとしたらB、B とは言わないまでもA
- be immune to ... …に影響されない
- geopolitical 地政学的な
- paralysis 停滞、まひ
- capture とらえる
- ground level work 基礎固めの作業・活動
- far more likely to *do* ～する可能性がはるかに高い
- escape 免れる

14
- substantive かなりの
- obstacle 障害
- insist on ... …を主張する
- prevail 優勢である
- shape 方向付ける
- hold A to B AをBに当てておく
- scrutiny 監視
- prefer 好む
- ruthlessness 冷酷さ
- expose 暴く
- for what it is 真の姿で、あるがままに

15
- justice 正義
- rubble 荒廃
- two decades 20年
- grim 厳しい
- reminder 思い起こさせるもの

ウクライナ侵攻 ❶ **Unite to protect Ukraine and the global order**

Like his fellow nationalists, Putin believes that Ukraine is not a real state but is an integral part of the Russian motherland. According to that logic, <u>any demand by it, or another similarly situated county — i.e., a former Soviet republic — for autonomy from Russia</u> must be the product of foreign subversion. **(Paragraph 5、1〜5行目)**

[名詞句の解析] any demand by it の it がウクライナを指すことがわかれば、その後の等位接続詞 or は it「ウクライナ」と another similarly situated country「ほかの同様の立場の国」を並列したものであることが理解できる。この2つは demand「要求」の主体を表現している。では「要求」の対象は何かという視点を持っておくと、ダッシュ（―）で囲まれた挿入部分の後に登場する for autonomy を見た時点で、これを demand と結び付け、demand for autonomy from Russia「ロシアからの自律を求める要求」とスムーズに解釈できる。

....

Intelligence officials reportedly believe Putin has not made a decision on how to proceed and will likely wait a few weeks before doing so. <u>Weighing heavily on his thinking are the upcoming Beijing Winter Olympic Games.</u> **(Paragraph 8、1〜4行目)**

[分詞句＋be＋Sの倒置] 下線部を Weighing heavily on his thinking という動名詞句を主語とする文だと考えてはいけない。be 動詞が are となり複数名詞に一致していることからも、この文の主語は後半の the upcoming Beijing Winter Olympic Games であり、「分詞句＋be＋S」という通常の語順と異なる倒置構文が用いられていることがわかる。プーチン大統領が出方を決めずに様子を見ているという直前の文の内容を受け、その既出情報と結び付きの強い his thinking「プーチン大統領の考え」を軸に、新たな情報である Beijing Winter Olympic Games「北京冬季オリンピック」という要因を文章中に導入する形である。

ウクライナ侵攻 2 Hold Russian soldiers and their leaders accountable for war crimes

Evidence is being collected by human rights groups, media organizations, independent observers, as well as governments and international institutions like NATO — and private satellite imagery has proven false Moscow's claims that bodies were planted after the withdrawal of its forces. (Paragraph 11、1〜5行目)

[Oの後置（SVCO）] 下線部の述語であるhas proven false Moscow's claims ...の部分について、falseをMoscow's claimsにかけて考え、「誤ったモスクワの主張を証明した」と解釈しないように。ここは、has proven (V) Moscow's claims that ... its forces (O) false (C)が基本にあり、そこから長い修飾語句を伴う名詞句のOが後置され、has proven (V) false (C) Moscow's claims that ... its forces (O)という形になったもの。SVOCの文のOが重い名詞句の場合に、Oを後置してSVCOの語順とするのはよくあるパターンである。

The only way that Putin and those around him face justice will be if they are turned over to a court by other Russians. That is possible only if pressure is intensified and the costs of refusal become too painful. (Paragraph 16)

[特殊なbe動詞の構文] ポイントは後半のif節の解釈である。be動詞の後ろにあるから「…かどうか」を意味する名詞節だと考えてしまうと意味がわからなくなる。ここで用いられているbe動詞はIt is ... that 〜の分裂文（強調構文）のbe動詞と同タイプのやや特殊なbeで、後ろに副詞的な要素も持ってくることができる。したがって、このif節は副詞節で「…する場合、…するケース」というくらいの意味に解釈できる。The only way that ... will[would] be if 〜 は「唯一…することがあるとすれば、〜する場合だ」という感じの訳がうまく当てはまることが多い。

The war has given policymakers and publics reason to believe that a nuclear arsenal contributes to national security. <u>If those conclusions go unchallenged, nuclear proliferation is likely to follow. Nothing could be more dangerous.</u> (**Paragraph 2**)

[goの使い方と比較構文] 下線部の2文にそれぞれポイントがある。第1文ではif節のgo unchallengedの部分。「…の状態のままである」を表す動詞としてはremainが有名だが、unnoticed, unchallenged, unrecognizedなどが後に続く場合、goを動詞に用いて、「気づかれないまま、異議を唱えられないまま、認識されないまま、進んでいってしまう」というニュアンスを表すことが多い。第2文はmore dangerousの後にthan thisを補って考え、「これほど危険なこともないだろう」と正しく理解すること。この場合、thisはもちろん直前の文の内容を指す。

Those remarks were only the most recent signs of Kim's determination to not only acquire, but hone, a nuclear capability. <u>North Korea has conducted 13 missile tests this year — a record — including in March what is thought to have been an ICBM capable of hitting any target in the United States.</u> (**Paragraph 10**)

[whatの使い方] 下線部の後半のincludingに続くwhat節に注意。この種のニュースでは日本語のメディアなどでも断定を避けるため「ミサイル<u>と見られる飛翔体</u>」といったぼかした言い方をされることが多いが、英語のメディアでも同様でwhat節を使った遠まわしな言い方が頻出する。パターンとしては、what is thought to be ...「…だと思われるもの」、what appear(s) to be ...「…と見られるもの」、what <u>人</u> claim to be ...「<u>人</u>が…だと主張するもの」などがある。

The stakes have only gotten higher following Russian President Vladimir Putin's remarks this week that his country "would use all the instruments at its disposal to counter a threat against its territorial integrity," a not-so-subtle reference to his readiness to use nuclear weapons if he felt a need to do so. (Paragraph 8、1〜5行目)

［名詞句による同格語］followingの後に続く名詞句が複雑で、全体が非常に息の長い文になっている。下線部のa not-so-subtle reference ...「必要を感じれば核兵器を用いる準備があるということをあからさまに示唆したもの」は、直前のthat節で表現されているプーチン大統領の言葉「領土の一体性が脅かされるなら使える手段はすべて行使する」を言い換えた同格語。このように前に出てきた節や述語の内容を名詞句の形で受けるパターンは時事英文で頻出の表現法で、本書のほかの記事にも見られるので注意してみよう。

Even if they don't prevail today, they shape the debate and hold to international scrutiny those who prefer a world in which power determines outcomes. (Paragraph 14、4〜6行目)

［Oの後置］下線部は、hold O to international scrutinyのOに当たる名詞句those who ... outcomesが長く重いために後置され、hold to scrutiny Oという形になったもの。「ウクライナ侵攻」2本目で確認したSVOC→SVCOの後置と原理としては同様の現象である。hold ... to international scrutinyは「…を国際社会の目を通じて厳しく監視する」という意味。a world in which power determines outcomesは直前の文のa world of equality, democracy and a world governed by rulesという表現との対比で用いられていることを理解したい。

世界はウクライナと国際秩序を守るために団結せよ

1　西側諸国は、30年前に冷戦が終結して以来、ロシアとの関係で最大の危機に直面している。

2　ロシアがウクライナとの国境に10万人を超える軍隊を集結させたことで、ヨーロッパ大陸で大規模な地上戦が起きる見込みが強く現実味を帯びてきた。ロシア政府は、米国をはじめとする西側諸国政府に対して多項目にわたる要求リストを提示したが、ロシアのウラジーミル・プーチン大統領にとって、要求の核心は単純だ。ロシアには、ほかのすべての国家の利害よりも自らの利害を優先させられる勢力範囲を持つ権利がある、という主張である。彼の考えでは、唯一そうした取り決めだけが、プーチンが自国にふさわしいと考える安全保障と地位を与えてくれるらしい。

3　このような要求は不当である。すべての国には安全保障を確保する権利があるが、ほかの国の主権を犠牲にして手にするものではない。プーチンが求めているのは、国際秩序のルールを書き換えることにほかならない。国際社会は彼に抵抗していかなければならない。

4　プーチンは、西側諸国の影響力がロシアの国境に向かって着実に東へと拡大していることに憤り、緩衝地帯を作り出そうと画策してきた。その地帯の国々の政府がプーチンに抵抗すれば、プーチンはそれらを潰そうとする。ウクライナの場合、同国政府が西側諸国との連携を強めていったことが引き金となり、プーチンは2014年にクリミアをロシアに再編入し、さらにウクライナ東部の政情不安をあおり、隙あれば同地域の分離独立を画策している。

5　プーチンは、彼と同類の国家主義者同様に、ウクライナは現実の国家ではなく、ロシア本国と不可分な、同国の一部であると信じている。その論理からすれば、ウクライナ、あるいは同様の立場にあるその他の国——すなわち以前ソビエト連邦を構成していた国々——がロシアからの自律を要求してきたとすれば、それは外国からの破壊工作の産物であるに違いない、となる。実際にロシア人の間では、そうした国々はロシアを包囲し、孤立させ、最後にはロシアの息の根を止める陰謀に加担しているという考えが蔓延しているのだ。

6　12月、ロシアは米国と北大西洋条約機構（NATO）に対して、相手国（ロシア）にとって脅威と考えられうる地域への軍隊、ミサイルシステム、航空機、軍艦の配

備に、法的拘束力のある制限を課すことを求める2つの条約案を提示した。この提案は、今後NATOの中・東欧諸国へのいかなる拡大も停止するよう求めているだけでなく、NATO加盟国と非加盟国の境界線を1990年代時点まで戻すことを要求している。その提案は、これらの国々が自衛のために西側から武器を購入する権利さえも否定するものとなっていた。

7 米国とその同盟国はこれらの要求を即座に拒否し、核軍縮や軍事演習の制限といったほかの問題についての交渉を提案した。ロシア政府側も同様にすぐさまその提案返しを拒否し、ロシアにとっての「本題」、すなわち同国のセルゲイ・ラブロフ外相が強調するところによると、ロシアを脅かしかねないNATOの「東方へのさらなる拡大と攻撃兵器の配備」に議論を絞るよう要求した。プーチン大統領の代弁者である同外相は、「楽観できる根拠はあまりない」とぶっきらぼうに言ったという。

8 伝えられるところによると、諜報機関の関係者は、プーチンがこの先どう進めるかはまだ決断しておらず、おそらくは2、3週間待って決断を下すだろうと考えている。近々開催される冬季北京オリンピックがプーチンの考えに大きく影響している。いかなるものであれ軍事的な行動を起こせば五輪に水を差すことになり、プーチンの大事な外交同盟相手であり相棒である中国の習近平国家主席の怒りを招くことになる。

9 当面優先されるべきは、ロシアが紛争を選択した場合に確実に報いを受けさせられるような、西側諸国の共同戦線を構築することである。平和を乱し、ヨーロッパを不安定に陥れ、国際秩序に喧嘩を売ったことに対して、ロシアも、プーチンも、そしてプーチン以外の主要な高官も罰を受ける必要がある。ウクライナには自衛手段が提供されるべきだ。そのような兵器がロシアの脅威になるという主張は荒唐無稽である。戦闘を起こす決定の背後にいる個々人に加え、ロシア経済の主要部門に対してもダメージを与える制裁措置を準備する必要がある。もしロシア政府が戦争を選択した場合にどのような結果が生じるか、疑問の余地がないようにしなければならない。

10 プーチンは、西側諸国の間で意見の一致も歩調を合わせた行動も不可能であると高をくくっている。どうやら彼はNATOという大西洋をまたいだ同盟は分裂しており、西欧諸国が国境を接する中・東欧諸国を守ろうとすればその利益が脅かされうる場合、中・東欧諸国の主権に対してNATOが実質的に関与してくることはないと考えているようである。プーチンは、特に自分の国が西欧諸国に供給するエネルギー資源に関しては、自分は相手を従わせられるカードを持っていると確信している。

世界はウクライナと国際秩序を守るために団結せよ

11 日本は、起ころうとしている紛争に関してこれまであまり目立った態度は示してこなかった。先週のビデオ会議で、岸田文雄首相とジョー・バイデン米大統領はロシアのウクライナに対する侵略行為を抑止するために緊密に連携していくと述べ、岸田首相は、いかなる攻撃に対しても米国やほかの友好国、そして国際社会と緊密に連携して強い行動をとっていくことを約束した。また先週、日本とフランスの外務・防衛担当大臣が２プラス２会合において、ウクライナの主権と領土の保全を全面的に尊重することを再確認した。

12 実際のところ、日本がウクライナ国内で、あるいはウクライナについてできることは、外交的支援を示すことと、西側諸国の決意と結束を明確にすることを除けば、あまり多くはない。ただ、日本がウクライナの問題に関わることは、ヨーロッパ諸国にインド太平洋地域の安全保障に参加するよう呼びかけることに匹敵する意味合いを持っており、これからも積極的に行っていくことを目指していかなければならない。

13 今回の危機的状況が生み出す結果は、ほかのすべての国と同様、日本にも影響を与える。プーチンは、国際政治の最も基本的なルールである「国家間の対等性」を書き換えようとしている。プーチンの世界では、対等な権利を持っている国とそうでない国があり、一等国の要求や懸念はほかのすべての国よりも優先されるべきものとなっている。彼の要求に屈服することは、ヨーロッパ内のパワーバランスを変容させるだけでなく、中国が行ってくるであろう主張に対して前例を作ることになってしまう。

14 もしそのような世界が現実のものとなってしまえば、日本は今よりも主権、独立性、そして自由がない国になってしまうだろう。それは受け入れられるものではない。

（訳・注　小川）

ロシア兵とその指導者に戦争犯罪の責任を負わせよ

1　その映像は凄惨で、身の毛もよだち、紛れもないものであった。

2　ロシアによるウクライナ侵攻中に戦争犯罪が行われており、証拠の量、それが国内各地で見つかっていること、そしてロシアの過去の行動から判断すると、残虐行為と違法行為はどうやら計画的な政策のように思われる。

3　日本政府は当然ながらこれらの行為を戦争犯罪と見なし、それらを糾弾するとともに、法の裁きを求めた。それは容易なことではないが、説明責任の追及は計画的かつ断固としてなされなければならない。犯人たちは発見され、罰せられなければならない。

4　その支配下にあった地域からロシア軍部隊が撤退するのに合わせて、恐ろしい残虐行為の証拠が増えつつある。今週の国連安全保障理事会での演説の締めくくりに、ウクライナのウォロディミル・ゼレンスキー大統領は国内各地の町におけるウクライナ一般市民の死体をとらえた短い映像を流した。ウクライナ政府は、ブチャの町ではロシア軍によって少なくとも300人の一般市民が拷問を受けて殺害されていて、これははるかに大規模で残虐的な軍事作戦の一部にすぎないと主張した。

5　映像は気分を悪くさせるような内容である。後ろ手に縛られて後頭部に一発の銃創がある人もいれば、両目を撃ち抜かれている人もいる。死体は切断され、焼かれていた。集団墓地もある。強姦や拷問の報告も複数ある。

6　この蛮行はこれまでにほかの場所でも見られた。たとえば、ロシア軍はシリア内戦中に一般市民を標的にしたとして告発された。国連人権理事会は2020年の報告書で、シリアでの一般市民を標的にした無差別攻撃は「戦争犯罪に相当する」としてロシア空軍を非難した。人権団体はジョージアやチェチェンでの戦争犯罪でもロシア軍を非難してきた。

7　松野博一官房長官はそうした行為を「戦争犯罪」と呼んだ。岸田文雄首相も同様にきっぱりと、一般市民の殺害は「非人道的な行為で国際法に違反しており、決して許すことはできない」と語った。

ロシア兵とその指導者に戦争犯罪の責任を負わせよ

8 NATOのイェンス・ストルテンベルグ事務総長は、NATOがブチャやほかのウクライナの都市で行われた戦争犯罪について信頼できる証拠を持っていると語った。アントニー・ブリンケン米国務長官はロシアによる戦争犯罪の報告を「十分に信頼に足る」と評し、「殺害、拷問、強姦、残虐行為のための意図的な作戦で……証拠は世界の誰の目にも明らかだ」と付け加えた。

9 ロシアは嫌疑を否定している。ワシリー・ネベンジャ国連大使は、ロシア軍は一般市民を標的にしていないと述べた。セルゲイ・ラブロフ外相は証拠を「フェイク」で「でっちあげ」だとはねつけ、ほかのロシア政府高官も非難はロシアの信用を失墜させるための「途方もない捏造」だと評した。

10 ゼレンスキー氏は、ロシアの戦争犯罪を調査して訴追するためにニュルンベルク裁判のような裁判を開くよう国連に要請し、またそのような行為を犯すようにと命令を発した、あるいはそれらを実行したすべての人間に対する法の裁きを求めた。ハーグにある国連の法的機関、国際刑事裁判所(ICC)は、3月に戦争犯罪の可能性があるとして調査を開始した。

11 証拠は各国政府やNATOのような国際機関のほか、人権団体、報道機関、独立系の監視団によって収集されている――また、民間の衛星画像は、死体が軍の撤退後に置かれたというロシア政府の主張が虚偽だということを証明した。G7外相会合は木曜日(4月7日)、各国政府がICCを支援すると表明した。

12 これから先、訴追が行われるのは確実だろう。それでも、被告人を発見して彼らに責任を負わせるとなると話は別である。犠牲者の数が多く、しかも部隊が頻繁に入れ替わるため、残虐行為の責任を負うべき兵士たちをとらえることは運次第という場合がしばしばだ。一般市民にテロ行為を働くという政策が実際に存在しているとすれば、身柄の拘束と裁判のリスクを減らすために部隊を移動させる動機がよりいっそう大きくなることだろう。

13 指揮系統の上にいる、命令を発した者たちは、引き金を引いた者たちと同罪だが、彼らを発見するのはさらに困難だろう。戦時国際法の「意図的な」違反が立証される必要がある。無差別な暴力行為を認める政策は証明が難しい。高官たちは指揮系統の下で起きていたことは知らなかったと主張できる。

14 ロシア政府の最上位の人間、つまりウラジーミル・プーチン大統領、ラブロフ外相、もしくはセルゲイ・ショイグ国防相を告発することは究極の難題である。米国のジョー・バイデン大統領はプーチン氏を「責任を問われるべき」人物で、「戦争犯罪人」と呼んだ。プーチン氏が戦争犯罪について知っていたと証明することは極めて難しいだろう。犯罪組織のトップがそうした命令を直接伝えることはめったにない。目配せやうなずきで意図を伝えるが、確実に否認できるようなやり方をとる。

15 プーチン氏をウクライナに対する「侵略戦争」を引き起こした罪に問うことはおそらく可能だろう。これは国連憲章およびICCの規則に従うと明らかな国際法違反に当たる（ただし、ロシアは2016年にICCを脱退した）。

16 プーチン氏とその周囲の人間に法の裁きを受けさせる唯一の方法は、彼らがほかのロシア人の手によって司法の場に引き渡される場合だろう。圧力が強化され、拒否の代償があまりにも痛みを伴うものになる場合にのみ、それは起こりうる。

17 岸田氏は「戦争犯罪を決して許さないというわれわれの決意」を示すために、日本が米国やほかの先進経済国と協調して追加の制裁を実施すると語った。ヨーロッパはロシアからのエネルギー供給の輸入を停止する方向に近づきつつあり、これはロシア経済にとって大きな打撃になるだろう。ただし、その限界点は大きく遅れるかもしれない。プーチン氏はこれをロシアにとっての生存戦争と見なしていて、制裁はその主張を補強している。

18 それでもなお、たとえ法の裁きが下される見込みが小さいとしても、われわれは試みなければならない。幸いにも、戦争犯罪に時効は存在しない。また、期待していい理由もある。それぞれセルビア、リベリア、コートジボワールの元大統領だったスロボダン・ミロシェヴィッチ、チャールズ・テイラー、ローラン・バグボといった指導者たちは、いずれも結局はICCの被告席に座ることになった。そのことは、われわれが説明責任への取り組みを明確に示す形で行動しなければならないことを意味する。

19 いつも通りのやり方はありえない。ウクライナで起きたことはあまりにもあからさまで、あまりにも恐ろしい。行動を怠れば、この暴挙――この非人道的行為――が繰り返されることになるだろう。　　　　　　　　　　　　　　（訳・注　桑田）

ウクライナ戦争から誤った核の教訓を学ぶ

1 ロシアのウクライナ侵攻がもたらした多くの不穏な遺産の中でも、最も警戒するべきことの一つは核兵器の実用性が確認されたと思われたことである。

2 この戦争は政策立案者らと国民に対して、核兵器の備蓄が国の安全保障に貢献すると信じる理由を与えた。そうした結論が疑問を持たれないままになれば、核の拡散がそれに続くことになるだろう。それ以上に危険なことはない。

3 核の影がウクライナ戦争に暗雲を投げかけてきた。侵攻の何週間も前に、ロシアは核戦力の大演習を実施し、それがウクライナとの国境への軍の動員と重なった時、そのことは総力を結集して戦うというロシア政府の姿勢を示した。侵攻が始まった直後、ロシアのウラジーミル・プーチン大統領は、自国の「抑止力」——核兵器——を「特別な警戒態勢」に置き、西側諸国による介入は「これまでに一度も見たことのない結果」につながるだろうと警告した。

4 ほかのロシア政府高官も自国の核の選択肢を強調した。国家安全保障会議のドミトリー・メドヴェージェフ副議長は世界に対して、ロシアの政策は通常兵器のみを使用する敵への核攻撃を認めていると念を押した。彼はまた、「われわれの国、およびその独立へのいかなる侵害に対しても相応の対応を与える用意がある」と付け加えた。

5 ロシアのセルゲイ・ラブロフ外相は、核戦争のリスクは今や「とても、非常に大きく、軽視されるべきではない」と述べる一方、セルゲイ・ショイグ国防相は核の「準備を整えること」が優先事項だと語った。ロシアは世界最大の核兵器の備蓄——約6,000発の弾頭——を有するため、そうした発言は真剣に受け止められなければならない。

6 ロシアがそのような兵器の使用に訴える可能性がある——自国の独立もしくは主権が脅かされる可能性があり、それを理由に核使用を正当化する——という考えは、馬鹿げているが同時にぞっとするものだ。兵器の備蓄と、これまでの戦局を通じてずっと明らかだった政府首脳の妄想力は、そうした警告が無視できないことを意味している。

7 脅しにはある程度の効果があった。核使用へと拡大していく可能性があることは、西側諸国が戦争により深く介入するのを控えさせた。自分たちの直接関与がプー

チン氏を恐ろしい決断に追い込みかねないと西側政府が信じているなら、彼らが抑止されたと主張しないことは難しい。

8 そのことが、この戦争を注視する他国の政府が学ぶであろう教訓になるのは確かだ。西側諸国が抑止されたのであれば、そうした国々は米国による安全保障の価値に疑問を抱くことだろう。核兵器を放棄するというウクライナの1994年の決定——ソビエト連邦が崩壊した後、ウクライナはソ連の核兵器の約3分の1を保有していた——は間違っていたのではないかと考えるだろう（発射コードがなかったので、そうした兵器の実用性は疑わしかった）。その論理はウクライナ副首相の外交政策顧問を務めるスヴィトラーナ・ザリシュク氏によって支持されていて、彼女は核兵器を放棄したことは誤りだったと語っている。

9 北朝鮮の金正恩最高指導者はウクライナの経験から何も学ばないだろう。むしろ、それは自身の——彼の父および彼の祖父の——核兵器の追求がずっと正しい戦略だったと裏付けるだろう。北朝鮮は政権の存続を確かなものにするために一貫して核兵器を保有しようとしてきた。今週の軍事パレードで演説した金氏は、「いかなる勢力であってもわが国の根本的な利益を侵害しようと試みるなら、われわれの核戦力は想定されていない2つ目の使命を断固として果たさなければならないだろう」と警告した。さらには、軍は「その特有の抑止力をいかなる時でも稼働させるために（中略）完璧に準備が整った状態にしておかねばならない」と述べた。

10 そうした発言は核能力を手に入れるだけでなく、それに磨きをかけるという金氏の強い決意を示す最新の兆候にすぎない。北朝鮮は今年、最多記録となる13回のミサイル発射実験を実施していて、その中には3月に行われた、米国内のいかなる目標にも到達可能なICBMと見られるものも含まれる。

11 北朝鮮が2017年に自主的な一時停止を宣言してから初めてとなる核実験を間もなく実施するとの兆候もある。実験は、金氏が2021年1月の演説で明らかにした「超現代的な戦術核兵器」を開発するという目的を実現させるために必要なものだと考えられる。

12 これについて「安心感を与えるような」説明は、金氏がジョー・バイデン米大統領を動かせずにいる自分にいら立ち、大統領に対して北朝鮮にもっと注意を払わせようとしている、というものだ。金氏は米国政府が北朝鮮を外交上優先し、その地位を回復させ、同国の懸念事項に対応してほしいと望んでいる。非核化への真摯な歩みを要求するバイデン氏の政策を金氏は「狭量なトリック」だとして相手にせず、自国に対して「長期的な対立」に備えるよう命じた。韓国での保守的な大統領の選

ウクライナ戦争から誤った核の教訓を学ぶ

出、韓国政府内の革新勢力の味方を失ったこと、そして来るべきバイデン氏のアジア歴訪が相まって、行動を起こさねばという金氏の決意を後押ししている。

13 より不安感を与えるような説明としては、金氏がおそらくウクライナの経験を参考にして、核能力についてより広い視野で考えているというものだ。この場合、西側政府が控えめな反応によってロシアに示した配慮が、北朝鮮の指導部に対して核兵器の抑止力よりも抑圧力——敵対国を意のままに屈服させるための力——を重視するよう促したことになる。一部の専門家が同国での「最初の戦術核兵器発射システム」の可能性があると考える4月の短距離ミサイル発射実験に金氏が立ち会っていたことは、この見解に信憑性を与える。

14 金氏の論理——および彼と同じように考える人たち——は2つの論点で間違っている。第一に、核兵器を誤って評価している。韓国と日本はウクライナとは異なり、米国の核の傘で明確に守られた条約同盟国である。米国を攻撃できる能力は、核兵器を使うことすらなく北朝鮮を完膚なきまでに破壊できる米国の能力を考慮すると、ほとんど意味がない。

15 第二に、彼らはそれらの兵器を手に入れるための代償を認識できていない。国際的な約束に背き、国際法に違反しながらの核能力の追求は、金氏と彼の国を無法者として確立させる。それに続く制裁と疎外化——プーチン氏とロシアが今それを実感し始めている——は、核兵器は国の安全保障を確かなものにするのではなく、それを危険にさらすという証拠になるだろう。

(訳・注　桑田)

岐路に立つ国連

1 国連がもしその有用性を発揮すべき時があるとすれば、それは加盟国がほかの加盟国に侵略され、その結果、国連システムの礎であるルールに基づいた国際秩序が脅かされていると考えられた時だろう。

2 しかし国連はぐらついており、加盟国や自らの機構そのもの、あるいはこの機構に意義と目的をもたらしている秩序を守る行動をとれないでいる。

3 岸田文雄首相は今週開かれた国連総会での演説で、国連の無力さを非難し、構造改革を訴えた。日本の首相がこのような主張をするのは初めてではないが、今ほど危機的で緊急性の高い時期だった例は少ない。

4 「国連憲章とそれが掲げる理想は危機にさらされている」というアントニオ・グテーレス国連事務総長の警告はもっともだ。年次総会の開会式で氏は「巨大な世界的機能不全」を嘆いたが、その原因はウクライナ戦争だけではない。戦争が引き起こしたインフレや、それに伴う世界的な食糧危機も包含する。気候変動が深刻化し、恐ろしい影響を及ぼしているにもかかわらず、対処できていないことも含まれる。人為的あるいは自然の原因が引き金となった、人々の大移動もある。不平等の拡大がその他あらゆる問題の影響を悪化させている状況もそうだ。

5 どの問題も、前例もなく予期できなかった、というものではない。われわれはその進行を見てきた。その拡大を許してきたのだ。グテーレス氏の結論は、否定しがたい。いわく、「まさに人類の未来と私たちの地球の運命を脅かしている」にもかかわらず、「国際社会には、私たちが生きる時代の非常に大きな課題に取り組む準備ができておらず、率先して取り組もうともしていない」。

6 岸田氏ら改革派にとって極めて重要な第一歩は、国連安全保障理事会の改革だ。国連安保理は国際秩序の混乱に対する防波堤の役割を担っているが、常任理事国5カ国の権限によってむしろ無力化している。拒否権を持っていることで、各々が自らの国益を損ねると見なす行動を許さないのだ。

7 したがって現在、ロシアは、自国が行った主権国家への侵攻を止めようとする動きを阻むことが可能で、またそうしてきた。岸田氏は、明らかな不正行為を前にこのまま行動を起こさなければ、「国連憲章の理念と原則を踏みにじり」、「国連の信頼性は危機に陥る」と警告した。さらに、今回の無茶な国際法違反は別の場所

岐路に立つ国連

で同様の行動をもくろむ、ほかの政府のタガを外してしまう恐れがある。フランスのエマニュエル・マクロン大統領も国連における演説で、世界は「主権と安全が武力、つまり軍隊の規模によって決定される」恒久的な紛争の時代に近づいていると厳然たる姿勢で警告した。

8 今週のロシアのプーチン大統領の発言を受けて、事態はより深刻となるばかりだ。ロシアは「領土保全が脅かされれば、持てるあらゆる手段を用いて対抗する」と、自身が必要だと思えば核兵器を使用する用意があることにあからさまに言及したのだ。このような核による脅迫は、到底容認できない。

9 だがこのような脅しは、独りよがりの歴史解釈と、ロシア帝国に対する常軌を逸した理想を原動力とした侵略が失敗した結果として考えれば、完全に予測できることだ。先月開催された核拡散防止条約（NPT）再検討会議が目に見える結果を残せず失敗に終わったことが、この脅迫を可能にしている。岸田氏は日本の首相で初めてこの会議に出席し、閉会時に共同声明の発表すらできなかったことをロシアの責任だと批判した。

10 核問題は岸田首相が熱意を注ぐ課題だ。第二次世界大戦で最初の原爆が投下された広島が選挙区である彼にとっては当然だろう。8月の演説で彼は「ヒロシマ・アクション・プラン」を発表、この構想は核の不使用・不拡散を強化し、核兵器の削減を促進し、兵器と関連物質の備蓄の透明性を高め、原子力の平和的利用を促すものだ。岸田氏は今週の総会で、「核兵器のない世界」のために闘い、「長崎を最後の被爆地とし続ける」と誓った。

11 国連改革を求める訴えの矛先は主に安全保障理事会に向けられている。提案されているのは、安保理の加盟国拡大、常任理事国の追加あるいは常任理事国5カ国の拒否権剥奪だ。しかし、どんな改革も手続き上のハードルが高い。国連憲章の改正には、常任理事国5カ国すべてを含む全加盟国の3分の2以上の批准が必要だ。

12 結局のところ、改革への望みは2つの単純な理由でかなえられていない。権限を持つ国がそれを手放すことを拒み、権限強化を求める国は二国間競争において不利益を被りたくないライバルに阻まれる。

13 多くの人にとっては、安全保障理事会に的を絞るのは見当違いなことだ。それよりも世界の何億、ひょっとしたら何十億という人々の日常生活に影響を及ぼす具体的な課題に取り組んでいる、国連システムの無数の機関に注意を向けるべきだろう。そういった機関は安保理がとらわれている地政学的な圧力や度重なる停滞と無縁ではないものの、草の根レベルの活動はそれらを免れる可能性がはるかに高い。

14 改革を阻む障害が多大であっても、望みを捨てねばならないわけではない。平等で民主主義の世界、そしてルールによって統治される世界を求める者は、自らが思い描く世界秩序を訴え続けるべきだ。たとえ今はかなわなくても、そういった人々が議論を方向付け、武力が結果を左右する世界を好む人々を国際的な監視下に置く。そうした人々が企てる秩序の冷酷さは、そのままの姿を白日の下にさらすべきである。

15 挫折感を抱くことになるだろうが、正義が容易に実現されることはまれだ。何といっても国連は、第一次世界大戦から20年もたたずに起きた第二次世界大戦の荒廃のさなかで生まれたのだ。国連の現状は、そこに懸かっているもの、およびその可能性について、厳しい現実を思い起こさせる。　　　　　（訳・注　宇都宮）

第 1 章 国際

9月19日、女王エリザベス2世の国葬が英国、ロンドンで執り行われた

An aging China poses new challenges

中国の高齢化がもたらす新たな課題

January 22, 2022　　　　　　　　　●Tracks 035-042 / 解説 p. 110、訳 p. 117

Track 035

1　China looks set to become the first country to get old before it gets rich.

2　Its declining birth rate looks almost impossible to reverse, a trajectory with profound implications for its economic and social prospects. The Chinese government is well aware of the problem and the dangers. Unfortunately, however, none of the responses looks like they will work.

Track 036

3　Japan too must be alert to the repercussions of China's aging. This country's experience with a graying population may provide some ways to work with its neighbor and ease the transition to a grayer society.

4　According to census data released earlier this week, China's birth rate fell for a fifth consecutive year to hit a record low in 2021. There were just 10.62 million births last year, according to China's National Bureau of Statistics, an 11.6% drop from 2020.

2021年、中国の出生数は5年連続で減少し、出生率は1949年の建国以来、最低となった。中国政府は少子高齢化に歯止めをかけようと対策を打ち出してきたが、功を奏していない。同じ問題を抱える日本や韓国と協力し、経済や社会への影響を抑えていく必要がある。

1
- ☐ [タイトル]pose 提起する
- ☐ look set to *do* 〜しそうである
- ☐ get old before it gets rich 未富先老→中所得国のまま高齢化が進むこと

2
- ☐ declining 減少している
- ☐ birth rate 出生率
- ☐ reverse 回復させる、逆転する
- ☐ trajectory 軌跡
- ☐ profound 深刻な
- ☐ implications 影響
- ☐ prospect 先行き
- ☐ well aware of ... …を十分承知して
- ☐ response 対応策

3
- ☐ alert 注意を払って
- ☐ repercussions 影響
- ☐ graying 高齢化の進む
- ☐ neighbor 隣国
- ☐ ease 緩和する
- ☐ transition 移行

4
- ☐ census 国勢調査
- ☐ release 発表する
- ☐ consecutive 連続した
- ☐ hit 記録する、…に達する
- ☐ record low 過去最低値
- ☐ National Bureau of Statistics 国家統計局

Track 037

5   While that is an improvement over the 18% fall from 2019 to 2020, it is still the lowest level since the founding of Communist China in 1949. Births outpaced deaths — barely — allowing the total population to increase by 480,000 to 1.4126 billion people. The country's natural growth rate has plunged to 0.034%; it was only lower during the Great Leap Forward, when tens of millions of people died as a result of Mao's disastrous economic policies.

6   Just 43% of the births were second children, a fall from 50% in 2017. Since a country needs a fertility rate (the average number of births per mother) of 2.1 to maintain the size of its population, China's rate of 1.3 in 2020 leads many demographers to believe that China's total population may have peaked.

Track 038

7   Even more ominous is the changing composition of the population. The share of working-age people under 60 has fallen from 70.1% a decade ago to 63.3% in 2020. Those aged 65 and older now constitute 13.5% of the total, up from 8.9%. The government predicts a loss of 35 million workers over the next five years and the share of working-age people could reach half the population by 2050.

8   This evolution will have powerful consequences. Wages will have to go up as the labor pool shrinks, payments to pension plans will decline and tax revenues will go down as demand for services rises. That last shift will be especially challenging. China today only spends about 7% of GDP on social welfare, substantially below the global average as calculated by the International Labor Organization, which is 12.8%. Even Brazil spends 17% of GDP on social welfare. Worse, it is estimated that the main pension fund for city dwellers could run out by 2035. Some experts fear social instability in a slowing economy.

5
- ☐ improvement 改善
- ☐ founding 設立
- ☐ Communist China 共産中国→中華人民共和国の俗称
- ☐ outpace 上回る
- ☐ barely かろうじて
- ☐ natural growth rate 自然増加率→出生率から死亡率を引いたもの
- ☐ plunge 急落する
- ☐ the Great Leap Forward 大躍進政策
- ☐ tens of millions 数千万
- ☐ Mao 毛沢東 (Mao Zedong) →中華人民共和国の初代国家主席
- ☐ disastrous 大失敗に終わった

6
- ☐ fertility rate 出生率→この場合は合計特殊出生率のこと
- ☐ per …につき
- ☐ maintain 維持する
- ☐ demographer 人口統計学者
- ☐ peak 頭打ちになる

7
- ☐ ominous 不穏な
- ☐ composition 構成
- ☐ decade 10年
- ☐ constitute 占める
- ☐ predict 予測する

8
- ☐ evolution 展開
- ☐ consequence 結果、影響
- ☐ wage 賃金
- ☐ labor pool 労働人口
- ☐ shrink 少なくなる
- ☐ pension plan 年金制度
- ☐ tax revenue 税収
- ☐ demand 需要
- ☐ challenging 厳しい
- ☐ GDP 国内総生産→gross domestic productの略
- ☐ social welfare 社会福祉
- ☐ substantially 大幅に
- ☐ average 平均
- ☐ calculate 計算する
- ☐ the International Labor Organization 国際労働機関
- ☐ estimate 推定する
- ☐ dweller 住民
- ☐ run out 底をつく
- ☐ social instability 社会不安

Track 039

9   Economists warn that China's plan to become "a rich and powerful country" by 2049, the 100th anniversary of the founding of the People's Republic of China, is imperiled. The International Monetary Fund has declared that China's economy is "unbalanced and momentum is slowing," and its shrinking workforce, declining productivity, the U.S.-China trade war and its decoupling from the international economy are all long-term threats to growth. The world must be ready for this adjustment in Chinese prospects, which has economic and military implications.

10   The reasons for the changing demographic structure are well known. Most fundamentally, as China develops, its citizens have better lives and better health care, allowing them to live longer. Families, and women in particular, are less inclined to have children. There are complaints about the costs of education — a big concern in a hypercompetitive child-rearing environment — and housing, the disproportionate burden born by women within the household, as well as fears that women lose opportunities for advancement when they take maternity leave.

Track 040

11   These issues prompted the government in 2016 to lift the "one-child policy," in force since 1980, and then last summer to allow families to have three children. The continuing decline in the birth rate shows that those moves had no impact. The recent crackdown on private education and the attempt to slow the rise in housing prices aim to ease the burden on families. More will be done. Housing subsidies, more generous maternity leave policies, increases in childcare centers and changes in income tax policies are being debated or attempted in pilot programs.

9
- [ ] warn …と警鐘を鳴らす
- [ ] ...th anniversary …周年
- [ ] imperil 危うくする
- [ ] the International Monetary Fund 国際通貨基金
- [ ] declare 発表する
- [ ] momentum 勢い
- [ ] decoupling 分断
- [ ] threat 脅威
- [ ] adjustment 変化

10
- [ ] fundamentally 根本的に
- [ ] in particular 特に
- [ ] be inclined to *do* ～する傾向がある
- [ ] complaint 不満
- [ ] concern 懸念
- [ ] hypercompetitive 競争の激しい
- [ ] child-rearing 子育ての
- [ ] disproportionate 過度の
- [ ] burden 負担
- [ ] bear 担う→bornは過去分詞形
- [ ] household 家庭
- [ ] advancement 昇進
- [ ] maternity leave 産休

11
- [ ] issue 問題
- [ ] prompt ... to *do* …に～させる
- [ ] lift 解除する
- [ ] in force 施行されて
- [ ] crackdown 取り締まり
- [ ] attempt 試み;試みる
- [ ] aim 目指す
- [ ] housing subsidies 住宅助成金
- [ ] generous 手厚い
- [ ] income tax 所得税
- [ ] pilot 試験的な

12 Three other changes are critical. The first is a redistribution of family responsibilities so that the mother's load is lightened. Both parents need to support the household. This should go hand in hand with workplace changes to better accommodate working mothers. A third step is last year's decision to raise the retirement age, a move that is politically charged.

Track 041

13 Still, most demographers believe these trajectories are nearly impossible to alter. Younger Chinese have ideas about "the good life" and having more children is not part of that vision.

14 Making a virtue of necessity, China's government last month unveiled a national plan to grow the country's robotics industry and upgrade equipment and processes in the manufacturing sector. Automation, powered by artificial intelligence, is intended to help address the country's productivity shortcomings and mounting demographic woes. It won't address the revenue issues, neither taxes nor pension payments.

Track 042

15 China's trajectory follows that of Japan. Currently, the pace of aging in China will overtake that in Japan in 2025; the share of the elderly in the total population will close in on that of Japan a decade later. The two countries have several bilateral forums in which demographics are discussed. They should do more to share their experiences addressing this transition. The potential range of conversations is vast, including national and local governments, businesses and civil society groups. South Korea is also experiencing the demographic trend and could join the discussions.

16 Aging has been part of the agenda at the trilateral summit. The urgency of this issue should demand more attention and spur more action. *(958 words)*

12
- [ ] critical 極めて重要な
- [ ] redistribution 再分配
- [ ] load 負担
- [ ] go hand in hand with ... …と並行する、連携する
- [ ] accommodate …に便宜を図る、適応させる
- [ ] retirement age 定年
- [ ] politically charged 政治がらみの

13
- [ ] alter 変える

14
- [ ] make a virtue of necessity せざるを得ないことを潔く行う
- [ ] unveil 公表する
- [ ] equipment 設備
- [ ] manufacturing sector 製造業
- [ ] power 推進する
- [ ] intended 意図された
- [ ] address …に対処する
- [ ] shortcomings 不足
- [ ] mounting 山積する
- [ ] woes 問題
- [ ] revenue 歳入

15
- [ ] overtake 追い越す
- [ ] the elderly 高齢者
- [ ] close in on ... …に近づく
- [ ] bilateral 二国間の
- [ ] potential 見込みのある
- [ ] range 範囲
- [ ] vast 幅広い
- [ ] civil society group 市民社会団体

16
- [ ] trilateral 三国間の
- [ ] urgency 緊急性
- [ ] demand attention 注目を要する
- [ ] spur 駆り立てる

Ukraine crisis pushes the world's hungry over the brink

ウクライナ危機が世界の飢餓を崖っぷちに追い込む

June 11, 2022　　　　　●Tracks 043-049 / 解説 p. 111、訳 p. 120

Track 043

1　The world is on the brink of a food crisis that could result in starvation for millions, unrest and mass migrations.

2　The immediate cause of this impending catastrophe is Russia's invasion of Ukraine and the resulting cutoff of their vital exports. That is not the entire story, however. Structural factors have exacerbated the shortages. All must be addressed to re-establish food security for those who will suffer despite no fault of their own. Most immediately, however, wealthy nations must accelerate efforts to get food into the hands of hungry populations around the world.

Track 044

3　Prior to the invasion, Ukraine and Russia were critical food exporters. As Hans-Werner Sinn wrote earlier this week, Ukraine accounted for 10% of global exports of wheat, 13% of barley, more than 50% of sunflower oil, 5% of rapeseed oil and 15% of corn. By one estimate, Russia and Ukraine accounted for 12% of all traded food calories; together they produce about 30% of global wheat exports. In addition, Russia is the world's largest producer of fertilizer.

小麦など穀物の生産・輸出大国であるロシアとウクライナ。欧米諸国による対ロシア禁輸措置やロシアによるウクライナの輸出港封鎖なども影響し、穀物価格が高騰した。加えて作物が特に飢えに苦しむ地域に届かず、世界全体の飢餓を加速する事態が起きている。

1
- [タイトル]push ... over the brink 崖から(奈落の底に)突き落とす
- [タイトル]the hungry → = hungry people
- on the brink of ... …の瀬戸際で
- starvation 飢餓

2
- immediate 直接の
- impending 差し迫った
- catastrophe 大惨事
- invasion 侵攻
- cutoff 途絶えること、途絶
- vital 極めて重要な、生命線の
- entire …全体
- structural 構造的な、元々ある
- exacerbate 悪化させる
- address …に対処する
- security 安全確保、安全保障→外交・軍事面での努力も含め主に外国から安定的に調達することを指す
- despite …にもかかわらず
- population 1つの国(・地域)の人々 →populations さまざまな国の人々

3
- prior to ... …以前は
- critical 極めて重要な
- Hans-Werner Sinn →ドイツの経済学者。IFO経済研究所所長
- account for ... …を占める
- barley 大麦
- sunflower ひまわり
- rapeseed 菜種
- food calorie カロリー数から見た食糧の量
- fertilizer 肥料

4   Production disruptions — or the threat of such interruptions — has pushed the U.N. Food and Agricultural Organization's global FAO food price index 30% higher year on year and 62% higher than in 2020 on average. The head of the World Food Program warns that 323 million people are "marching toward starvation," while the Red Cross anticipates that rising food prices will mean that 47 million people face acute hunger.

Track 045

5   If the prospect of mass starvation in distant countries is not horrific enough to motivate the world to take action, self-interest should. Hunger frequently leads to mass protest and instability. The Arab Spring was set off by skyrocketing food prices. Those conflagrations are seldom contained. It is estimated that every 1% increase in hunger leads to a 2% increase in migration.

6   The cause of this dangerous situation rests squarely on the shoulders of Russian President Vladimir Putin. The invasion of Ukraine is expected to cause a one-third reduction in its wheat production. A Russian naval blockade has prevented crops from being shipped; reportedly some 20 million tons of wheat is trapped in silos or on ships that cannot reach foreign markets. Grain storage facilities have been targeted for attack. There are reports of grain being stolen. U.S. Secretary of State Antony Blinken was succinct: "The Kremlin is exporting starvation and suffering well beyond Ukraine's borders."

Track 046

7   Putin counters that the West is to blame. He insists that the Western sanctions campaign prevents Russia from exporting its food and fertilizer. He is being disingenuous and trying to deflect attention for the many cruelties of his war.

4
- □ disruption 中断、途絶えること
- □ threat 恐れ、ネガティブな可能性
- □ interruption 中断、途切れ
- □ the U.N. Food and Agricultural Organization 国連食糧農業機関
- □ index 指数
- □ year on year 前年比で
- □ the World Food Program 世界食糧計画→必要とする食糧や発展の支援を飢餓に苦しむ国や被災国などに行う国連機関。2020年ノーベル平和賞受賞
- □ march toward ... …に突き進む
- □ the Red Cross 赤十字社→本来は戦争や災害時の傷病者救護支援を活動の中心とする世界的人道・医療支援組織
- □ anticipate 予想する
- □ acute 深刻な

5
- □ motivate ... to *do* …に～させる動機付けになる、…を～する気にさせる
- □ self-interest 私利私欲、個人の利害
- □ instability 社会の不安定、政情不安
- □ the Arab Spring アラブの春→2010～12年にかけアラブ諸国で広がった民主化などを求める反政府デモ・騒乱
- □ set off ... …の引き金となる
- □ skyrocket 高騰する
- □ conflagration 燃え広がり、運動拡大
- □ contain 封じ込める、抑え込む

6
- □ rest on the shoulders of ... …の責任・原因である
- □ squarely 間違いなく、まさに
- □ be expected to *do* ～することが予想されている
- □ one-third 3分の1の
- □ naval 海軍による
- □ blockade 封鎖措置、妨害
- □ ship 輸送する→現代では「船で輸送する」という意味に限らない
- □ reportedly 報道によると、伝えられているところでは
- □ some ... [数字の前で]約…
- □ trap 動かせない状態に置く
- □ grain 穀物
- □ Secretary of State 国務長官
- □ succinct 簡明・端的に表現した
- □ the Kremlin ロシア政府、ロシア中枢部
- □ suffering 苦しみ、困窮状態

7
- □ counter …と反論する
- □ the West 西側諸国
- □ ... is to blame …に責任がある
- □ sanction 制裁
- □ disingenuous 不誠実な、腹黒い
- □ deflect そらす
- □ cruelty 残虐行為

8   The loss of those two suppliers is enough to cause a global crisis. The shortages have been exacerbated, however, by other policies and practices. For example, land once used to grow food is increasingly devoted to the production of biofuels. It is estimated that 4% of the world's agricultural land is used for growing biofuels and 40% of U.S. corn production is used to make ethanol. Rising fuel prices have sparked a frantic search for alternative energy sources and those crops are increasingly attractive.

`Track 047`

9   The prospect of shortages has prompted some food exporters to hoard their supplies. A growing number of governments have cut off exports of staples like grains and cooking oil. The decision by Indonesia, the world's leading exporter of palm oil, to restrict shipments means that more than 40% of international vegetable oil sales are now off-limits. It is estimated that the war in Ukraine has prompted 23 countries to embrace food protectionism.

10   Then there is the spiraling inflation that is pushing up food prices, imperiling the lives of the world's poorest citizens. The World Bank reckons that already nearly 700 million people live in extreme poverty, or under ¥250 ($1.86) a day. For this swath of humanity, even tiny increases in the cost of food are life threatening.

`Track 048`

11   There are a number of steps that can be taken to ease this crisis. The first and most obvious is for Putin to quit holding the world hostage to his imperial dreams, to end the invasion or, at the very least, to allow Ukraine to resume shipments of grain and other food supplies. Even if Black Sea ports remain closed, alternative export routes should be opened as part of humanitarian aid and relief.

8
- [ ] supplier(s) 供給国→ロシアとウクライナのこと
- [ ] practice 行為、慣行
- [ ] once かつて
- [ ] be devoted to ... …の用途に充てられる
- [ ] biofuel バイオ燃料→バイオマス(動植物)を原料とする燃料。カーボンニュートラルで注目
- [ ] agricultural land 農地
- [ ] ethanol エタノール→工業原料や医療(消毒)用に加えバイオ燃料としても需要が高まっている
- [ ] spark …(ブームなど)に火をつける
- [ ] frantic 狂ったような、血まなこの
- [ ] search 探し求めること、争奪戦
- [ ] alternative 代替の、代わりとなる

9
- [ ] prompt ... to *do* …が〜する誘因となる
- [ ] hoard ためこむ、出し惜しみする
- [ ] supply (供給できる)在庫
- [ ] a growing number of ... *do* 〜する…がだんだん増えてきている
- [ ] cut off 絶つ、止める
- [ ] staple 主要産品、常食される食品
- [ ] palm oil ヤシ油、パーム油
- [ ] shipment 出荷
- [ ] off-limits 絶たれて(= inaccessible)
- [ ] embrace (方針・主義を)とる
- [ ] protectionism 保護主義

10
- [ ] then それに加えて
- [ ] spiral 急激に進行する
- [ ] imperil 危険にさらす
- [ ] citizen (一般)市民
- [ ] the World Bank 世界銀行→途上国に融資や資金援助、技術支援を行う国際金融・支援機関。特にグループ内の国際復興開発銀行と国際開発協会を指す
- [ ] reckon …と考える、見なす
- [ ] extreme 極度の
- [ ] swath of ... ある一定の数の…
- [ ] humanity 人間、人間性

11
- [ ] a number of ... いくつかの…
- [ ] take steps 手段を講じる
- [ ] ease 緩和する
- [ ] quit *doing* …することをやめる
- [ ] hold .. hostage …を人質にする
- [ ] imperial 帝国[他国侵略]主義的な
- [ ] at the very least 最低限でも
- [ ] Black Sea 黒海→ウクライナの南方
- [ ] humanitarian 人道(主義)的な
- [ ] relief 救済(措置)

12 Governments that have the mistaken impression that food protectionism provides them greater security need to be disabused of that idea. Local agricultural production has to increase. That means turning to new crops, perhaps genetically modified ones. And more has to be done to combat soil erosion and the reliance on fertilizer imports must also be reduced.

Track 049

13 Last month, the Group of Seven leading industrialized nations launched, with the World Bank, the Global Alliance for Food Security to "catalyze an immediate and concerted response to the unfolding global hunger crisis." This effort will accelerate and Japan should be ready to push it further when it takes the chair of the G7 next year.

14 Support must also be given to the other international organizations that have long fought hunger and promoted agricultural production, like the World Food Program, like the International Fund for Agricultural Development and like the Food and Agriculture Organization. They are on the front lines of the battle to prevent the Ukrainian crisis from becoming a global humanitarian catastrophe.

(887 words)

12
- ☐ disabuse A of B AからBという誤解を解く
- ☐ turn to ... …に切り替える
- ☐ genetically modified 遺伝子組み換えをした
- ☐ more has to be done = more effort should be made
- ☐ combat …に立ち向かう
- ☐ soil erosion 土壌侵食→風雨・洪水や乱開発で土壌が流出・失われること

13
- ☐ the Group of Seven ... nations 主要先進7カ国、G7
- ☐ the Global Alliance for Food Security →ロシアのウクライナ侵攻を受け今年6月のG7サミットに先駆けた会合で創設が打ち出された協調運動
- ☐ catalyze 促進する
- ☐ concerted 協調した、連携した
- ☐ unfolding 進行中の、拡大中の
- ☐ push ... further …を推し進める
- ☐ take the chair 議長（国）を務める

14
- ☐ promote 促進する、向上させる
- ☐ the International Fund for Agricultural Development 国際農業開発基金→途上国の農業生産拡大のための融資を行う国連機関
- ☐ the Food and Agriculture Organization 食糧農業機関→人類の飢餓からの解放と世界経済発展を目指す
- ☐ the front line （最）前線

Execution of Myanmar democracy activists reveals junta's true colors

ミャンマーの民主化運動家の処刑により露呈する軍事政権の本質

July 30, 2022　　　　　　　　●Tracks 050-056 / 解説 p. 113、訳 p. 123

Track 050

1　The military junta that rules Myanmar has again confirmed its brutality by executing four democracy activists.

2　Cloaked in opaque legal procedures, hidden not only from the public but also from the families of the accused, these are state-sanctioned murders. They prove once again the regime's utter disregard for human rights and the rule of law. They underscore the need for a united international response to these atrocities. The Myanmar government must be ostracized, isolated and sanctioned until it reverses course, releases its political prisoners and hands power to a duly elected government.

Track 051

3　Since seizing power in a coup on Feb. 1, 2021, rejecting the results of the November 2020 election that handed its political proxies a crushing defeat, Myanmar's military has waged a bloody war against democratic forces and a variety of militia groups. In February, the United Nations human rights office said that it had documented 1,500 people known to have been killed in protests against the coup, a death toll that does not include thousands more who have died as a result of ethnic violence. The U.N. spokesperson said that 200 of those deaths were "due to torture in military custody."

4　Nearly 12,000 others have been detained, of which 8,792 remain in custody. These arrests resulted from "voicing their opposition to the military, whether in peaceful protests or through online activities even."

▼ About This Editorial ▼

2015年、ミャンマーでは民主化を掲げアウン・サン・スーチー氏率いる国民民主連盟（NLD）が総選挙で圧勝し、2020年秋の選挙でも躍進。さらに民主化が進むと思われた。ところがその結果に納得しない軍部が翌年2月クーデターを決行、以降民主運動勢力や国民に対し残虐な殺戮行為を続け、圧政を敷いている。

1
- [タイトル]true colors 本性、本質
- [タイトル](military) junta 暫定（軍事）政権
- confirm 証明する、確信させる
- brutality 残忍性
- execute 処刑する

2
- cloak 隠す、秘密に包む
- opaque 半透明の、不透明な
- the accused 被告人、被告たち
- sanction 許可する、制裁を加える→まったく違う2つの意味に注意
- regime 政権
- utter まったくの
- disregard for ... …を無視すること
- rule of law 法の支配
- underscore …の重要性を明確にする
- atrocity 残虐行為
- ostracize （国際社会から）追放する
- isolate 孤立させる
- reverse course 方向転換する
- hand 手渡す、移譲する
- power 権力、政権
- duly 正当な手段で

3
- coup クーデター→発音は /kuː/
- hand A B AにBを下す・与える
- political proxy 政治代理人→軍部が推す候補者
- crushing 壊滅的な、惨敗の
- wage a war 戦争を仕掛ける
- bloody 残虐な、多数犠牲者の出る
- force 勢力
- militia （国の正規軍に対し）市民軍
- the United Nations human rights office 国連の人権機関→ここは国連人権高等弁務官事務所（OHCHR）を指す
- document 正式に把握する
- protest 抗議
- death toll 死者数
- thousands more さらに数千人の人
- ethnic （少数）民族に対する、民族主義的な
- spokesperson 広報官、報道官
- torture 拷問
- in military custody 軍による拘束中

4
- detain 拘留する
- of which ... その中で…が
- arrest 逮捕、拘束
- result from ... …が原因で起こる
- voice 表明する、…と声を上げる
- opposition 反対
- the military 軍部、軍事政権
- ... even ただ…（をしただけ）でも

71

Track 052

5 According to the Assistance Association for Political Prisoners, a nonprofit organization that tracks and attempts to verify the status of individuals detained by the junta, 117 people have been sentenced to death in Myanmar in the past year as well and as many as 40 face imminent execution.

6 The four killed last weekend included Phyo Zeya Thaw, a National League for Democracy lawmaker and hip-hop artist who had a strong following among the country's youth, and Kyaw Min Yu, a prominent pro-democracy activist known as Ko Jimmy. They were convicted of terrorism charges last year. The other two men, Hla Myo Aung and Aung Thura Zaw, were alleged to have been involved in the killing of a police informant.

Track 053

7 All the men were tried and sentenced to death in secret trials closed to the public and international observers. As yet more proof of the junta's inhumanity, the prisoners were allowed to speak to relatives last weekend for the first time in months but no one was told if or when the executions would occur. After the murders were announced, family members were not allowed to see or reclaim the bodies.

5
- [ ] the Assistance Association for Political Prisoners →ミャンマーの政治犯支援協会。亡命先での活動も盛んでタイのメイソットに拠点がある
- [ ] track 調査する、…の居所を突き止める
- [ ] verify 確認する
- [ ] sentence ... to death …に死刑判決を下す
- [ ] as many as ... …もの数の
- [ ] imminent 間近に迫った

6
- [ ] National League for Democracy 国民民主連盟（NLD）
- [ ] lawmaker （国会）議員
- [ ] following 支持、支持者数
- [ ] prominent 著名な
- [ ] pro-democracy 民主化推進派の
- [ ] convict A of B AにBの罪で有罪判決を下す
- [ ] charge 罪
- [ ] allege ... to have *done* （証拠はなく）…に～したとする疑いをかける
- [ ] be involved in ... …に関与する
- [ ] police informant 警察への情報提供者、密告者

7
- [ ] try 裁判にかける
- [ ] trial 裁判
- [ ] closed to ... …には非公開の
- [ ] observer 観察者、監視者
- [ ] as …として
- [ ] yet more ... さらなる…
- [ ] proof 証拠
- [ ] inhumanity 非人道性
- [ ] for the first time in ... …ぶりに
- [ ] if …かどうか
- [ ] the murders →4名の処刑を指す
- [ ] reclaim …の返還を要求する
- [ ] body 遺体

8　The killings have rightly received international condemnation. A joint statement released by Japan, Australia, Britain, Canada, New Zealand, Norway, South Korea, the United States and the high representative of the European Union called the executions "reprehensible acts of violence that further exemplify the regime's disregard for human rights and the rule of law." The signatories went on to "urge the regime to release all those unjustly detained, grant full and independent access to prisons" and to "end the use of violence, respect the will of the people and restore the country's path toward democracy."

Track 054

9　Foreign Minister Yoshimasa Hayashi said that Japan "deeply deplores" the actions by the military, expressed the nation's "deepest condolences" to the families of those who lost their lives following the coup and warned that the killings will "lead to deeper conflict due to the hardening of public sentiment and further isolation of Myanmar from the international community."

10　Even Southeast Asian nations, known for their reluctance to interfere in the internal affairs of neighboring states, have spoken out. Cambodian Prime Minister Hun Sen, chair of the Association of Southeast Asian Nations (ASEAN), last month sent a letter to military leader Min Aung Hlaing asking him not to carry out the executions.

8
- □ the killings →4名の処刑を指す
- □ rightly 当然
- □ condemnation (強い)非難
- □ joint statement 共同声明
- □ high representative 高位の代表者→ ここではEUの外相に当たる上級代表の こと
- □ reprehensible とがめるべき
- □ further 今まで以上に、さらに
- □ exemplify 例証する、…の一例となる
- □ signatory 署名者→共同声明参加国の こと
- □ go on to *do* さらに(進んで)~する
- □ urge ... to *do* …に~するよう強く促す
- □ release 釈放する
- □ unjustly 不当に
- □ grant 授ける、認める
- □ access to ... …に立ち入れる権利
- □ respect 尊重する
- □ will 意思
- □ restore 回復する、取り戻す
- □ path 道筋、方向性

9
- □ Foreign Minister 外務大臣
- □ deplore 嘆く、非難する
- □ express 表明する
- □ condolences 哀悼の気持ち、弔意
- □ following …以降
- □ deeper より深刻な、より根深い
- □ conflict 対立、(政府と民衆の)抗争
- □ hardening (態度などの)硬化
- □ public sentiment 国民感情
- □ isolation 孤立化

10
- □ Southeast Asian 東南アジアの
- □ reluctance to *do* なかなか~したがら ないこと、~に二の足を踏むこと
- □ interfere in ... …に干渉する
- □ internal affairs (各国の)内政(問題)
- □ neighboring 近隣の、国境を接する
- □ speak out 明確に態度を表明する
- □ chair 議長
- □ ASEAN 東南アジア諸国連合
- □ carry out ... …を実行する

Track 055

11   ASEAN's foundational principle of noninterference assumes that instability can be contained. Yet even Hun Sen, who rules his country with an iron fist, knows that the junta's policies will only further destabilize Myanmar. Already more than 275 militias operate across the country under the command of democratic forces; when combined with ethnic armies fighting for their rights, they control about half the country. The risk of violence spilling over borders is real.

12   The disregard for those pleas, the disdain for the rule of law and the denial of any humanity to the victims or their families are proof that Myanmar's junta understands only brute force. Condemnation is not enough. It is well past time for the community of nations to impose sanctions against the military government, its members and key supporters. These should bear the imprimatur of the United Nations to give them authority and legitimacy.

Track 056

13   Thus far, Japan has not adopted that hard line. Talk about a "rules-based order" in the Indo-Pacific is empty in this case, as the Japanese government ignores the blatant illegality that sustains military rule. Tokyo has tempered criticism of the junta, fearful that tough words would push it closer to China. There has been no pressure from Japan on the military regime or its enablers and no support for the shadow National Unity Government that is composed of the democratic forces opposed to the junta. This prevarication must stop.

11
- □ foundational principle 基礎的な原理
- □ noninterference 非干渉（主義）
- □ assume 前提とする、想定する
- □ instability 不安定、政情不安
- □ contain 抑え込む
- □ iron fist 鉄拳、暴力手段、圧政
- □ destabilize 不安定化させる
- □ operate 活動する
- □ command 指揮（系統）、命令
- □ spill over ... …からこぼれ出る、…を越えて広がる

12
- □ plea 嘆願、意思表示
- □ disdain for ... …を見下すこと
- □ denial of A to B Bに対してAを否定すること
- □ humanity 人道的な対応、人道主義
- □ brute force 残忍な暴力
- □ it is well past time for ... to *do* …が～する段階はとっくに過ぎている
- □ impose A against B BにAを課す
- □ supporter 支持者、支援国
- □ bear たずさえる、付与される
- □ imprimatur お墨付き、正式な認可
- □ authority 権威
- □ legitimacy 正当性

13
- □ thus far これまでのところ
- □ hard line 強硬路線
- □ rules-based ルール［国際法］に基づく
- □ Indo-Pacific インド太平洋地域
- □ empty 虚しい、意味のない
- □ blatant あからさまな
- □ illegality 違法性、法律無視
- □ sustain 存続させている
- □ military rule 軍事政権による支配
- □ Tokyo 日本政府
- □ temper 和らげる、抑える
- □ enabler それを可能にしている存在
- □ shadow 影の、非正規で組まれた
- □ National Unity Government (of Myanmar) （ミャンマー）国民統一政府
- □ prevarication 逃げ口上、弱腰の対応

14 Japan must join the chorus of condemnation. Then it should impose penalties on the government, its leaders and their top supporters. Myanmar should be denied arms and businesses tied to the rogue government should be sanctioned. Executions must be stopped and the junta compelled to hand power back to the rightfully elected stewards of the nation.

(909 words)

14
- □ chorus of ... 声を合わせた…
- □ deny A B A に B を与えない
- □ arms 武器
- □ business 企業
- □ tied to ... …と関係がある

- □ rogue ならず者の、非人道的な
- □ be compelled to ... …を余儀なくされる→直前の junta の後に must be が省略されている
- □ rightfully 正当な手順で
- □ steward 世話役、（政権の）担い手

Revered and reviled, Mikhail Gorbachev remade the world

称賛と非難をともに浴びたミハイル・ゴルバチョフ氏は世界を作り変えた

September 3, 2022　　　　　　　●Tracks 057-065 / 解説 p. 114、訳 p. 126

Track 057

1　Few people can claim to have truly changed the world.

2　Mikhail Gorbachev, the last leader of the Soviet Union, is on that short list. Gorbachev, who died this week at the age of 91, will be remembered by history as the man who ended the Soviet Union and the Cold War — and helped walk the world back from the brink of nuclear annihilation as a result.

Track 058

3　The latter was intended; the former was not. For those reasons, Gorbachev is revered around the world and reviled at home. Yet even foreigners must also recognize the unintended effects of his tenure. He provided a powerful lesson to autocrats about the consequences of reform and the apparent need to rule with an iron fist.

4　Ironically for a man who engineered the demise of his party and its system of governance, Gorbachev was a loyal communist. Despite firsthand knowledge of the excesses of the regime — not only did he witness the horrors of forced collectivization of farms but both grandfathers were persecuted by Stalin — he joined the party and rose through the ranks of the Komsomol, the Communist youth organization, attending university and studying law.

ソビエト連邦の最後の指導者だったゴルバチョフ氏は、冷戦を終結させた人物として、またソ連を崩壊させた人物として、故国の外と内で対照的な評価を受けた。当時を振り返っても、そして今なお残るその余波を見ても、彼が世界を変えた人物だったのは間違いない。

1
□ [タイトル]revere 称賛する、尊敬する
□ [タイトル]revile 非難する

2
□ walk A back from B AをBから引き戻す
□ brink 瀬戸際
□ annihilation 壊滅

3
□ the latter 後者→冷戦に幕を下ろしたこと
□ the former 前者→ソビエト連邦に幕を下ろしたこと
□ home 故郷、本国
□ unintended 意図しない
□ tenure 在任
□ autocrat 独裁者、専制君主
□ consequence 影響、結果
□ iron fist 鉄拳、暴力手段、圧政

4
□ ironically 皮肉にも
□ engineer もたらす
□ demise 終焉
□ party 政党
□ system of governance 統治体制
□ communist 共産主義者
□ firsthand 直接に、実体験からの
□ excess 行きすぎた行為
□ regime 体制、政権
□ forced 強制的な
□ collectivization of farms 集団農場化
□ persecute 迫害する
□ rise through the ranks of ... …で出世する
□ Komsomol →旧ソ連共産党の青年組織

Track 059

5	He began his political career in earnest in 1956, when he was named first secretary of the Komsomol for the Stavropol region. He performed well and eventually became party chief for the region. His job allowed him to interact with visiting Soviet leaders — many at the very top of the party — and they were very impressed with him. Key figures such as Mikhail Suslov, a top party official and ideological hard-liner, and KGB head and future Communist Party General Secretary Yuri Andropov became his patrons.

6	That performance and those contacts resulted in him being called back to Moscow in 1978, where he continued his ascent. He became the central committee secretary, a member of the party's most elite, and a full member of the Politburo in 1980. A generation younger than virtually all other members of the Politburo, he watched and waited as three other men — "one leader who was half dead, and another who was half alive, and another who could hardly speak" — held the country's top post and died in succession.

Track 060

7	Andrei Gromyko, the frosty foreign minister, assuaged whatever doubts his peers may have harbored about Gorbachev, telling them that he had "a nice smile, but he has iron teeth." More important than his dentistry was his vision. He saw clearly the flaws of the Soviet system and the rot that had penetrated its core.

8	Gorbachev knew firsthand the corruption that consumed the party and the way it demoralized the public, deprived the workforce of motivation and crippled the economy. His reformist zeal produced missteps, however, and the sheer size of the vested interests he challenged — 18 million party members alone — forced him to zigzag on policy, frustrating allies and confusing the public.

5
- ☐ in earnest 本格的に
- ☐ name A B AをBに指名する
- ☐ first secretary 第一書記
- ☐ eventually やがて
- ☐ interact with ... …と交流する
- ☐ be impressed with ... …に感銘を受ける
- ☐ figure 人物
- ☐ official 高官
- ☐ ideological イデオロギーの
- ☐ hard-liner 強硬派
- ☐ KGB →旧ソ連の国家保安委員会
- ☐ General Secretary 書記長
- ☐ patron 後援者

6
- ☐ contact 接点、関係
- ☐ result in him being called back to ... 彼が…へと呼び戻されることにつながる
- ☐ ascent 昇進
- ☐ Politburo 政治局→旧ソ連共産党の重要機関
- ☐ virtually 実質的に、ほぼ
- ☐ watch and wait …の成り行きを見つめる
- ☐ one leader ... →ゴルバチョフ以前の三人の共産党書記長、ブレジネフ(1906-1982)、アンドロポフ(1914-1984)、チェルネンコ (1911-1985) 各氏のこと。後者二名は就任後１年強で死去し、短期政権となった
- ☐ in succession 続けざまに

7
- ☐ frosty 冷徹な
- ☐ assuage 和らげる
- ☐ peer 同僚
- ☐ harbor (よくない思いを)抱く
- ☐ dentistry 歯学
- ☐ flaw 欠陥
- ☐ rot 腐敗
- ☐ penetrate …に浸透する
- ☐ core 芯

8
- ☐ corruption 腐敗
- ☐ consume 消耗する、食い尽くす
- ☐ demoralize …の士気を喪失させる
- ☐ deprive A of B AからBを奪う
- ☐ workforce 労働者たち
- ☐ cripple まひさせる
- ☐ reformist 改革主義者の
- ☐ zeal 熱意
- ☐ misstep 過ち
- ☐ sheer (大きさや程度が)巨大な
- ☐ vested interest 既得権益
- ☐ zigzag ジグザグに進む
- ☐ frustrate いら立たせる
- ☐ ally 支持者

Track 061

9   Through it all, however, Gorbachev sought to save the Communist Party, not to destroy it. If his package of reforms, known as *perestroika*, was to have any chance of success, Gorbachev knew he needed a more benign international environment. He could not rebuild the Soviet economy if huge chunks of labor and capital had to be devoted to an insatiable, all-consuming military machine.

10   That pushed him to withdraw Soviet forces from the ruinous invasion of Afghanistan. It drove him to negotiate with U.S. President Ronald Reagan the first arms control agreement that eliminated an entire class of nuclear weapons and began the withdrawal of most Soviet tactical nuclear weapons from Eastern Europe. His 1989 summit with U.S. President George H.W. Bush effectively put an end to the superpower standoff.

Track 062

11   He backed talks with action. He ended the Brezhnev Doctrine, which gave Moscow the right to intervene in the affairs of states in its sphere of influence. The Warsaw Pact quickly unraveled, as communist regimes throughout the region were ousted and once Soviet states claimed their independence. The map of Europe was transformed.

12   Gorbachev rose above historical fears and prejudice and agreed to the unification of Germany within NATO, a move that allowed Europe to emerge as a power in a new multipolar world order. On that day of the agreement, Gorbachev announced that "We are leaving one epoch in international relations and entering another, a period, I think, of strong, prolonged peace."

9
- ☐ through it all その間ずっと
- ☐ seek to *do* 〜しようとする→sought はseekの過去形
- ☐ package of reforms 一連の改革
- ☐ benign 好意的な
- ☐ huge chunks of ... …の巨大な塊、相当量の…
- ☐ capital 資本（金）
- ☐ be devoted to ... …に割り当てられる
- ☐ insatiable 飽くことのない
- ☐ all-consuming すべてを食い尽くす

10
- ☐ withdraw A from B AをBから撤退させる
- ☐ ruinous 破滅的な
- ☐ negotiate with ... …と交渉する
- ☐ arms control agreement 軍縮協定
- ☐ eliminate 全廃する
- ☐ class 種類
- ☐ withdrawal 撤去
- ☐ tactical nuclear weapon 戦術核兵器
- ☐ effectively 実質的に
- ☐ put an end to ... …を終わらせる
- ☐ superpower 超大国
- ☐ standoff にらみ合い、膠着状態

11
- ☐ back A with B AをBで裏付ける
- ☐ doctrine 政策、ドクトリン
- ☐ intervene in ... …に介入する
- ☐ sphere of influence 勢力圏
- ☐ unravel 瓦解する
- ☐ oust 追放する
- ☐ claim *one's* independence 独立を宣言する
- ☐ transform 一変させる

12
- ☐ rise above ... …を乗り越える
- ☐ prejudice 先入観
- ☐ unification 統一
- ☐ emerge as ... …として台頭する
- ☐ multipolar 多極的な
- ☐ epoch 時代
- ☐ prolonged 長期にわたる

Track 063

13 We in the West applauded and celebrated Gorbachev's vision and courage. He was lionized and won the Nobel Peace Prize in 1990. At home, his image was different. It was often said that Gorbechev could be elected president anywhere but the Soviet Union.

14 For Vladimir Putin, the collapse of the Soviet Union was the "greatest geopolitical catastrophe of the century." His entire tenure as leader of Russia has been devoted to regaining the power and status Moscow once possessed. The invasion of Ukraine is an attempt to undo that legacy.

Track 064

15 For the leadership of the Chinese Communist Party, Gorbachev served up an indelible lesson. Economic reform was permissible as long as it was tightly controlled and the party oversaw the process. Political liberalization, however, was beyond the pale.

16 For the mandarins in Beijing there could be no loosening of the Communist Party's grip on power. The forces he unleashed were too powerful and the unraveling of the Soviet Union foreshadowed the fate of China as well if they made his mistakes. The actions of the CCP indicate that it studied his history well and will not do as he did.

Track 065

17 The dogged and unflinching rejection of that agenda is proof of just how important and influential Gorbachev's decisions were. Even if he did not — could not — better the lives of the Russian people, his actions did improve those of millions of others around the globe.

13
- [ ] applaud 称賛する
- [ ] celebrate 祝福する
- [ ] lionize もてはやす

14
- [ ] collapse 崩壊
- [ ] geopolitical 地政学的な
- [ ] catastrophe 大惨事
- [ ] regain 取り戻す
- [ ] possess 保有する
- [ ] undo 元に戻す

15
- [ ] the Chinese Communist Party 中国共産党
- [ ] serve up ... …を提供する
- [ ] indelible 消去できない
- [ ] permissible 許容できる
- [ ] tightly 厳しく
- [ ] oversee 監視する→oversawは oversee の過去形
- [ ] liberalization 自由化
- [ ] beyond the pale 範囲の外で→この pale は「杭、柵」の意味

16
- [ ] mandarin 大物、重要人物
- [ ] there could be no loosening of ... …を緩めることはありえなかった
- [ ] grip on ... …の掌握
- [ ] unleash 解き放つ
- [ ] unraveling 解体
- [ ] foreshadow 予兆する

17
- [ ] dogged 執拗な
- [ ] unflinching 断固とした
- [ ] rejection 拒絶
- [ ] agenda 課題
- [ ] better 改善する

18   He ended the suppression of democratic impulses throughout Europe, dispersed the cloud of nuclear destruction that hung over the entire world and offered hope that autocrats could see beyond their narrow interests and speak to those of their nation. For that, he will be rightly honored around the world.

(1,002 words)

18
- □ suppression 抑圧
- □ impulse 衝動
- □ disperse 消し去る
- □ hang over ... …を覆う
- □ see beyond ... …の先に目を向ける
- □ narrow interest 私利私欲
- □ speak to ... …を論じる

Queen Elizabeth II: The end of an era for Britain and the world

エリザベス2世逝去：英国そして世界にとっての一時代の終焉

September 17, 2022 　　　　●Tracks 066-074 / 解説 p. 115、訳 p. 129

Track 066

1 　The death of Queen Elizabeth II marks the end of an era, not only for the United Kingdom, but for the entire world. She was a remarkable woman, steadfast in her commitment to duty — to her country and her Commonwealth — who exuded both confidence and a certain humility. As queen, she invariably put the demands of her position — it feels tawdry to call it "a job" — above whatever personal impulses she might have felt.

2 　As the longest-serving monarch in British history, she witnessed extraordinary events. Since ascending to the throne, however, perhaps the most enduring trend has been her country's struggle to find its place in the world.

Track 067

3 　The second half of the 20th century has not been kind to Great Britain. The Commonwealth, of which she was a symbol, has been transformed, and her passing has, amidst the outpouring of grief, also prompted a spirited debate about the meaning of the British Empire and her — and her family's — role within it.

4 　Elizabeth was an unexpected monarch. Her uncle, Edward VIII, abdicated the throne to pursue American socialite Wallis Simpson. Her father took his place, ruling as George VI until his death in 1952. Elizabeth ascended to the throne, although her coronation was held the following year.

数カ月前に在位70年を祝った女王エリザベス2世が96歳で逝去した。色鮮やかな衣装に身を包んだ女王のほほえみとユーモアは、英国国民と世界に慈しみと安心感を与え続けてきた。この世界にとっても大きくかけがえのない存在であり続けた君主の逝去を皆で悼みたい。

1
- □ [タイトル]Queen Elizabeth II →II は the Second と読む
- □ mark 示す
- □ steadfast 揺るぎない
- □ commitment to ... …への献身
- □ the Commonwealth (of Nations) コモンウェルス→旧称イギリス連邦。旧大英帝国を構成した諸国の多く(現在56カ国)で構成される経済同盟
- □ exude 体からにじみ出させる
- □ humility 謙虚さ
- □ invariably 変わることなく
- □ put A above B AをBに優先させる
- □ tawdry 安っぽい
- □ impulse 衝動

2
- □ longest-serving 在位期間が最長の →serveは「(君主として)国民に仕える」
- □ monarch 君主
- □ witness 目撃する
- □ extraordinary 尋常ではない
- □ ascend to the throne 女王に就任する→throneは「女王・国王の地位」
- □ enduring 長期にわたる

3
- □ be kind to ... …にとってよい時代だ
- □ ..., of which she was a symbol 彼女がその象徴であった…→コモンウェルスは英国君主がその長を務め、君主制をとる加盟国(20カ国)のうち15カ国は形式上英国君主をその君主に戴く
- □ be transformed 変容する
- □ passing 逝去、崩御
- □ amidst …のさなかで = amid
- □ outpouring of ... あふれるほどの…
- □ spirited 活発な、熱烈な
- □ the British Empire 大英帝国→英国と旧植民地の(現在は象徴的な)まとまり

4
- □ VIII = the Eighth
- □ abdicate (王位などを)放棄する
- □ pursue 追い求める→エドワード8世は王太子時代に見初めたウォリスと結ばれるため英国政府や国民の反対を押して325日で王位を退いた
- □ socialite 社交界の花形
- □ take *one's* place 〜の後を継ぐ
- □ rule 統治する、王位に就く
- □ coronation 戴冠式

Track 068

5   During her reign, Britain had 15 prime ministers, among them Winston Churchill, Anthony Eden, Margaret Thatcher and Boris Johnson. One of her last official acts was meeting Liz Truss, the newly selected prime minister, and asking her to form a government.

6   As a girl, Elizabeth was a figure of quiet courage and fortitude, offering encouragement, solace and thanks to the people of Britain as they endured World War II. As queen, she witnessed a decade later the humiliation of the Suez Crisis and the nadir of British power.

Track 069

7   While on the throne, more than 20 countries left the British Empire to claim their independence. She watched Britain join the European Communities and then leave it 47 years later. She lost family — her second cousin, Lord Mountbatten — to "The Troubles" when he was assassinated by members of the Provisional Irish Republican Army.

8   Her personal life was no less tumultuous. In sharp contrast to the stoicism and calm that she demonstrated, family dramas played out in the public eye. Her children and grandchildren had messy and acrimonious marriages, divorces and affairs. There was no doubt about her devotion to them, however, and that love was another, formidable component of her image.

5
- □ reign 治世
- □ (Sir) Winston Churchill →軍人出身で第二次大戦中および戦後辣腕を振るった
- □ Anthony Eden →軍人出身でスエズ危機（第二次中東戦争）勃発時の首相
- □ Margaret Thatcher →1980年代を中心に強硬な政策で停滞した英国経済を再建。「鉄の女（Iron Lady）」と呼ばれた
- □ official act 公務
- □ form a government 組閣する

6
- □ as a girl 少女時代は
- □ figure 人物
- □ fortitude 不屈の精神
- □ solace 慰め
- □ thanks 感謝の気持ち
- □ endure …に耐える
- □ humiliation 屈辱→スエズ危機では米国のエジプト加担で英仏イスラエル側が敗退、英仏はスエズ運河を失った
- □ nadir 最低点、どん底

7
- □ claim 手に入れる、主張する
- □ watch （在位中に）見守る、体験する
- □ the European Communities 欧州共同体→石炭鉄鋼・原子力・経済の3共同体からなり、後のEUの基礎となる
- □ lose A to B AをBで失う
- □ second cousin はとこ、またいとこ
- □ The Troubles →英国・アイルランド間の「北アイルランド紛争」
- □ Provisional Irish Republican Army 暫定アイルランド共和軍→北アイルランド解放を目指す民族主義的過激組織

8
- □ no less ... それに劣らず…
- □ tumultuous 波乱万丈の
- □ stoicism ストイックさ、堅忍主義
- □ demonstrate 示す、他人に見せる
- □ play out 派手に展開される、（出来事が）起きる
- □ messy 不道徳な、厄介な
- □ acrimonious 言い争いに満ちた
- □ affair 情事、不倫
- □ devotion 愛情、献身
- □ formidable 比類ない、強力な
- □ component 構成要素

Track 070

9   While duty and service were the hallmarks of her life and reign, those who knew Elizabeth best also spoke of her "wicked sense of humor." The world was given two glimpses of that side of her: once in a video for the opening ceremony of the 2012 London Olympic Games in which she appeared to jump out of a helicopter with James Bond, and in a second video to mark her Platinum Jubilee in 2022 with Paddington Bear, during which she confessed to having her own secret stash of marmalade sandwiches.

10   There has been an outpouring of grief and sympathy at her death around the world. The British Embassy in Tokyo daily has had flowers left at its gates and there continue to be lines to sign the book of condolences.

Track 071

11   Members of Japan's imperial family have their own memories of the queen. She met three generations, starting with Akihito, then crown prince, who attended Elizabeth's coronation on behalf of his father, Hirohito, in June 1953. Both Emperor Naruhito and Empress Masako studied in Britain before their marriage — the crown prince met the queen while there — and they will be attending the funeral.

12   Any honest assessment of the queen's reign must also acknowledge the extraordinary costs extracted by the empire over which she ruled. She was not responsible for the excesses of the British Empire or the colonial system, but she sat at its apex.

9
- ☐ duty 道義、責任感
- ☐ service 献身、（国民への）奉仕
- ☐ hallmark 特質
- ☐ speak of ... …に言及する
- ☐ wicked 茶目っ気のある
- ☐ glimpse 垣間見ることのできる例
- ☐ the Olympic Games オリンピック
  →the Olympicsとも称されるが複数の競技が一堂に行われるため必ず複数形
- ☐ James Bond →英国の国民的映画「007シリーズ」の主人公スパイ
- ☐ Platinum Jubilee 在位70周年記念（式典）→2022年7月初旬を中心に祝われた
- ☐ Paddington Bear →世界中で人気の童話シリーズの主人公である子熊
- ☐ confess to ... …を告白・白状する
- ☐ stash 隠し持っていること
- ☐ marmalade →パディントンの大好物

10
- ☐ sympathy お悔み
- ☐ Embassy 大使館
- ☐ have A left at B AがBに残されていた
- ☐ there continue to be ... →there areにcontinue to が合わさった形
- ☐ condolence(s) お悔み（の言葉）

11
- ☐ imperial family 皇族
- ☐ Akihito →現在の上皇
- ☐ then その当時の
- ☐ crown prince 皇太子
- ☐ on behalf of ... …の名代として
- ☐ Hirohito →昭和天皇
- ☐ Naruhito →今上天皇
- ☐ Emperor 天皇
- ☐ Empress 皇后

12
- ☐ honest 率直な
- ☐ assessment 評価
- ☐ cost 負担、犠牲
- ☐ extract 引き出す、（金品を）出させる
- ☐ empire →大英帝国やコモンウェルス
- ☐ rule over ... …を統治する
- ☐ excess 度を過ぎた行為（搾取や非人道的統治など）
- ☐ colonial 植民地（時代）の
- ☐ apex 頂点

Track 072

13   The very idea of a monarchy is redolent of privilege, class and a huge bureaucracy that is at some point — many points — indifferent to its subjects. That Elizabeth strove to rise above that — and succeeded — does not negate its existence or the pain it created. Nor does the mass outpouring of grief and sense of loss many feel at her death.

14   Her son and successor, Charles III, inherits the throne of a country in turmoil. He has been prepared, not only studying but standing in for his mother, but for some things there can be no real preparations.

Track 073

15   The United Kingdom has a new prime minister, its fourth in six years; a revolving door in the office of a country's top leader is never a good sign. The decision to leave the European Union continues to be a subject of passionate debate as many of its promised rewards remain distant prospects. The economic difficulties created by Brexit have been magnified by the COVID-19 pandemic and Russia's invasion of Ukraine. Many Britons worry about being able to pay their heating bills as winter approaches.

16   Brexit has also reopened questions about Northern Ireland, and many in Scotland now call for a second referendum on independence. The existence of the United Kingdom itself may well be at stake.

13
- ☐ monarchy 君主制、王政
- ☐ be redolent of ... …のにおいがぷん ぷんする、…を強く想起させる
- ☐ class 階級
- ☐ bureaucracy 官僚制度
- ☐ be indifferent to ... …に無関心だ
- ☐ subject 臣民、（君主国家の）国民
- ☐ strive 奮闘する
- ☐ rise above ... …を乗り越える
- ☐ negate 否定する、無効にする
- ☐ nor does ... …もまた（否定するもので は）ない

14
- ☐ successor 後継者
- ☐ inherit 受け継ぐ
- ☐ ... in turmoil 混乱の中にある…
- ☐ not only A but B Aに加えてBも
- ☐ stand in for ... …の代理を務める→母 親の存命時から時に公務を務めていた
- ☐ there can be no preparations 準備 ができない（可能性もある）

15
- ☐ fourth in six years 6年間で4人目
- ☐ revolving door 回転ドア→ここでは トップが目まぐるしく変わることを表す
- ☐ office 執務室、官職
- ☐ sign 兆候、傾向
- ☐ the European Union 欧州連合、EU →英国のEU脱退はBrexitと呼ばれ 英国内外で多くの議論を呼んできた
- ☐ subject 対象、話題
- ☐ promised 約束された→EU離脱によっ て確実に得られるとされたこと
- ☐ reward 利益、恩恵
- ☐ distant prospect 遠い将来にやっと得 られる見込みのもの
- ☐ magnify 増幅・拡大させる
- ☐ Briton イギリス人
- ☐ being able to do …できるかどうか
- ☐ heating bill 暖房費

16
- ☐ reopen 再燃させる
- ☐ Northern Ireland 北アイルランド →1921年の同地区以南（アイルランド 自由国。現在はアイルランド共和国）の 独立以降、独立をめぐり英国と流血の 紛争を繰り返している
- ☐ referendum 国民投票
- ☐ may well do ～してもおかしくない
- ☐ at stake 危険にさらされて

Track 074

17 Queen Elizabeth, with her unyielding sense of duty and commitment to service, helped fill the gaps as her countrymen grappled with these questions. Amid the many memorials and remembrances, one phrase has been repeated time and time again: "She was the glue that held the nation together." That glue is now gone at a time when Britain may need it most. She will be missed.

(921 words)

17
- □ unyielding 不屈の
- □ sense of duty 使命感
- □ fill the gaps 溝を埋める
- □ countryman 国民→女性も含む
- □ grapple with ... …に立ち向かう
- □ memorial 追悼（の言葉）

- □ remembrance 回顧（の言葉）
- □ time and time again 何度も何度も
- □ glue 接着剤
- □ hold ... together …を1つに保つ
- □ miss いなくなったことを悲しむ

9月9日、前日のエリザベス女王逝去を受け、1面で報じた英国各紙。女王の棺は14日から19日朝までウェストミンスター宮殿内のホールに安置され、訪れた一般弔問客は25万人に上ったという。

Time for Japan and China to get their relationship right

日本と中国は関係を正すべき時を迎えている

October 1, 2022　　　　　　　　　●Tracks 075-083 / 解説 p. 116、訳 p. 132

Track 075

1　Fifty years ago this week, on Sept. 29, 1972, Japan and China normalized their relationship.

2　It has been a turbulent half century since with ties oscillating between hot and cold, calm and contentious. That is to be expected. The two countries are neighbors, with deeply intertwined histories, cultures and economies. Both nurture ambitions for regional leadership — and both offer radically different visions of regional order. That is a formidable obstacle to building a truly forward-looking and productive partnership. It can and should be overcome.

Track 076

3　Japan was stunned — as was most of the world — when U.S. President Richard Nixon made his historic visit to China in February 1972. The Japanese government moved quickly to normalize ties with Beijing. They terminated the state of war between the two countries and ended diplomatic recognition of the Nationalist government that fled to Taiwan in 1949 after losing the civil war to the communist guerrillas.

▼ **About This Editorial** ▼

国交正常化から50年を迎え、日中関係とそれを取り巻く情勢は大きく変化した。日本の経済援助を受ける側だった中国は、今や世界一の経済大国の地位を視野に、国際的な立場を強めている。隣国として、主要な貿易相手国として、今後も日中関係の重要性は変わらない。

1 □ normalize 正常化する

2 □ turbulent 波乱の
□ tie 結び付き、関係
□ oscillate between A and B AとBの間を揺れ動く
□ contentious 対立的な
□ intertwined 結び付いた、絡み合った
□ nurture 心に抱く

□ radically 根本的に
□ formidable 途方もない
□ obstacle 障害
□ forward-looking 前向きな
□ partnership 協力関係
□ overcome 克服する

3 □ be stunned 驚愕する
□ terminate 終結させる
□ the state of war 戦争状態
□ diplomatic 外交的な
□ recognition 承認
□ the Nationalist government 国民政府

□ flee to ... …に逃れる→fledはfleeの過去形
□ civil war 内戦
□ communist guerrilla 共産党ゲリラ

4   Economic ties quickly expanded. The common threat posed by the Soviet Union provided the glue for the relationship and the prospect of shared prosperity motivated both to work closely together. Japan offered a model for economic development and the capital to see it realized. Throughout this "honeymoon period," both governments sought and were able to minimize divisive issues, such as disputes over history and territory. Instead, they spoke of mutual benefits and worked to achieve them.

`Track 077`

5   The collapse of the Soviet Union in 1991 ended that happy interlude. The glue that united the two countries evaporated and those contentious issues assumed prominence and power in the relationship. China proved too apt a pupil. Its breakneck economic development propelled China into the ranks of leading nations. It surpassed Japan as the world's second largest economy in 2010 and there are forecasts that it will overtake the U.S. as number one within a decade.

6   Chinese technology is world class and on several metrics its capabilities exceed those of Japan. Most alarming is the growth in the country's military. The People's Liberation Army is a formidable force, with strengths in every domain.

`Track 078`

7   Economic prowess, aggressive diplomacy and a powerful military are three pillars of the national ambition to become a world leader by the 100th anniversary of the founding of the People's Republic of China in 1949. This vision is understandable but its contours and content spell trouble for Japan.

4
- [ ] expand 拡大する
- [ ] threat 脅威
- [ ] pose 提起する
- [ ] glue 接着剤
- [ ] prospect 可能性
- [ ] prosperity 繁栄
- [ ] capital 資本
- [ ] see it realized それが実現されるのを見届ける
- [ ] honeymoon period 蜜月期間→関係が良好な期間のこと
- [ ] minimize 最小限に抑える
- [ ] divisive 見解が分かれる
- [ ] dispute 紛争
- [ ] mutual 相互の

5
- [ ] collapse 崩壊
- [ ] interlude 合間の時間
- [ ] evaporate 消滅する
- [ ] assume prominence 前面に出る →assumeは「帯びる、手にする」
- [ ] apt 物覚えのよい
- [ ] breakneck 猛烈な
- [ ] propel A into B AをBに進ませる
- [ ] surpass 上回る
- [ ] economy 経済圏
- [ ] forecast 予測
- [ ] overtake 追い抜く

6
- [ ] metric 基準
- [ ] capability 能力
- [ ] exceed 超える
- [ ] alarming 警戒するべき
- [ ] the People's Liberation Army 人民解放軍
- [ ] domain 領域→ここでは陸・海・空などの区別のこと

7
- [ ] prowess 優秀さ
- [ ] diplomacy 外交(術)
- [ ] pillar 柱
- [ ] anniversary …周年
- [ ] the People's Republic of China 中華人民共和国
- [ ] contours 輪郭、形
- [ ] spell trouble for ... …にとって問題になる

8   That is why it is so important for our two countries to create a
relationship that works — for both nations. Two issues currently
get in the way. The first is the Senkakus, a group of islands in the
East China Sea held by Japan but claimed by China under the
name of Diaoyu. The power of that longstanding dispute intensified
in 2012 when Japan nationalized the islands. Since then, China
has regularly sent vessels into waters surrounding the islets — on
Wednesday Chinese coast guard vessels intruded in the area — to
assert Chinese claims.

Track 079

9   The second issue is Taiwan, which China claims is a renegade
province and demands that it be united with the mainland. While
Japan adheres to the "one-China" policy — the 1972 Joint
Communique says there is one China and that Taiwan is an
inalienable part of China — Tokyo also believes that disputes
between Beijing and Taipei must be resolved peacefully and that
China has threatened peace and stability with its military exercises
and bellicose statements. The launch of missiles that flew over
Taiwan to land in Japan's exclusive economic zone, allegedly as a
message to Tokyo, was an especially chilling move. Claims that
Taiwan's security impacts that of Japan and efforts by the Self-
Defense Forces to be better prepared for a Taiwan Strait
contingency fuel Chinese unease and the belief that Tokyo is
determined to prevent unification.

10   At first glance, the problems in the relationship are essentially
territorial disputes. In fact, the animating forces are the different
and competing visions of regional order. For Japan, the most
important principle is a rules-based process for dispute resolution
that is open, transparent and treats all participants equally. For
China, size and power should trump all other considerations.

8
- get in the way 妨げになる
- the East China Sea 東シナ海
- claim …の領有権を主張する
- longstanding 長年にわたる
- intensify 激化する
- nationalize 国有化する
- vessel 船舶
- waters surrounding ... …の周辺海域
- islet 小島
- coast guard 沿岸警備隊
- intrude 侵入する
- assert 主張する

9
- renegade 反抗的な、反逆した
- province 属州
- mainland 本土
- adhere to ... …を支持する
- joint communique 共同声明
- inalienable 不可分の
- threaten 脅かす
- stability 安定
- military exercise 軍事演習
- bellicose 好戦的な
- fly over ... …の上空を飛行する
  →flewはflyの過去形
- exclusive economic zone 排他的経済水域
- allegedly …だとされている
- chilling ぞっとするような
- security 安全保障
- impact …に影響を与える
- the Self-Defense Forces 自衛隊
- be better prepared for ... …に対して入念に備える
- strait 海峡
- contingency 不測の事態、有事
- fuel あおる
- unease 不安
- be determined to *do* ～すると固く決意している
- unification 統一

10
- at first glance 一見したところ
- territorial 領土の
- animating 動かしている
- competing 競合する
- principle 原則
- rules-based ルールに基づいた
- transparent 透明な
- participant 参加者、当事者
- trump …に勝る
- consideration 考慮、判断

Track 080

11 There are ways to ensure that these differences do not result in conflict. Most importantly, we must install guardrails to prevent provocations from sparking confrontation. This requires a multidimensional response.

12 First, resume top-level discussion. There have been no face-to-face meetings between the two countries' leaders since then Prime Minister Shinzo Abe visited China in December 2019. Chinese President Xi Jinping was supposed to reciprocate the following year, but the COVID-19 pandemic intervened.

Track 081

13 Prime Minister Fumio Kishida and Xi have spoken on the phone just once, in October 2021 when the Japanese leader took office. There are hopes that the two men will meet later this year, either at the Group of 20 meeting set for Bali, Indonesia, or at the Asia-Pacific Economic Cooperation forum in Bangkok. Once, or even twice, is not enough. Regular meetings are needed to signal their determination to forge a working relationship and convince their bureaucracies and their publics to make that real.

14 A priority is the opening and use of military-to-military communication mechanisms. There must be ways for the two armed forces to talk, set rules of the road and understand the signals they are sending. Transparency is to be encouraged.

Track 082

15 Second, our two countries must figure out how to cooperate on issues of shared concern. We should be able to work together to facilitate development in the region, pooling capital and expertise to ensure that aid gets to those who need it and is used most efficiently. We should be promoting sustainability, social resilience and the connectivity that creates collective and shared interests.

11
- ☐ ensure 保証する、確実にする
- ☐ install 設置する
- ☐ guardrail ガードレール
- ☐ prevent ... from *doing* …が〜するのを防ぐ
- ☐ provocation 挑発
- ☐ spark …の口火を切る
- ☐ confrontation 対立
- ☐ multidimensional 多元的な

12
- ☐ resume 再開する
- ☐ face-to-face 1対1の、対面の
- ☐ then 当時の
- ☐ reciprocate 返礼する→ここではお返しに訪問するという意味
- ☐ COVID-19 新型コロナウイルス感染症
- ☐ pandemic パンデミック、(疫病の)世界的大流行
- ☐ intervene 邪魔をする

13
- ☐ take office 就任する、公職に就く
- ☐ the Group of 20 G20
- ☐ set for ... …で予定されている
- ☐ the Asia-Pacific Economic Cooperation アジア太平洋経済協力
- ☐ signal 合図する、意思表示する
- ☐ determination 強い決意
- ☐ forge 築く
- ☐ working 実務的な、うまくいく
- ☐ convince 納得させる
- ☐ bureaucracy 官僚
- ☐ make ... real …を実現させる

14
- ☐ military-to-military 軍と軍の間の
- ☐ communication mechanism 通信機構
- ☐ armed forces 軍隊
- ☐ rules of the road 道路交通法[ルール]
- →ここでは比喩的に使われ「(軍事当局同士のやりとりに関する)基本ルール」を表す
- ☐ transparency 透明性
- ☐ be encouraged 推奨される

15
- ☐ figure out how to *do* 〜するための方法を見つけ出す
- ☐ cooperate 協力する
- ☐ facilitate 促進する
- ☐ pool 共同で提供する
- ☐ expertise 専門知識
- ☐ get to ... …に届く
- ☐ efficiently 効率的に
- ☐ sustainability 持続可能性
- ☐ resilience 回復力
- ☐ connectivity 接続性
- ☐ collective 集団的な、共同の

16 Economic ties are a vital component of the bilateral relationship. China is Japan's biggest trading partner, with total trade reaching ¥38.4 trillion last year, according to data released by the Finance Ministry; Japan is China's fourth largest trade partner. Despite the sharpening economic competition between Japanese and Chinese businesses, we should still be able to develop and sustain a division of labor that allows both countries' businesses to prosper. For all its growth, China faces domestic economic challenges and will need help.

Track 083

17 Working together does not mean that Japan should turn a blind eye to Chinese misbehavior. Japan must safeguard its national interests with determination. Only that will convince the leadership in Beijing of our seriousness and credibility as a partner.

18 In his message to the event commemorating the 50 years of normalization, Kishida spoke of his desire for "constructive and stable" ties between the two countries. Given the current state of relations, that is an understandable and achievable goal. Given the potential of the Japan-China relationship, it is the bare minimum that should be expected — and a damning commentary on the first half century.

(1,118 words)

16
- ☐ component 構成要素
- ☐ bilateral 二国間の
- ☐ trillion 兆
- ☐ according to ... …によると
- ☐ the Finance Ministry 財務省
- ☐ sharpening 激しくなりつつある
- ☐ sustain 維持する
- ☐ division of labor 分業
- ☐ prosper 繁栄する
- ☐ for all ... …にもかかわらず
- ☐ domestic 国内の

17
- ☐ turn a blind eye to ... …に目をつぶる
- ☐ misbehavior 不正
- ☐ safeguard 保護する
- ☐ national interest 国益
- ☐ with determination 断固として
- ☐ seriousness 真剣さ
- ☐ credibility 信頼性

18
- ☐ commemorate 記念する
- ☐ normalization 正常化
- ☐ constructive 建設的な
- ☐ achievable 実現可能な
- ☐ given …を考慮すると
- ☐ bare minimum 必要最小限のこと
- ☐ damning 痛烈な
- ☐ commentary 指摘

国際 **1** An aging China poses new challenges

> Families, and women in particular, are less inclined to have children. There are complaints about <u>the costs of education</u> — a big concern in a hypercompetitive child-rearing environment — and <u>housing</u>, <u>the disproportionate burden born by women within the household</u>, as well as <u>fears that women lose opportunities for advancement when they take maternity leave.</u> **(Paragraph 10、4~9行目)**

[並列関係] 下線部のabout以下は、列挙されている名詞句がどういう並びになっているかに注意が必要。educationの後に続くダッシュ（—）で囲まれた場所を挿入句として一度、かっこに入れて考えると、the costs of education ... and housingという流れが見える。the costs「費用」とhousing「住居」が同列に置かれるのは奇妙なので、the costs (of education and housing)「教育と住居の費用」という結び付きだとわかる。さらに後ろには、the disproportionate burden ...とfears that ...という大きい名詞句が2つ、as well asを挟んで続いている。housingとthe disproportionate burdenの間に接続詞がないため、文法的にはas well asが等位接続詞のandのように用いられ、<u>the costs ...</u>, <u>the disproportionate burden ...</u> as well as <u>fears that ...</u>という形で3つの名詞句を結んでいると考えるのが理に適っているように思えるが、the costsとthe disproportionate burdenが外的な要因であるのに対し、fearsは感情を述べたものであるので意味的には少しバランスが悪い。意味を重視するなら、上の接続詞の問題はあるものの、as well asは以下のようにcomplaintsとfearsを並列させていると考えるほうが自然かもしれない。

There are

　　　{ complaints about { the costs of <u>education</u> — ... — and <u>housing</u>,
　　　　　　　　　　　　　　 the disproportionate burden ... the household,
　　　 as well as
　　　 fears that women lose ... take maternity leave.

国際 1 An aging China poses new challenges

- The two countries have several <u>bilateral</u> forums in which demographics are discussed. **(Paragraph 15、4〜5行目)**
- Aging has been part of the agenda at the <u>trilateral</u> summit. **(Paragraph 16、1行目)**

[接頭辞のbi-とtri-] bilateral「二国間の」は政治、経済などを語る文脈で頻出の語。「二」を表すラテン語のbi-と「側の」を表すlateralが結び付いている。この成り立ちを知っていれば、unilateral「一方的な、片側の」や、2つ目の例にあるtrilateral「三国間の、三者の」といった語もすんなりと理解できるだろう。では「四者協議」なら「四」を表すquadr-という接頭辞を使ったりするのだろうかと思いついた人は鋭い。「クアッド (Quad)」と略される「日米豪印戦略対話」の正式名称は、<u>Quadrilateral</u> Security Dialogueである。

国際 2 Ukraine crisis pushes the world's hungry over the brink

A growing number of governments have cut off exports of staples like grains and cooking oil. <u>The decision by Indonesia, the world's leading exporter of palm oil, to restrict shipments means that more than 40% of international vegetable oil sales are now off-limits.</u> **(Paragraph 9、2〜6行目)**

[名詞句の解析] 直前の内容から、輸出停止を行っている政府の例としてthe decision by Indonesiaが挙げられていることがわかる。しかし、「インドネシアによる決定」だけでは、具体的に何を決定したのかが見えてこない。決定の内容を説明する語句が後から出てくるはずだという意識で読み進め、The decision ... to restrict shipments「出荷を制限するという決定」という結び付きを把握する。decision「決定、決定すること」のような名詞を見た際には、「誰が」「何を」決定することを指しているのか、主体と対象を考えるようにしたい。

There are a number of steps that can be taken to ease this crisis. <u>The first and most obvious is for Putin to quit holding the world hostage to his imperial dreams, to end the invasion or, at the very least, to allow Ukraine to resume shipments of grain and other food supplies.</u>
(Paragraph 11、1〜5行目)

[to不定詞の意味上の主語] 下線部はbe動詞を用いたSVCの文だが、The first and most obvious (step)がS、isがVであるのはよいとして、Cに当たる部分がfor Putinという前置詞句から始まっていることに少し戸惑う人もいるかもしれない。「for＋名詞句」がto不定詞の意味上の主語を表現できるということを今一度確認しておこう。ここのfor Putin to ..., to ... or, at the very least, to...は「プーチン氏が…するか、…するか、あるいは少なくとも…すること」という意味。たとえば、For that to be true would mean all events have been cancelled.「それが本当だとすれば、すべてのイベントがキャンセルされたということだ」のように、意味上の主語を持つto不定詞句が文全体の主語になる場合もある。

Execution of Myanmar democracy activists reveals junta's true colors

The military <u>junta</u> that rules Myanmar has again confirmed its brutality by executing four democracy activists. **(Paragraph 1)**

[頻出の借用語] 下線部のjuntaは「（主にクーデター後の）臨時政権、暫定政権」を表す語で17世紀にスペイン語から借用された。元々はナポレオン時代にフランス侵略軍と戦ったスペイン各地の政権の名称として知られ、日本語でも「フンタ」と言うとこれらを意味する外来語である。時事英語では国を一時的に支配する軍事政権などを表す際によく用いられる。『ランダムハウス英和大辞典 第2版』（小学館）によると、英語に入った後、発音が英語化し /dʒʌ́ntə/ となったものの、スペイン語の発音との関連で20世紀以降、特にアメリカでは /hʌ́ntə/ のほうが優勢となっているとされている。

<u>As yet</u> more proof of the junta's inhumanity, the prisoners were allowed to speak to relatives last weekend for the first time in months but no one was told if or when the executions would occur.
(Paragraph 7、2〜5行目)

[例の熟語？] 下線部をどう読むかがポイント。as yetには「今までのところは、まだ」を表す熟語的な副詞句の用法がある。だが、このAs yetをそういう副詞句として解釈すると、この文にはthe prisonersという明白な主語名詞句があるため、more proof of the junta's inhumanityという部分の名詞句が浮いてしまう。ここから、このAsは「…として」を表すシンプルな前置詞であり、yetはasではなくmoreと結び付いて比較級を強めているということに気づけたかどうか。そう解釈すれば、As ... inhumanityまでを「軍事政権の非人道さを示すいっそうの証拠として」という前置詞句のカタマリとして理解することができる。

> Despite firsthand knowledge of the excesses of the regime — <u>not only did he witness the horrors of forced collectivization of farms but both grandfathers were persecuted by Stalin</u> — he joined the party and rose through the ranks of the Komsomol, the Communist youth organization, attending university and studying law. **(Paragraph 4、3〜7行目)**

[挿入節と否定語句] 文頭の Despite ... という前置詞句と文の主語である he の間にダッシュ（－）で挟まれた大きいカタマリ（下線部分）が挿入されていて、しかも、それ自体が主語と動詞を持つ節を形成している。さらに、この挿入節では not only という否定語句が文頭に出て、後ろが did he witness ... という疑問文と同じ形になっている点にも注意したい。英語では否定語句や only を含む副詞要素、また、「so ＋形容詞／副詞」などが文頭に出ると、助動詞や be 動詞と主語が入れ替わったり、do が挿入されたりして疑問文と同じ形になるというルールがあるためだ。意味的には、下線部分が直前で言及されているゴルバチョフの経験の内容を具体的に説明する役割を果たしている。

> <u>If his package of reforms, known as *perestroika*, was to have any chance of success</u>, Gorbachev knew he <u>needed</u> a more benign international environment. **(Paragraph 9、2〜4行目)**

[if 節の be to] 1つ目の下線部は if 節の中に was があるが、仮定法ではなく単なる過去形であることに注意したい。また、was to have ... と「be to ＋不定詞」の形になっているという点がポイント。if 節の中で「be to ＋不定詞」が用いられた場合、「もし…しようとするならば」という意味を表し、帰結節ではそれに呼応して「…しなければならない」を意味する need や must などといった表現が出てくることが非常に多い。今回の例でも、if 節に対する実質的な帰結節の2つ目の下線部でやはり needed が使用されている。

As queen, she invariably put the demands of her position — it feels tawdry to call it "a job" — above whatever personal impulses she might have felt. **(Paragraph 1、5〜7行目)**

[動詞と前置詞句の結び付き] she (S) ... put (V) というのが文の中心となるSVであることはすぐにわかるはずだが、このputを確認した時点で、後ろに場所や空間を表す表現が出てくることを予想したい。put「置く」は空間を表す副語句とともに用いて、「…に置く、…に配置する」という意味を表す動詞だからである。この予想があれば、離れた位置にあるabove ... feltがputを修飾する語句になっていることもすんなりと読み取れるだろう。なお、put A above B「Bの上にAを置く」は、比喩的に「BよりもAを優先する」という意味でよく用いられる。

The United Kingdom has a new prime minister, its fourth in six years; a revolving door in the office of a country's top leader is never a good sign. **(Paragraph 15、1〜3行目)**

[政治関連の比喩表現] 下線部のa revolving door「回転ドア」は一国の政治情勢などを説明する際によく見られる語句。行政機関、立法機関と民間企業を行ったり来たりすることを指し、「天下り」のような意味で用いられる場合もあるが、今回のような文脈では「指導者やトップがコロコロ入れ替わること」を指す。「国内政治・外交」4本目の記事では、日本のかつての状況（首相がたびたび変わること）を説明するためにこの表現が使用されている。

It has been a turbulent half century <u>since</u> with ties <u>oscillating</u> between hot and cold, calm and contentious. **(Paragraph 2、1〜2行目)**

［副詞 since と「揺れ動き」を表す重要単語］1つ目の下線部の since は前置詞ではなく、単体で「それ以来」を意味する副詞の用法である点に注意したい。なお、since にはさらに、long since で「ずっと前に」を表す用法もある。2つ目の下線部の元になっている動詞の oscillate はあるものが一定の周期で揺れ動くことを表し、「振り子」などの動きを表現する際にも用いられる。一方、類義語の vacillate は2つのものの間で不安定に揺れ動くというニュアンスが強い。双方とも人が2つの選択肢の狭間で揺れ動く様子を描写する際にも使用されるが、vacillate には vacillant「動揺した、ぐらついた」という形容詞形もある。

Claims that Taiwan's security impacts that of Japan and efforts by the Self-Defense Forces to be better prepared for a Taiwan Strait contingency fuel Chinese unease and the belief that Tokyo is determined to prevent unification. **(Paragraph 9、10〜14行)**

［長い主語名詞句と意外な動詞］まずは文頭にある長い名詞句を正しく理解することがポイント。Claims の内容を表す that 節は that of Japan まであり、後ろの and は Claims と efforts を結び付けていることを把握したい。この efforts から始まる名詞句の範囲をしっかり確定しないと混乱することになる。a Taiwan Strait contingency「台湾海峡の不測の事態」は1つの意味を持った語句なので、その後の fuel が動詞であると見極め、Claims ... and efforts ... (S) fuel (V) Chinese unease and the belief ... (O) という文の骨格を把握する。fuel については「燃料」を意味する名詞の用法を最初に思い浮かべる人も多いかもしれないが、「あおる、たきつける」という意味の動詞としても用いられる。

中国の高齢化がもたらす新たな課題

1　中国は、豊かになる前に高齢化する初めての国となりそうだ。

2　減少する出生率の回復はほとんど不可能なようで、その軌道は経済・社会の先行きに深刻な影響を及ぼすだろう。中国政府は、この問題と危険性を十分に認識している。しかし残念ながら、どの対応策もうまくいきそうにない。

3　日本もまた、中国の高齢化がもたらす影響に注意しなければならない。日本の高齢化の経験は、隣国と協力してさらなる高齢化社会への移行を緩和する何らかのすべを示すことができるかもしれない。

4　今週発表された国勢調査のデータによると、中国の出生率は5年連続で減少し、2021年に過去最低を記録した。中国国家統計局によると、昨年の出生数はわずか1,062万人で、2020年に比べ11.6%減っている。

5　その割合は2019年から2020年にかけての18%減少よりは改善したものの、1949年の共産中国建国以来、最低の水準であることに変わりはない。出生数が死亡数をかろうじて上回ったため、総人口は（前年比）48万人増の14億1,260万人となった。自然増加率は0.034%に落ち込んだ。これより増加率が低かったのは大躍進政策の時代だけで、当時は毛沢東主席による経済政策の大失敗で数千万人が死亡している。

6　昨年生まれた子供のうち第2子はわずか43%で、2017年の50%に比べ減少した。国が人口規模を維持するためには出生率（母親一人当たりの平均出生数）2.1が必要なことから、1.3という2020年の中国の出生率は、多くの人口統計学者に中国の総人口は頭打ちとなったのではないかという思いを抱かせている。

7　さらに不穏なのは、人口構成の変化だ。60歳未満の労働年齢人口が全体に占める割合は、2020年に10年前の70.1%から63.3%に低下している。65歳以上は8.9%から増加し、今や全体の13.5%を占める。政府は、今後5年間で3,500万人の働き手が失われ、2050年までに労働年齢層の割合は人口の半分になる可能性があると予測している。

中国の高齢化がもたらす新たな課題

8 こうした展開は、重大な結果をもたらすだろう。労働人口が減少すれば賃金は上昇せざるを得ず、年金制度への納付は減少して税収が落ち込む一方で、社会福祉への需要が増大する。この最後の変化は、特に厳しいものとなるだろう。中国は現在、社会福祉にGDPの約7%しか充てておらず、国際労働機関（ILO）が算出した世界平均の12.8%を大幅に下回っている。ブラジルでさえGDPの17%を社会福祉に費やしている。さらに悪いことに、都市生活者のための主要な年金基金が2035年までに枯渇する可能性があると推定されている。経済が減速する中での社会不安を懸念する専門家もいる。

9 中華人民共和国建国100年に当たる2049年までに「豊かで強力な国」になるという中国の目標は危うくなっていると、経済学者らは警告する。国際通貨基金（IMF）は、中国経済は「バランスを欠き、勢いが落ちている」と断言しており、労働人口の減少、生産性の低下、米中貿易戦争、国際経済からの分断はいずれも、成長を長期的に脅かすとしている。中国の見通しの変化は経済的、軍事的影響を及ぼすため、世界の国々はそれに備えなければならない。

10 中国の人口構造が変化している理由は周知の通りだ。何よりも根本的に、中国が発展するにつれて国民はよりよい生活と医療を手に入れ、長生きできるようになった。家庭では特に女性が子供を持つことを望まない傾向にある。激しい競争にさらされる子育て環境において大きな懸念となっている教育費のほか、住宅費、家庭内で女性が引き受ける負担の偏りといった不満に加え、産休取得で昇進の機会を失う不安もある。

11 これらの問題がきっかけとなって政府は2016年に、1980年以降実施していた「一人っ子政策」を撤廃し、さらに昨夏には家庭が子供を3人もうけることを容認するようになった。相変わらずの出生率低下は、そういった対策が何の影響も及ぼさなかったことを示している。私教育に対する近年の取り締まりや、住宅価格上昇を抑制する試みは、家庭の負担軽減を目的としたものだ。今後さらなる対策が実施されるだろう。住宅助成金や、より手厚い産休制度、保育所の増設、所得税政策の変更などが議論され、また試験的なプログラムとして実施されている。

12 さらに3つの改革が重要だ。まず、母親の負担が軽くなるよう、家事を再分配することである。両方の親が家庭を支えなければならない。これと並行して実施すべきなのは職場改革で、働く母親にもっと適応させたものにする必要がある。第3のステップは、昨年決定された定年退職年齢引き上げで、これは政治がらみの動きだ。

13 それでも、人口統計学者の多くはこれらの軌道を変えるのはほぼ不可能だと考えている。中国の若者たちには「豊かな暮らし」のイメージがあり、子供を増やすことはそのビジョンに含まれていない。

14 避けがたい事態に前向きに取り組もうと、中国政府は先月、国内のロボット産業を成長させ、製造業の設備と工程を改善する国家計画を発表した。人工知能を活用した自動化は、中国の生産力不足と山積する人口問題への対処を目的としている。税金や年金の支払いなど、歳入の問題への対応策とはならない。

15 中国の軌道は、日本の軌道をたどっている。今のところ、中国の高齢化の速度は2025年に日本を追い抜き、その10年後には総人口に占める高齢者の割合が日本に迫ると言われている。日本と中国は、人口動態について議論する二国間フォーラムをいくつか開催している。移行期に対処する両国の経験をもっと共有していくべきだ。国や地方自治体、企業、市民社会団体など、非常に幅広い対話の可能性があるだろう。韓国もまたこのような人口動態の傾向を抱えており、議論への参加が考えられる。

16 高齢化は日中韓サミットの議題の一つとなっている。いっそうの注目と対応を要する喫緊の課題だ。　　　　　　　　　　　　　　　　　　　　　（訳・注　宇都宮）

ウクライナ危機が世界の飢餓を崖っぷちに追い込む

1 世界は食糧危機にひんしており、その結果、何百万人もの人々が飢えに苦しみ、社会不安と大量の移民が生じる可能性がある。

2 この差し迫った大惨事の直接の原因はロシアによるウクライナ侵攻と、それが生み出す、両国の生命線ともいえる輸出の途絶にある。ただ、それが事態の全容ではない。構造的な要因が食糧不足を悪化させている。自身に何の落ち度もないのに苦しむであろう人々に食糧安全保障を再確立するために、あらゆる問題に対処していく必要がある。とはいえ豊かな国々は今すぐに、世界中の飢えた人々の手に食糧を届ける努力を加速させなければならない。

3 侵攻前、ウクライナとロシアは極めて重要な食糧輸出国だった。今週ハンス・ヴェルナー・ジンが書いているように、ウクライナは世界全体の輸出量において小麦の10％、大麦の13％、ひまわり油の50％超、菜種油の5％、そしてトウモロコシの15％を占めている。ある推計によれば、ロシアとウクライナは貿易で取引される全食糧カロリーの12％を占め、両国合わせて世界の小麦輸出量の約30％を生産している。加えて、ロシアは世界最大の肥料生産国でもある。

4 生産の中断、もしくはそうした中断の脅威は、国連食糧農業機関の世界FAO食品価格指数を前年比30％増、平均で2020年比62％増に押し上げている。世界食糧計画の代表は、3億2,300万人が「飢えに向かって突き進んでいる」と警告し、一方赤十字社は食糧価格の上昇により4,700万人が深刻な飢餓に直面すると予想している。

5 遠くの国々で数多くの人々が飢餓に苦しむという見通しが、世界に行動を起こす気にさせるのに十分な恐怖ではないなら、一人ひとりの利害がその役割を果たすはずだ。飢餓はしばしば大規模な抗議運動や政情不安を引き起こす。「アラブの春」は食糧価格の高騰が引き金となった。こうした炎のようなうねりはめったに抑え込めるものではない。飢餓が1％増加するごとに、移民が2％増加すると推計されている。

6 この危険な状況の原因はまさにロシアのウラジーミル・プーチン大統領にある。ウクライナへの侵攻が同国の小麦生産量を3分の1減少させることになると予想されている。ロシア海軍による封鎖で農作物の出荷ができず、伝えられるところによれば、約2000万トンの小麦がサイロや船に積まれたままで海外市場に届かない状

態にあるという。穀物の貯蔵施設も攻撃の対象となっている。穀物が盗まれたという報告がある。米国のアントニー・ブリンケン国務長官は、「ロシア政府はウクライナの国境のはるか先まで飢餓と苦しみを輸出している」と端的に述べた。

7　プーチンは、責められるべきは西側諸国だと反論している。その主張によれば、欧米の制裁措置がロシアの食糧と肥料の輸出を妨げている。彼は不誠実な態度を取り、彼が起こした戦争における多くの残虐行為から耳目をそらそうとしているのだ。

8　この2つの供給国を失うことは、世界的な食糧危機を引き起こすのに十分である。だが、ウクライナ侵攻以外のさまざまな政策や慣行が食糧不足に輪をかけている。たとえば、かつて食糧の栽培に使われていた土地がバイオ燃料の生産に充てられることが増えてきている。世界の農地の4%がバイオ燃料の栽培に使われ、米国のトウモロコシ生産の40%がエタノールの製造に使われていると推定される。燃料価格の上昇が代替エネルギー源の血まなこの争奪戦に火をつけて、そうした作物はますます魅力的なものとなった。

9　不足が予想されることから、一部の食料輸出国は在庫を出し惜しみするようになった。穀物や食用油といった主要生産物の輸出を停止する政府も増えている。世界有数のパーム油輸出国であるインドネシアが出荷制限を決定したことは、世界の植物油販売の40%超が断たれたことを意味する。ウクライナでの戦争がきっかけとなって、23カ国が食糧保護主義をとるようになったと推計されている。

10　それらに加えてインフレの急激な進行が、食料価格を押し上げて世界で最も貧しい人々の生活を脅かす。世界銀行の推計によると、極度の貧困状態、すなわち1日250円（1.86ドル）未満で生活している人がすでに7億人に迫っているという。このような層に属する人々にとっては、ほんのわずかな食料価格の上昇であっても生命を脅かすことになる。

11　この危機を緩和するために講じることのできる措置はいくつかある。まず何よりも最も明白なものは、プーチンが世界を自らの帝国主義の野望の人質とすることをやめ、侵攻を終わらせるか、最低限ウクライナが穀物やその他食料品の出荷を再開できるよう認めることである。たとえ黒海の港が閉鎖されたままでも、人道的な支援や救済措置の一環として、代替の輸出ルートを開くべきである。

ウクライナ危機が世界の飢餓を崖っぷちに追い込む

12 食糧保護主義によって、自国はより大きな食糧安全保障が得られるという間違った印象を持っている各国政府は、その考えを改める必要がある。各国の農業生産を増やす必要がある。その場合、新しい作物、おそらくは遺伝子組み換え作物に目を向けることになるだろう。土壌侵食をなくすためにより多くのことを行う必要があるし、肥料の輸入への依存も減らしていかなければならない。

13 先月、G7は世界銀行とともに「食料安全保障のためのグローバル・アライアンス」を打ち出した。これは、「進行中の世界的飢餓の危機に対して速やか、かつ協調的な対応を促進する」ための枠組みである。この取り組みは加速することが見込まれ、日本が来年G7の議長国を務める際には、それをさらに推進していく意気込みを持つべきだ。

14 長年にわたり飢餓と戦い、農業生産を促進してきた、世界食糧計画、国際農業開発基金、食糧農業機関といった、ほかの国際機関にも支援を提供していくことが肝要だ。そうした組織は、ウクライナの危機が世界的な人道的大惨事になることを防ぐ闘いの最前線にいるのである。 （訳・注　小川）

ミャンマーの民主化運動家の処刑により露呈する軍事政権の本質

1　ミャンマーを統治する軍事政権は、4人の民主化運動家を処刑し、またもやその残虐性を証明することとなった。

2　不透明な法的手続きに阻まれ、国民だけでなく被告人の家族からも隠ぺいされているこれらの出来事は、国家公認の殺人だ。これらはミャンマー軍事政権が人権と法の支配を完全に無視することを再び証明している。また、こうした残虐行為に対して、国際社会の一致団結した対応が必要だとわれわれに訴えかけている。ミャンマー政府は、その方針を転換し、収監されている政治犯を釈放し、正当に選挙で選ばれた政府に権力を渡すまで、国際社会から排斥され、孤立させられ、制裁を加えられなければならない。

3　2021年2月1日のクーデターで、自らが推す候補者らが大敗を喫した2020年11月の選挙結果を拒否して政権を奪取して以来、ミャンマー軍部は民主勢力やさまざまな民兵組織に対して多くの血が流れる武力衝突を仕掛けてきた。この2月、国連人権高等弁務官事務所は、クーデターへの抗議活動で殺害されたとされる1,500人を正式に把握したと発表したが、この死者数には、少数民族への暴力により死亡した、それ以外の何千人もの人々は含まれていない。国連の報道官は、そうした死亡者のうち200人は「軍による拘束下での拷問が原因」だと述べている。

4　ほかにも12,000人近くが拘留され、そのうち8,792人が今も拘束されたままである。これらの逮捕は、「平和的な抗議行動であれ、単にネット上での行為であれ、軍に反対する声を上げたこと」が理由だった。

5　軍事政府に拘束された人々を追跡し、状況の確認を試みる非営利団体「政治犯支援協会」によると、同様に過去1年間にミャンマーで117人が死刑を宣告され、40人もの人々の死刑執行が間近に迫っている。

6　先週末に処刑された4人の中には、国民民主連盟所属の議員で、同国の若者から強い支持を得ていたヒップホップアーティストのピョ・ゼヤ・トー氏と、コ・ジミーとして知られる著名な民主化運動家のチョウ・ミン・ユー氏が含まれていた。彼らは昨年、テロリズムの罪で有罪判決を下された。ほかの2名の男性、フラ・ミョ・アウン氏とアウン・トゥラ・ゾー氏は、警察への情報提供者の殺害に関与した疑いが持たれていた。

ミャンマーの民主化運動家の処刑により露呈する軍事政権の本質

7　彼ら全員が、国民や国際社会の監視機関に公開されない秘密裁判で裁かれ、死刑を宣告された。軍事政権の非人道的さを示すさらなる証拠として、囚人たちは先週末、数カ月ぶりに親族と話すことを許されたものの、処刑が行われるかどうか、あるいはいつ行われるかは誰にも知らされなかった。処刑が発表された後、家族は遺体を見ることも引き取ることも許されなかった。

8　この殺害は当然、国際的な非難を浴びた。日本、オーストラリア、英国、カナダ、ニュージーランド、ノルウェー、韓国、米国、そしてEU上級代表により発表された共同声明は、これらの処刑を「人権と法の支配に対する軍事政権の軽視をさらに例証した、非難すべき暴力行為」であるとした。共同声明に署名した各国やEUはさらに、「不当に拘束されたすべての人々を解放し、刑務所への完全かつ独立した立ち入りを認め」、なおかつ「暴力の行使を止め、国民の意思を尊重し、ミャンマーの民主主義への道を回復する」よう、軍事政権に強く求めた。

9　林芳正外務大臣は、日本がミャンマー軍部による行動を「深刻に憂慮する」と述べ、クーデター以降命を落とした人々の家族に「心からの深い哀悼の意」を表明し、今回の処刑が「国民感情の硬化とミャンマーの国際社会からのさらなる孤立により、より深い対立をもたらす」と警告した。

10　近隣諸国の内政に干渉したがらないことで知られる東南アジアの国々でさえ、はっきりと声を上げた。東南アジア諸国連合（ASEAN）の議長であるカンボジアのフン・セン首相は先月、軍司令官のミン・アウン・フライン氏に対し、処刑を実施しないよう求める書簡を送っている。

11　ASEANの基礎原則である非干渉主義は、情勢不安は抑え込むことができることを前提としている。しかし圧政で国を支配しているフン・セン氏でさえ、軍事政権が掲げる政策はミャンマーをさらに不安定にするだけであることを知っている。すでにミャンマー全体で275を超える民兵組織が民主主義勢力の指揮下で動いている。自らの権利を求め戦う民族的軍事組織と合わせると、両者は国土の約半分を支配下に収めている。暴力が国境を越えて広がる危険性は現実のものとなっている。

12 こうした意思表示を無視し、法の支配をないがしろにし、犠牲者やその家族に対する人道的対応を否定することは、ミャンマーの軍事政権が残忍な暴力しか理解する気のないことの証しである。非難するだけでは不十分だ。国際社会が軍事政権およびそれを構成する人間と主要な支援者らに制裁を課すという段階は、もうとっくに過ぎている。それらの制裁には権威と正当性を付与すべく国連のお墨付きが必要だろう。

13 これまでのところ、日本はそのような強硬路線をとっていない。インド太平洋地域における「ルールに基づく秩序」に関する話し合いも今回の事例では空虚だ。日本政府が、ミャンマー軍部による支配を存続させている、あからさまな違法性を無視しているからである。日本政府は、軍事政権を厳しく批判すれば軍部が中国に接近することになると恐れ、二の足を踏んできた。軍事政権やそれを支えている勢力に対して日本からの圧力はまったくなく、また、反軍事政権の民主勢力による影の国民統一政府への支援も行っていない。このような弱腰の対応はやめなければならない。

14 日本は国際社会と協調した非難の大合唱に参加すべきだ。そして、ミャンマー政府、その指導者ら、そして主要な支援者たちに対して、罰則を科していくべきである。ミャンマーは武器を与えられてはならないし、ならず者の政府とつながりのある諸企業は制裁を受けるべきだ。処刑はやめさせなければならないし、また軍事政権には選挙で正当に選ばれた国の導き手に政権を返上させなければならない。

（訳・注　小川）

称賛と非難をともに浴びたミハイル・ゴルバチョフ氏は世界を作り変えた

1 本当の意味で世界を変えたと主張できる人はほとんどいない。

2 ソビエト連邦の最後の指導者だったミハイル・ゴルバチョフ氏はその短いリストに名前が載っている。今週91歳で死去したゴルバチョフ氏は、ソビエト連邦と冷戦に幕を下ろした人物として——そして結果的に世界を核による壊滅の瀬戸際から引き戻すのを助けた人物として、歴史に記憶されることだろう。

3 後者は意図したことだったが、前者はそうではなかった。そうした理由から、ゴルバチョフ氏は世界各地で称えられ、故国では非難されている。しかしたとえ外国人であっても、彼の在任がもたらした予想外の影響は認識しなければならない。彼は改革による影響と、圧政が必要だと思われる点に関して、独裁者たちに強力な教訓を提供した。

4 自らの党とその統治体制に終焉をもたらした人物にとっては皮肉にも、ゴルバチョフ氏は忠実な共産主義者だった。体制の行きすぎた行為を実体験から知っていた——彼は強制的な集団農場化の恐怖を目の当たりにしただけでなく、二人の祖父のいずれもがスターリンによる迫害を受けた——にもかかわらず、ゴルバチョフ氏は党に加わり、大学に通って法律を学びながら、共産党青年団のコムソモールで出世の階段を上った。

5 彼が本格的に政治活動を始めたのは1956年、スタブロポリ地方のコムソモールの第一書記に指名された時だった。成果を残し、やがて同地方の党のトップの地位に就いた。同地を訪れるソ連の指導者たち——多くは党中央のトップに位置する人物——との交流がその仕事を通じて生まれ、その人物たちは彼を高く評価した。党の高官でイデオロギーでの強硬派だったミハイル・スースロフ氏や、KGBの議長で後の共産党書記長のユーリ・アンドロポフ氏などの重要人物が、ゴルバチョフ氏の後援者となった。

6 その実績とこれらの人々との関係から、ゴルバチョフ氏は1978年にモスクワへ呼び戻されることになり、同地で昇進を続けた。党エリートの中のエリートとされる中央委員会書記になり、1980年には党政治局員になった。政治局のほかのほぼすべての局員よりも1世代若かった彼は、3人のほかの人物——「半分死んでいた一人の指導者、半分だけ生きていたもう一人、ろくにしゃべれなかったもう一人」——が国家のトップの座を占め、相次いで死去するのを見つめてきた。

7 冷徹な外務大臣だったアンドレイ・グロムイコ氏は、同僚たちがゴルバチョフ氏に対して抱いていたかもしれない疑念を、彼は「すてきな笑顔と鉄の歯」を持っていると述べて和らげた。歯学よりも重要だったのはゴルバチョフ氏の洞察力だった。彼はソ連のシステムの欠陥と、その芯にまで浸透していた腐敗をはっきりと見抜いていた。

8 ゴルバチョフ氏は党を食い尽くしていた腐敗と、それがどのような形で国民の士気を喪失させ、労働者たちから意欲を奪い、経済をまひさせていたかを、実体験から知っていた。しかし彼の改革主義者としての熱意は過ちを生み、挑んだ既得権益のあまりの大きさ——党員だけで1,800万人——のせいで政策は揺らぐことを余儀なくされ、それが支持者たちをいら立たせ、国民を混乱させた。

9 けれどもその間ずっと、ゴルバチョフ氏は共産党を破壊しようとするのではなく、救おうとした。「ペレストロイカ」として知られる彼の一連の改革に少しでも成功の望みがあるとすれば、より好意的な国際環境が必要だと彼はわかっていた。労働力と資本の相当量が、飽くことなくすべてを食い尽くす軍部に割り当てる必要のある状況では、ソビエト経済を再建することなどできなかった。

10 そのことが、ゴルバチョフ氏にアフガニスタンの泥沼の侵攻からソ連軍を撤退させた。彼はロナルド・レーガン米大統領と最初の軍縮協定を交渉し、協定によって核兵器の一種類が全廃され、ソ連のほとんどの戦術核兵器について東ヨーロッパからの撤去作業が始まった。1989年のジョージ・H・W・ブッシュ米大統領との首脳会談で、超大国同士のにらみ合いに実質的に終止符が打たれた。

11 ゴルバチョフ氏は発言を行動で裏付けた。彼はソ連の勢力圏内の国の内政に介入する権利をソ連政府に与えたブレジネフ・ドクトリンに終止符を打った。地域内の各国で共産党政権が追放され、当時のソビエト連邦内の国家が独立を宣言したため、ワルシャワ条約はたちまち瓦解した。ヨーロッパの地図は一変した。

12 ゴルバチョフ氏は歴史的な恐怖と先入観を乗り越え、NATOの枠内でのドイツの統一に合意し、その動きはヨーロッパを新たな多極的な世界秩序における一大勢力として台頭させた。その合意当日、ゴルバチョフ氏は「われわれは国際関係の1つの時代を離れ、別の時代に入った。私が思うに、それは強い長期にわたる平和の時代である」と宣言した。

称賛と非難をともに浴びたミハイル・ゴルバチョフ氏は世界を作り変えた

13 西側に暮らすわれわれはゴルバチョフ氏の先見の明と勇気を称賛し、祝福した。彼はもてはやされ、1990年にノーベル平和賞を受賞した。国内では彼のイメージは別物だった。ゴルバチョフ氏はソ連以外ならばどこでも大統領に選ばれるとしばしば言われたものだ。

14 ウラジーミル・プーチン氏にとって、ソ連の崩壊は「20世紀で最大の地政学的な大惨事」だった。彼のロシアの指導者としての全在任期間は、ロシアがかつて保有していた権力と地位を取り戻すことに捧げられてきた。ウクライナ侵攻は崩壊の遺産をなかったことにするための試みだ。

15 中国共産党の指導部にとって、ゴルバチョフ氏は消し去ることのできない教訓を提供した。厳しく統括され、また党がその過程を監視するという条件において、経済改革は許容できた。だが、政治的な自由化はその範囲を外れたものだった。

16 北京の大物たちにしてみれば、共産党の権力掌握を緩めることなどありえなかった。ゴルバチョフ氏が解き放った勢いはあまりにも強力で、ソビエト連邦の解体は、彼と同じ過ちを犯した場合の中国の運命を予兆するものであった。中国共産党の行動は、党が彼の歴史を十分に学習していて、彼が行ったようにはしないつもりだということを示している。

17 その課題の執拗で断固とした拒絶は、ゴルバチョフ氏の決断がいかに重要で影響力があったのかを物語る証拠である。彼がロシア国民の生活を改善しなかった──改善できなかった──としても、彼の行動は世界各地のほかの何百万人もの人たちの生活を向上させた。

18 ゴルバチョフ氏はヨーロッパ全土で民主的衝動の抑圧を終わらせ、全世界を覆っていた核による破壊の雲を消し去り、独裁者でもその私利私欲を超えた先を見据え、国民の利益を論じることができるという希望をもたらした。そのことによって、彼は世界中で適切に評価されることだろう。　　　　　（訳・注　桑田）

エリザベス2世逝去：英国そして世界にとっての一時代の終焉

1 エリザベス2世の逝去は、英国のみならず、世界全体にとっても1つの時代の終わりを示すものだ。女王は祖国およびコモンウェルス（旧英国連邦）への使命に常に献身し、自信と一定の謙虚さをまとった非凡な女性だった。女王として、彼女は常にその地位（それを彼女の「仕事」と呼ぶのは無粋な気がするが）に求められるものを、感じたことがあったかもしれない個人的衝動が何であれ、それよりも優先させてきた。

2 英国史上最も長く国民に仕えてきた君主として、彼女はいくつもの尋常ならざる出来事に立ち会ってきた。しかしながら、彼女が女王の地位に就いて以来、おそらく最も長く続いてきた趨勢は、英国が世界の中でその居場所を見つけるために苦闘してきたことだった。

3 20世紀後半は、英国にとって決して優しい時代ではなかった。エリザベス女王が象徴としての役割を果たしてきたコモンウェルスは変貌を続け、女王の死は、あふれんばかりの哀悼の中で、大英帝国の意味と、帝国における女王そして王室の役割について活発な議論も促した。

4 エリザベスは予期せず即位した君主だった。彼女の叔父であるエドワード8世は、米国社交界の花だったウォリス・シンプソンを追いかけて王位を放棄した。エリザベス女王の父親は、エドワード8世の後継となり、1952年に亡くなるまで国王ジョージ6世として英国を統治した。エリザベスはその後を継いだが、戴冠式は翌年に行われた。

5 彼女の在位期間中、英国は15人の首相を擁したが、その中にはウィンストン・チャーチル、アンソニー・イーデン、マーガレット・サッチャー、ボリス・ジョンソンなどがいた。女王の最後の公務の一つは、新しく選ばれた首相であるリズ・トラスに会い、彼女に組閣を依頼することだった。

6 少女時代のエリザベスは、静かな勇気と不屈の精神を持った人物で、第二次世界大戦を耐え抜いた英国民に励ましと慰めと感謝の言葉を贈った。女王として、彼女は10年後にスエズ危機の屈辱とこれ以上なく落ちた英国の影響力を目にすることになった。

エリザベス2世逝去：英国そして世界にとっての一時代の終焉

7 在位中、20以上の国が大英帝国から離脱し、独立を手にした。彼女は英国が欧州共同体に加盟し、47年後に（EUを）脱退する様子も見守った。いわゆる「北アイルランド紛争」の中で彼女のまたいとこだったマウントバッテン卿がアイルランド暫定共和軍のメンバーたちによって暗殺されるという出来事が起こり、親族を失ったこともあった。

8 彼女の私生活も同様に波乱に満ちたものだった。彼女が見せたストイックさや冷静さとはまったく対照的に、親族の数々のドラマが衆目の見守る中で派手に展開されることになった。子供や孫たちは、厄介で言い争いの絶えない結婚をし、離婚をし、浮気をしてきた。ただ、親族への女王の献身は疑いようもなく、そうした慈愛もまた、彼女のイメージを形作る比類ない構成要素であった。

9 責任感と献身が彼女の人生と治世の特質であった一方で、エリザベスを最もよく知る人々はまた、彼女の「茶目っ気に満ちたユーモアのセンス」についても語っている。世界は2度、彼女のそうした側面を垣間見ている。一度目は2012年のロンドン・オリンピックの開会式の映像の中で、ジェームズ・ボンドと一緒にヘリコプターから飛び降りたように見えた場面、そして二度目は2022年の在位70周年を記念して、くまのパディントンと共演した映像の中で、マーマレード・サンドイッチをひそかに隠し持っていることを告白した場面である。

10 彼女の死に際し、世界中であふれるばかりの悲しみと哀悼の意が示されてきた。東京の英国大使館の複数の門には毎日花が手向けられ、弔問の記帳本に署名するための人の列が途切れることはない。

11 日本の皇室方も、女王とはそれぞれの思い出を持っている。女王は1953年6月、父・裕仁天皇陛下の名代としてエリザベスの戴冠式に出席した当時の明仁皇太子殿下に始まり、3世代にわたって皇室の方々と会っている。徳仁天皇陛下と雅子皇后陛下は結婚前に英国に留学をされており、徳仁皇太子殿下（当時）は留学中に女王に会われていて、今回の葬儀にもご出席される予定である。

12 女王の治世を正直に評価するなら、女王が統治した大英帝国によって途方もない負担がかかったことも認めなければならない。手を広げ過ぎた大英帝国や植民地制度の責任は女王にあったわけではないが、その頂点にいた存在であったことは事実である。

13 君主制という概念自体には、特権、階級、そしてある時点、あるいは多くの時点で、国民に対して無関心な巨大官僚機構といったイメージがつきまとう。女王がそうしたイメージを乗り越えようと奮闘し、成功したことは、君主制の存在やそれが生み出す痛み（負の部分）を無効にするわけではない。また、彼女の死に際し、多くの人が感じている、大量にあふれ出る悲しみや喪失感もまた、その負の部分を消すわけではない。

14 彼女の息子であり継承者であるチャールズ３世は、混乱の中にある国の王位を受け継ぐことになった。彼は自ら勉強をする一方、母親の代わりを務めて、これまで受け継ぐ準備はしてきたが、いくつかのことに関しては本当の意味での準備ができないものもあるだろう。

15 英国では、６年間で４人目の新しい首相が誕生した。一国のトップを担う者が目まぐるしく変わることは決して良い兆候ではない。EU離脱の決定は、確実に得られると約束されたはずの恩恵の多くがまだ遠い先の話であるため、依然として熱い議論の対象となっている。ブレグジットによって生じる経済の苦境は、新型コロナウイルスの大流行とロシアのウクライナ侵攻によってさらに拡大している。多くの英国人は冬が近づく中、暖房費が支払えるかどうかを心配している。

16 ブレグジットはまた、北アイルランドに関する問題を再燃させ、スコットランド人の多くは現在、独立に関する２度目の住民投票を求めている。英国の存在そのものが危うくなってもおかしくない状況にある。

17 エリザベス女王は、その不屈の使命感と奉仕に身を捧げることによって、英国民がこれらの問題に立ち向かう時にその溝を埋める役割を果たした。多くの追悼文や回顧の言葉の中で、幾度となく繰り返されている１つの言葉が「彼女は国をまとめる接着剤だった」というものだ。エリザベス女王という接着剤は、英国が最もその接着剤を必要とする時に失われてしまった。彼女は今後も長く惜しまれることだろう。

（訳・注　小川）

日本と中国は関係を正すべき時を迎えている

1 50年前の今週、1972年9月29日に、日本と中国は国交を正常化した。

2 その後は関係が温と冷、静と動の間を揺れ動く、波乱の半世紀だった。それは予想されたことだ。2つの国は隣同士で、深く結び付いた歴史、文化、経済を持つ。両国とも地域の主導権への野望を抱いている——そして根本的に異なる地域秩序の構想を提示している。真に前向きで生産的な協力関係を築くうえで、そのことは途方もない障害だ。それは克服することが可能だし、克服しなければならない。

3 リチャード・ニクソン米大統領が1972年2月に歴史的な中国訪問を行った時、日本は——そして世界のほとんども——驚愕した。日本政府はすぐさま中国政府との国交正常化に動いた。二国間の戦争状態を終結させ、共産党ゲリラとの内戦に敗れて1949年に台湾へと逃れた国民政府の外交承認を打ち切った。

4 経済的な関係はすぐに拡大した。ソビエト連邦によってもたらされた共通の脅威が関係のための接着剤となり、共有された繁栄の可能性が、緊密に協力する動機を両国に与えた。日本は経済発展のためのモデルと、その実現のための資本を提供した。この「蜜月期間」を通じて、両国政府は歴史と領土に関する議論などの見解が分かれる問題を最小限に抑えようと試み、そうすることができた。その代わりに両国は相互利益について語り、その実現に取り組んだ。

5 1991年のソビエト連邦の崩壊がそんな幸せな短い時間の終わりを告げた。両国をつないでいた接着剤が消滅し、対立をもたらす問題が関係の前面に出て力を持つことになった。中国は生徒としては物覚えがよすぎたのだ。猛烈な経済発展により、中国は主要国の仲間入りをした。2010年には日本を上回って世界2位の経済大国になり、10年以内に米国を抜いて1位になるだろうとする予測もある。

6 中国の技術は世界レベルで、いくつかの基準ではその能力は日本を超える。何よりも警戒するべきは同国の軍の成長だ。人民解放軍は手強い軍隊で、すべての領域で強さを誇る。

7 経済的な優秀さ、強引な外交、そして強力な軍が、1949年の中華人民共和国の建国から100周年を迎えるまでに世界のリーダーになるという、国家の野望の3本の柱である。この構想は理解できるが、その前のめりな姿勢と中身は日本にとって問題となる。

8   だからこそ、われわれ2つの国が双方に利益のある関係を作り出すことが非常に重要だ。現在、2つの問題が妨げになっている。1つ目は尖閣諸島で、日本が領有している東シナ海の島々だが、中国は釣魚島の名前で領有権を主張している。その長年にわたる論争の勢いが激化したのは2012年、日本が尖閣諸島を国有化した時だった。それ以降、中国は自らの権利を主張するため、島々の周辺海域に船舶を定期的に送り込んできた——水曜日（9月28日）には中国の沿岸警備艇が周辺に侵入した。

9   2つ目の問題は台湾で、中国は台湾が反抗的な属州だと主張し、本土に併合することを要求している。日本は「1つの中国」の方針を支持する——1972年の共同声明には、中国は1つで、台湾は中国の不可分の一部だとある——一方で、日本政府は、中国政府と台湾政府の問題が平和的に解決されなければならず、中国は軍事演習と好戦的な発言で平和と安定を脅かしてきたと考えている。台湾の上空を飛行して日本の排他的経済水域に着水したミサイルは、日本政府に向けたメッセージだとされていて、特にぞっとする動きであった。台湾の安全保障は日本の安全保障に影響するという主張と、台湾海峡での有事に対して入念に備える自衛隊の取り組みが、中国側の不安と、日本政府は統一を阻止しようと決意しているのだという中国の考えを強めている。

10   一見したところ、二国の関係の問題は本質的に領土をめぐる争いに思える。実際、動機になっているのは地域秩序についての別個の競合する構想だ。日本にとって最も重要な原則は、紛争解決のためのオープンかつ透明な、すべての当事者を平等に扱うルールに基づいたプロセスである。中国にとっては、大きさと力がほかのすべての判断に勝るべきだとなる。

11   これらの相違点が紛争に至らないようにするための方法がいくつかある。何よりもまず、挑発が対立の口火となるのを防ぐためのガードレールを設置しなければならない。これには多元的な対応が必要とされる。

12   第一に、首脳レベルの議論を再開することだ。2019年12月に当時の安倍晋三首相が中国を訪問して以来、両国の首脳による1対1の会談は行われていない。中国の習近平国家主席は翌年に返礼訪問を実施する予定だったが、新型コロナウイルス感染症のパンデミックが邪魔をした。

13 岸田文雄首相と習氏は、岸田氏が首相に就任した2021年10月に電話で一度話を
しただけだ。二人が今年の後半、インドネシアのバリで予定されているG20の会
合、もしくはバンコクでのアジア太平洋経済協力のフォーラムで会談するのではな
いかとの期待がある。一度や二度では十分ではない。良い関係を築くという強い
決意のシグナルを送り、官僚と国民にその実現を納得してもらうためには、定期
的な会談が必要だ。

14 優先事項の一つは軍と軍の間の通信機構の開設と使用だ。両国の軍が話し合い、
基本ルールを定め、お互いが送る信号を理解するための方法がなくてはならない。
透明性が推奨されることになるだろう。

15 第二に、われわれの2つの国が共有する懸念について協力するための方法を見つ
け出さなければならない。支援が必要とする人に届き、かつ最も効率的に使われ
るために、資金と専門知識を共同で供出して、地域の発展を促進する目的で一体
となることができるはずだ。共同で共通の利益を創出する持続可能性、社会的回
復力、接続性を促進するべきだ。

16 経済的な結び付きは二国間関係の重要な構成要素である。中国は日本の最大の貿
易相手国で、財務省が公表したデータによると昨年の貿易総額は38兆4,000億
円に達した。日本は中国にとって4番目に大きな貿易相手国だ。日本と中国の企
業の間で激しくなりつつある経済競争にもかかわらず、われわれは今もなお、両
国の企業が繁栄できるような分業を作り上げて維持できるはずだ。成長の一方で
国内の経済的な難題に直面している中国には援助が必要になるだろう。

17 協力することは、日本が中国の不正に目をつぶるという意味ではない。日本は断
固として国益を保護しなければならない。そうすることによってのみ、中国政府の
首脳にわが国の真剣さとパートナーとしての信頼性を納得してもらえるだろう。

18 日中国交正常化50周年の記念イベントに寄せたメッセージで、岸田氏は二国間の
「建設的で安定した」関係への願望を語った。関係の現状を鑑みると、それは理解
できるとともに実現可能な目標である。日中関係の潜在的可能性を考えれば、そ
れは期待されるべき必要最小限のことだ──そして最初の半世紀に関する痛烈な
指摘でもある。　　　　　　　　　　　　　　　　　　　　　　（訳・注　桑田）

第 **2** 章 　国内政治・外交

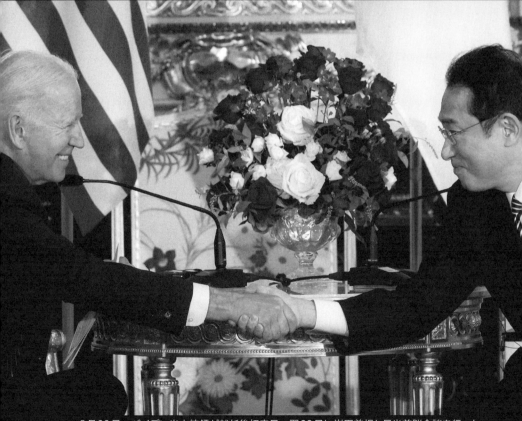

5月22日、バイデン米大統領が就任後初来日。翌23日に岸田首相と日米首脳会談を行った

Japan needs a real economic security strategy

日本には真の経済安全保障戦略が必要

January 8, 2022

●Tracks 084-090 / 解説 p. 172、訳 p. 177

`Track 084`

1   The government of Prime Minister Fumio Kishida is committed to an expansive conception of national security that focuses on economic issues.

2   After taking office, Kishida emphasized that economic security would be a top priority of the National Security Strategy that is anticipated to be released this year, created the post of minister for economic security and promised that his administration would submit an economic security promotion bill to this year's ordinary session of the Diet.

`Track 085`

3   Economic security is key to Japan's national security but it is also an amorphous concept that is easily abused. The challenge for the Japanese government is crafting a strategy that truly advances the nation's security and isn't just a fig leaf for protectionism, mercantilism and the expansion of bureaucratic power.

4   The government's thinking about economic security has been shaped by the work of the Strategic Headquarters on the Creation of a New International Order, a study group that Kishida chaired as head of the Liberal Democratic Party's Policy Research Council. It concluded that Japanese national strength and standing in an evolving world order depended on the vitality and innovative capacity of its economy.

岸田政権は安全保障政策として経済安全保障を積極的に推進している。世界情勢が不安定さを増す中、「新しい資本主義」を掲げる首相の戦略が保護貿易主義や偏った利益の配分に陥ることなく、各国と協調し、すべての国民に享受されるものになることを望む。

1
- □ [タイトル]strategy 戦略
- □ be committed to ... …に尽力する
- □ expansive 包括的な
- □ conception 構想
- □ focus on ... …に焦点を当てる

2
- □ take office 就任する
- □ emphasize 強調する
- □ priority 優先事項
- □ the National Security Strategy 国家安全保障戦略
- □ be anticipated to *do* ～すると見込まれる
- □ administration 政権
- □ promotion 推進
- □ ordinary session of the Diet 通常国会→「国会」の意味では必ず the Diet となる

3
- □ amorphous 無定形の、漠然とした
- □ abuse 乱用する
- □ craft (巧みに)作り出す
- □ advance 推進する
- □ fig leaf 隠れみの→「イチジクの葉」が
- 本来の意味
- □ protectionism 保護貿易主義
- □ mercantilism 重商主義
- □ expansion 拡大
- □ bureaucratic 官僚の

4
- □ the Strategic Headquarters on the Creation of a New International Order 新国際秩序創造戦略本部
- □ chair …の議長を務める
- □ the Liberal Democratic Party's Policy Research Council 自由民主党政務調査会→このトップが政調会長
- □ standing 地位
- □ evolving 発展する、変化する
- □ vitality 活力
- □ innovative capacity 革新力

Track 086

5   Economic security, the study group concluded, rests on two pillars: strategic autonomy and strategic indispensability. The first requires Japan to have the means to ensure the economic well-being of its citizens and national social and economic capacity. This reflects fears of vulnerability created by dependence on other countries for key economic inputs.

6   Long inchoate, this concern took concrete shape in 2010 when China cut off exports of rare earths to Japan during a confrontation over the Senkaku Islands. Since then, the entire world has awakened to China's central position in global production chains and the power that bestows upon Beijing in international disputes.

Track 087

7   The second pillar demands that Japan have industrial capacity in fields considered important to international society. In other words, Japan should make products that the rest of the world needs so that this country is considered an integral partner. This dovetails nicely with the country's long-standing preference for self-sufficiency in key technologies, semiconductors among them. It has given policymakers in Tokyo additional impetus to encourage companies to reroute supply chains through Japan.

8   Along with a ¥200 billion fund for Japanese companies, the government has provided enough money to tempt Taiwan Semiconductor Manufacturing Company to construct a semiconductor plant in Kumamoto Prefecture — while also setting aside funds to develop new technologies and to impose new or tighter controls on existing ones. This last item will include the creation of secret patents to keep especially sensitive new technologies from prying eyes.

5
- ☐ rest on ... …に基づく
- ☐ pillar 柱
- ☐ autonomy 自律性
- ☐ indispensability 不可欠性
- ☐ require ... to *do* …に〜することを求める
- ☐ means 方法、手段
- ☐ ensure 保証する、確保する
- ☐ well-being 幸福
- ☐ vulnerability 脆弱性
- ☐ dependence 依存
- ☐ input 投入物

6
- ☐ inchoate はっきりしない
- ☐ take concrete shape 具体化する
- ☐ cut off ... …を停止する
- ☐ rare earth レアアース
- ☐ confrontation 対立
- ☐ awaken to ... …に気づく
- ☐ bestow A upon B AをBに与える
- ☐ dispute 紛争

7
- ☐ in fields considered important to ... …にとって重要と見なされる分野
- ☐ in other words 言い換えれば
- ☐ integral 欠くことのできない
- ☐ dovetail with ... …と一致する
  →dovetailは木材を接合する手法の「あり継ぎ」のこと
- ☐ long-standing 長年の
- ☐ preference 好み、選択
- ☐ self-sufficiency 自給(自足)
- ☐ semiconductor 半導体
- ☐ policymaker 政策立案者
- ☐ additional 追加の
- ☐ impetus 弾み
- ☐ reroute …のルートを切り替える
- ☐ supply chain 供給網、サプライチェーン

8
- ☐ along with ... …とともに
- ☐ tempt ... to *do* …を〜する気にさせる
- ☐ Taiwan Semiconductor Manufacturing Company(, Ltd.) 台湾積体電路製造、TSMC
- ☐ set aside ... …を確保する
- ☐ impose A on B AをBに課す
- ☐ existing 既存の
- ☐ patent 特許
- ☐ keep ... from prying eyes …を詮索の目から守る
- ☐ sensitive 機密性の高い

Track 088

9 In addition to promoting supply chain resilience and developing and protecting new technologies, the new economic security legislation will also protect critical infrastructure. Governments are acutely attuned to threats to the most important elements of social and economic infrastructure, such as financial institutions, telecommunications networks and power grids. Japanese authorities will be working closely with the companies and authorities running these services to ensure that they are safe and secure. Again, there is a fear that Chinese-made components will be vulnerable to espionage or disruption.

10 A genuine economic security strategy will go beyond those technological components and identify ways that Japan can use its economic power to advance its national interests. For example, there should be discussion of the ways that Tokyo can leverage economic assistance and aid to maximize its influence in other capitals. There should be efforts to modernize international trade and investment regimes to promote the interests and values, such as transparency and economic liberalism, that Japan prioritizes. Energy and attention should also be given to institutions that set standards, especially those dealing with digital technologies and connectivity.

Track 089

11 In all those endeavors, Japan should work closely with like-minded governments, such as the United States, Australia, Canada and members of the European Union. In fact, one of the driving forces behind Japan's emphasis on economic security has been closer alignment with the U.S., which increasingly relies on economic statecraft in its strategic competition with China. Japan created an economic security bureau within the National Security Secretariat to facilitate policy coordination with the U.S.

9
- [ ] in addition to ... …に加えて
- [ ] resilience 回復力、強靭性
- [ ] legislation 法律
- [ ] infrastructure インフラ
- [ ] be attuned to ... …に順応する、理解している
- [ ] acutely 強く、鋭く
- [ ] financial institution 金融機関
- [ ] telecommunications network 通信ネットワーク
- [ ] power grid 送電網
- [ ] authorities 当局
- [ ] component 部品
- [ ] be vulnerable to ... …に脆弱だ
- [ ] espionage スパイ活動
- [ ] disruption 途絶

10
- [ ] genuine 真の
- [ ] go beyond ... …にとどまらない
- [ ] identify 特定する
- [ ] national interest 国益
- [ ] leverage 利用する
- [ ] maximize 最大限にする
- [ ] capital 首都→ここではその首都がある国、政府の意味
- [ ] modernize 最新化する
- [ ] investment regime 投資制度
- [ ] transparency 透明性
- [ ] prioritize 優先する、重視する
- [ ] deal with ... …を手がける
- [ ] connectivity 接続性

11
- [ ] endeavor 努力
- [ ] like-minded 同じような考えを持つ →-mindedは「…の考えの」
- [ ] driving force 原動力
- [ ] emphasis 重視
- [ ] alignment 連携
- [ ] increasingly ますます
- [ ] rely on ... …に依存する
- [ ] statecraft 国策
- [ ] competition 競合
- [ ] bureau (事務)局
- [ ] the National Security Secretariat 国家安全保障局
- [ ] facilitate 円滑にする
- [ ] coordination 協調

12　As an example of such multilateral cooperation, Japan should be leading efforts to forge a broad coalition to combat the uses of economic coercion. Some form of "insurance" or swap arrangement should be considered.

Track 090

13　While action is needed, caution is in order, too. Economic security is a pliable concept and there is a desire in parts of the government to control and direct national development and economic activity. There is fear that a national economic security strategy will reinvigorate protectionist and mercantilist impulses. That temptation is evident in the list of businesses originally subject to the enhanced scrutiny of foreign investment in revisions to the Foreign Exchange and Foreign Trade Act. That list includes hot springs operators, pen manufacturers and baseball stadium managers. It is essential then that vital economic interests be defined narrowly.

14　A final element of the strategy is a conspicuous effort to energize the country's economy. This is obvious but it is also easily overlooked. Japan needs steady growth to ensure that its citizens are happy and secure in their own lives. By this logic, Prime Minister Kishida's commitment to "new capitalism" is an integral part of Japan's economic security. A growing economy whose returns are not enjoyed by all Japanese will not be stable nor will it offer security to the people or the state.

(904 words)

12
- □ multilateral 多面的な
- □ forge 築く
- □ coalition 連携
- □ coercion 強制、強要
- □ insurance 保険
- □ swap arrangement スワップ協定→自国の通貨・金融危機に備えて市場の安定に必要な互いの通貨を融通し合う仕組み

13
- □ caution 慎重さ
- □ be in order 適切だ、ふさわしい
- □ pliable 融通の利く
- □ reinvigorate 再び活性化させる
- □ protectionist 貿易保護論者
- □ mercantilist 重商主義者
- □ impulse 勢い、衝動
- □ temptation 誘惑
- □ subject to ... …の対象で
- □ enhanced 強化された、拡張された
- □ scrutiny 精査
- □ revision 改正
- □ the Foreign Exchange and Foreign Trade Act 外国為替及び外国貿易法
- □ define 定義する
- □ narrowly 狭く

14
- □ conspicuous 目に見える
- □ energize 活気づける
- □ overlook 見落とす
- □ steady 着実な
- □ commitment 取り組み
- □ stable 安定した

Time for Japan to embrace realism in dealings with Russia

日本はロシアとの対応で現実主義を受け入れるべき時だ

March 26, 2022　　　　　　　　●Tracks 091-099 / 解説 p. 173、訳 p. 180

Track 091

1　Russia's decision to suspend negotiations on a formal peace treaty to end World War II is an opportunity for Japan.

2　That is because the move obliges the Japanese government to reassess its policy and strategy, to recognize the bitter truth about Russian thinking and dispense with the unreasonable expectations that have guided decision making in Tokyo.

Track 092

3　Since the end of World War II, the Japanese government has sought to sign a peace treaty with its counterpart in Moscow and secure the return of the islands of Kunashiri, Etorofu, Shikotan and the Habomai islets — collectively known as the Northern Territories — which were seized by Soviet forces in the closing days of that conflict.

4　Progress has been slow and begrudging, with anticipation well outpacing developments. In 1956, the two countries issued a joint declaration ending the state of war between them and Moscow agreed to return the Habomai islets and Shikotan once a peace treaty was signed.

ロシアによる一方的な交渉中断の通告で、平和条約締結と北方領土返還への期待がしぼむことになった。ロシアは日本の制裁を理由に挙げるが、そもそもの原因はロシアのウクライナ侵攻にある。日本は揺さぶりに屈することなく、毅然とした姿勢を維持するべきだ。

1
- [タイトル]embrace 受け入れる
- suspend 中断する
- negotiation 交渉

2
- oblige ... to *do* …に〜することを強いる
- reassess 再評価する
- recognize 認識する
- dispense with ... …をなしにする
- unreasonable 不合理な
- decision making 意思決定

3
- seek to *do* 〜しようと模索する → sought は seek の過去分詞形
- counterpart in Moscow モスクワの同等のもの → ロシア政府のこと
- secure 保証する、確保する
- collectively 一括して
- the Northern Territories 北方領土
- seize 奪う
- in the closing days of ... …の最後の数日間に
- conflict 紛争、戦争

4
- begrudging 不本意な、しぶしぶと
- anticipation 期待
- outpace 上回る
- development (事態の)進展
- joint declaration 共同宣言
- state of war 戦争状態

Track 093

5 In 1964, they agreed to let former Japanese residents visit the graves of family members. In 1992, visa-free travel to and from the islands was approved for cultural exchanges and to foster relations. Seven years later, the two governments reached yet another deal that allowed former residents of the four islands to make periodic visits. In addition, Tokyo and Moscow have agreed to various joint economic activities on the islands.

6 Hopes bloomed after a 2018 meeting in Singapore between then Prime Minister Shinzo Abe and Russian President Vladimir Putin, at which they agreed to accelerate negotiations over a bilateral peace treaty based on the 1956 joint declaration. A 2020 change to the Russian constitution that prohibited the transfer of territory ended that moment of optimism.

Track 094

7 Now, after Japan has joined Western sanctions to punish Russia for invading Ukraine, the Russian government has made the unstated perfectly clear: It has suspended the peace talks, ended the travel programs and shut down the economic activities. Russian's Foreign Ministry blames Japan's "openly unfriendly positions and attempts to damage the interests of our country."

8 Prime Minister Fumio Kisihida rightly responded that "This entire situation has been created by Russia's invasion of Ukraine," and called the attempt to blame Tokyo "extremely unfair and completely unacceptable." And he added, "Japan must resolutely continue to sanction Russia in cooperation with the rest of the world."

5
- [ ] let ... *do* …に〜することを認める
- [ ] visa-free ビザなしの→ -freeは「…がない」の意味
- [ ] to and from ... …への行き来
- [ ] cultural exchange 文化交流
- [ ] foster 育む
- [ ] yet another さらにもう1つの
- [ ] periodic 定期的な
- [ ] in addition それに加えて

6
- [ ] bloom 花が咲く、花開く
- [ ] then 当時の
- [ ] accelerate 加速させる
- [ ] bilateral 二国間の
- [ ] based on ... …に基づいて
- [ ] constitution 憲法
- [ ] prohibit 禁止する
- [ ] transfer 譲渡

7
- [ ] sanction 制裁
- [ ] make ... clear …を明らかにする
- [ ] the unstated 暗黙の意図
- [ ] shut down ... …を停止する
- [ ] openly あからさまに

8
- [ ] respond …と反応する
- [ ] entire 全体の
- [ ] extremely 極めて
- [ ] unacceptable 容認できない、受け入れられない
- [ ] resolutely 断固として
- [ ] in cooperation with ... …と協調して

Track 095

9   This tough line — Tokyo has imposed sanctions on scores of Russian individuals, seven banks and other institutions, implemented export bans and plans to revoke the country's most-favored-nation trade status — must come as a surprise to Moscow. Over the past decade, Japan has overlooked every other transgression as it sought rapprochement with Russia. Following the 2014 annexation of Crimea, Japan shied away from sanctions and Abe met with Putin numerous times in an attempt to forge a personal relationship that might lead to progress.

10   Abe had several motivations. As a conservative nationalist, he sought the return of territory he deemed an integral part of Japan; success would have been a cornerstone of his legacy; and Japan has always eyed the vast resources of the Russian Far East, its energy supplies in particular, and he hoped that a good relationship would ensure access to them.

Track 096

11   Equally powerful were strategic considerations. A relationship that resulted in the return of the territory would have signaled a transformation in the strategic environment. It would have meant that relations with Moscow were secure enough to divert military attention from the north and focus more on the southern approaches.

9
- [ ] tough line 強硬路線
- [ ] impose A on B AをBに課す
- [ ] scores of ... 多数の…
- [ ] individual 個人
- [ ] institution 機関
- [ ] implement 実施する
- [ ] export ban 輸出禁止
- [ ] revoke 取り消す
- [ ] most-favored-nation trade status 最恵国待遇
- [ ] overlook …に目をつぶる
- [ ] transgression 違反
- [ ] rapprochement 関係改善
- [ ] annexation 併合
- [ ] shy away from ... …を避ける
- [ ] numerous 数多くの
- [ ] in an attempt to *do* 〜しようとして
- [ ] forge 築く

10
- [ ] motivation 動機
- [ ] conservative 保守的な
- [ ] nationalist 国家主義者
- [ ] deem A B AをBと見なす→ここでは Aに当たるthe return of territoryが 前に出ている
- [ ] cornerstone 基盤、礎
- [ ] eye …に目をつける
- [ ] ensure 保証する

11
- [ ] strategic 戦略的な
- [ ] consideration 考慮
- [ ] result in ... …をもたらす
- [ ] transformation 転換
- [ ] environment 環境
- [ ] divert そらす、転じる
- [ ] focus on ... …を重視する
- [ ] approach 進入路、通じる道

12 That is no abstract concern. In the first nine months of 2021, Japan scrambled 199 times because of the presence of Russian aircraft, including just a few weeks ago when a Russian helicopter violated Japanese airspace. Earlier this month, several Russian Navy ships transited the Tsugaru Strait, which separates the main islands of Honshu and Hokkaido. In February, 24 Russian ships took part in a joint training exercise in the Sea of Okhotsk with Chinese naval vessels, which followed the voyage last year of 10 Russian and Chinese ships that sailed together around the Japanese archipelago.

Track 097

13 Abe hoped to put distance between Moscow and Beijing. He reached out to Putin to give the Russian president choices and prevent the consolidation of a revisionist axis between the two neighbors. It's a laudable goal. China and Russia have become increasingly close and the joint declaration they issued last month signals a partnership with "no limits." Viewed through the prism of their expanding military cooperation, that is worrisome.

14 While Abe's successors have not been as driven to solve the Russia problem, they adopted his policies to win his support and because Japanese public opinion largely backed those positions. That policy became unsustainable following the invasion.

Track 098

15 There must also be limits to Japan's tolerance of Russian misbehavior, however. The invasion of a sovereign country is well beyond them. That reassessment is even more compelling given the lack of progress resulting from engagement. Russia appears to be stringing Japan along, taking whatever it can while making no concessions. Meanwhile, Moscow is doing its best to drive its own wedge between Tokyo and Washington, insisting that their alliance is an obstacle to a resolution of the territorial dispute.

12
- [ ] abstract 抽象的な、理論上の
- [ ] scramble スクランブル発進する
- [ ] violate 侵犯する
- [ ] airspace 領空
- [ ] transit 通過する
- [ ] strait 海峡
- [ ] separate 隔てる
- [ ] take part in ... …に参加する
- [ ] training exercise 演習
- [ ] vessel 船舶
- [ ] voyage 航行
- [ ] sail 航海する
- [ ] archipelago 列島

13
- [ ] put distance between A and B A とBの間に距離を置く
- [ ] reach out to ... …に接触する
- [ ] consolidation 統合
- [ ] revisionist 修正主義者の
- [ ] axis 枢軸
- [ ] two neighbors 2つの隣国→ロシアと中国のこと
- [ ] laudable 称賛に値する
- [ ] increasingly ますます
- [ ] through the prism of ... …の視点で、…の見地から
- [ ] expanding 拡大する
- [ ] worrisome 気がかりな

14
- [ ] successor 後継者
- [ ] driven 意欲的な
- [ ] adopt 採用する
- [ ] public opinion 世論
- [ ] back 支持する
- [ ] unsustainable 維持できない

15
- [ ] tolerance 容認
- [ ] misbehavior 不法行為
- [ ] sovereign country 主権国
- [ ] reassessment 再評価、見直し
- [ ] compelling やむを得ない
- [ ] given …を考慮すると
- [ ] result from ... …に由来する
- [ ] engagement 関わること→ここではロシアとの交渉を指す
- [ ] string ... along …をだまし続ける
- [ ] take whatever ... can …が取れるものは何でも取る
- [ ] concession 譲歩
- [ ] drive *one's* own wedge between A and B AとBの間に自らの楔を打ち込む、AとBの仲を裂く
- [ ] obstacle 障害
- [ ] dispute 紛争、論争

16   It has been reported that the new National Security Strategy, currently under review, will label Russia a "security challenge" in contrast to the "partner" identified in the last strategy — a change that is long overdue. The Japanese government must show Russia that the invasion of Ukraine is unacceptable and business as usual is not an option. Tokyo must make clear that there can be no hope of splitting the nations fighting this gross violation of human rights and international law.

Track 099

17   For Japan, it's now time to look clearly at its relations with Russia and acknowledge Moscow's behavior for what it is: empty rhetoric, tactical tricks and bullying.

(964 words)

16
- [ ] the National Security Strategy 国家安全保障戦略
- [ ] currently 現在のところ
- [ ] under review 見直し中
- [ ] label 分類する
- [ ] in contrast to ... …とは対照的に
- [ ] be long overdue 遅きに失している
- [ ] business as usual いつも通りのやり方
- [ ] make clear that ... …だと表明する
- [ ] split 分裂させる
- [ ] gross 重大な
- [ ] violation 侵害

17
- [ ] acknowledge 認識する
- [ ] for what it is ありのままの、真の姿で
- [ ] rhetoric 美辞麗句
- [ ] tactical 戦術的な
- [ ] bullying 弱い者いじめ

Biden's visit takes the Japan-U.S. partnership to new heights

バイデン大統領訪日で日米パートナーシップはさらなる高みへ

May 28, 2022 ●Tracks 100-107 / 解説 p. 174、訳 p. 183

Track 100

1 Prime Minister Fumio Kishida and Japan could not have hoped for a better and more comforting visit by U.S. President Joe Biden.

2 The list of deliverables was long and meaty. As important, though, was confirmation that Japan remains a priority for the United States, the alignment of the two men's visions for global order and the affirmation of Japan's critical role in the region and beyond.

Track 101

3 As this country's only ally, reiteration of the longstanding U.S. position that the bilateral alliance is "the cornerstone of peace and prosperity in the Indo-Pacific" is more than diplomatic boilerplate. Biden's statement that "the U.S. remains fully committed to Japan's defense" matters greatly as countries like China and Russia seek to rewrite rules and redraw borders through the use of force. His pledge that the two countries will "face the challenges of today and in the future together" takes on a greater meaning following reports that Chinese and Russian aircraft conducted joint operations in skies near Japan as the two men met.

4 Central to the alliance is the belief among potential adversaries that the U.S. will use the full range of its capabilities, including nuclear weapons, to defend Japan. Therefore, deterrence is invariably a priority in leadership discussions and this meeting was no different.

バイデン米大統領が5月22日から3日間、就任後初めて訪日。日米同盟の抑止力と対処力を強化する方針を確認、またインド太平洋経済枠組み（IPEF）の立ち上げを発表して、地域への確固たる関与を表明した。日米首脳会談は大きな成果を残したといえる。

1
- □ [タイトル]take ... to new heights … を新たな高みへと導く
- □ comforting 励みになる

2
- □ deliverables 成果物
- □ meaty 内容の濃い
- □ confirmation 確証
- □ priority 優先事項
- □ alignment 一致
- □ order 秩序
- □ affirmation 確認
- □ critical 非常に重要な

3
- □ ally 同盟国
- □ reiteration 再表明
- □ longstanding 長年にわたる
- □ bilateral 二国間の
- □ alliance 同盟
- □ cornerstone 礎
- □ prosperity 繁栄
- □ Indo-Pacific インド太平洋地域
- □ diplomatic 外交の
- □ boilerplate 決まり文句
- □ fully committed to ... …に全力を尽くして
- □ matter 重要である
- □ redraw （境界線などを）引き直す
- □ pledge 誓約
- □ face …に立ち向かう
- □ take on a greater meaning より大きな意味を持つ
- □ joint operation 共同演習

4
- □ central to ... …の中核をなして
- □ adversary 敵対国
- □ capability 能力
- □ deterrence 抑止政策
- □ invariably 常に

Track 102

5 Kishida and Biden pledged to work together to "continually modernize the alliance, evolve bilateral roles and missions and strengthen joint capabilities including by aligning strategies and prioritizing goals together."

6 That cooperation extends beyond the two nations. The two leaders agreed to work together to promote capacity building in third countries, an effort that would rely on coast guards, as well as to cooperate in outer space and cyberspace — two domains increasingly critical to national security.

Track 103

7 While the U.S. role is crucial, even more important are Japan's own efforts. This country's national defense is first and foremost a Japanese responsibility. Equally significant, Japanese efforts signal to the United States Tokyo's seriousness and its credibility as a partner. Thus, Prime Minister Kishida stated his determination to fundamentally reinforce his country's defense capabilities and secure substantial increases in the defense budget to make sure that happens.

8 An area of expanding cooperation is economic issues. This was once a source of dangerous friction in the relationship; now the two countries are working together in this central arena of geopolitical competition. Biden and Kishida promised to collaborate in protecting and promoting critical technologies and to work to ensure that supply chains are resilient and stable. One key agreement was establishing a joint task force to explore development of next generation semiconductors, based on the Basic Principles on Semiconductor Cooperation adopted in the Japan-U.S. Commercial and Industrial Partnership.

5
- ☐ modernize 現代化する
- ☐ evolve 進化させる
- ☐ align 整合させる

6
- ☐ capacity building 能力強化
- ☐ effort 取り組み
- ☐ coast guard 沿岸警備隊
- ☐ outer space 宇宙空間
- ☐ cyberspace サイバー空間→コンピュータ・ネットワークが作り出す仮想空間
- ☐ domain 分野、領域

7
- ☐ national defense 国防
- ☐ first and foremost 何よりもまず
- ☐ significant 重要な
- ☐ signal A to B AをBに示す→Aに当たるTokyo's ... partnerが長いので後ろに置かれている
- ☐ Tokyo 日本政府
- ☐ credibility 信頼性
- ☐ determination 決意
- ☐ fundamentally 抜本的に
- ☐ reinforce 強化する
- ☐ substantial 大幅な
- ☐ defense budget 防衛費

8
- ☐ issue 問題
- ☐ source 原因
- ☐ friction 摩擦
- ☐ arena 舞台、場
- ☐ geopolitical 地政学的な
- ☐ collaborate 連携する
- ☐ critical technology 基幹技術
- ☐ ensure 保証する
- ☐ resilient 強靭な
- ☐ next generation semiconductor 次世代半導体
- ☐ Basic Principles on Semiconductor Cooperation 半導体協力基本原則→2022年5月4日に日米が協力し半導体サプライチェーンを構築することが合意された
- ☐ adopt 採択する
- ☐ Japan-U.S. Commercial and Industrial Partnership 日米商務・産業パートナーシップ（JUCIP）→2021年11月に日米の産業力強化のために設立することが合意された

Track 104

9 The two countries should follow up on the newly passed economic security legislation and identify additional ways to cooperate and strengthen economic security. That subject is certain to be taken up in the Economic Consultative Committee, the economic "two-plus-two" meeting that is supposed to be launched this summer.

10 Biden's announcement of the Indo-Pacific Economic Framework (IPEF) is a welcome sign of U.S. commitment to and engagement with the region. Its membership roster is longer than anticipated and includes not only all U.S. allies in the region, but important Southeast Asian nations as well such as Singapore, Indonesia and Vietnam. India's decision to join is especially gratifying, given New Delhi's refusal to join the Regional Comprehensive Economic Partnership agreement.

Track 105

11 While we would prefer that the U.S. reconsider membership in the Comprehensive and Progressive Agreement for Trans-Pacific Partnership, we recognize that is unlikely. IPEF is a good step although much — if not virtually everything — depends on what the framework negotiations yield.

12 Over five days in Japan and South Korea, President Biden demonstrated the seriousness of his commitment to the Indo-Pacific region. Not only is the U.S. steadfast in its alliances, but it is determined to work with allies and partners to set the rules for the 21st century. As the two leaders' joint statement declared, both countries will "play an active role in addressing the challenges most salient for the global community — whether the emergence of new technologies, the impact of climate change, or transnational threats such as infectious disease."

9
- [ ] follow up on ... …を実行に移す
- [ ] economic security 経済安全保障
- [ ] legislation 法律
- [ ] identify 明らかにする、特定する
- [ ] take up 取り上げる
- [ ] Economic Consultative Committee 経済政策協議委員会
- [ ] two-plus-two 2プラス2(ツープラスツー)の→主に安全保障分野での外務・防衛トップの会合の通称
- [ ] launch 開始する

10
- [ ] Indo-Pacific Economic Framework インド太平洋経済枠組み
- [ ] commitment to ... …への献身、参加
- [ ] engagement 関与
- [ ] roster 名簿
- [ ] anticipate 予測する
- [ ] gratifying 喜ばしい
- [ ] New Delhi インド政府
- [ ] refusal 拒否
- [ ] Regional Comprehensive Economic Partnership 地域的な包括的経済提携(RCEP)

11
- [ ] prefer 望む
- [ ] reconsider 考え直す
- [ ] Comprehensive and Progressive Agreement for Trans-Pacific Partnership 環太平洋パートナーシップに関する包括的及び先進的な協定(CPTPP)
- [ ] recognize 認識する
- [ ] unlikely 見込みが薄い
- [ ] virtually 事実上
- [ ] yield 生み出す

12
- [ ] steadfast 不動の
- [ ] joint statement 共同声明
- [ ] declare 宣言する
- [ ] address …に対処する
- [ ] challenge 課題
- [ ] salient 顕著な
- [ ] emergence 出現
- [ ] transnational 国境を越えた
- [ ] threat 脅威
- [ ] infectious disease 感染症

13 Fortunately, there is almost no gap in Japanese and U.S. thinking about what those challenges are. It is a long list, but both governments place at its top the threats posed by revisionist governments and the need to think creatively and act to address those dangers. That is an invaluable prerequisite and the foundation of the expanding partnership.

14 During Biden's stay in Tokyo, he also made clear the role he expects Japan to play. He expressed support for Japan's permanent membership on a reformed Security Council — and repeated time and again the importance of enhanced coordination among democracies and like-minded partners to tackle contemporary challenges. Japan is expected to stand with the U.S. as they provide development aid, build regional infrastructure, promote cybersecurity and build safe and secure 5G telecommunications systems.

15 This is a vote of confidence in Japan and in Prime Minister Kishida. The prime minister is emerging from the shadow of former Prime Minister Shinzo Abe, building on his work while also putting his own mark on Japan's foreign and national security policy. Hosting President Biden and other leaders for "the Quad" and the various bilateral meetings is proof not only of the priority he attaches to an ambitious regional security agenda but the readiness of those officials to work with him to achieve those objectives.

(908 words)

13 □ place 位置づける
□ pose 提示する、（脅威を）与える
□ revisionist 修正主義的な
□ invaluable 非常に重要な
□ prerequisite 前提条件

14 □ permanent membership 常任理事国であること
□ Security Council 安全保障理事会
□ time and again 繰り返し、何度も
□ enhanced 強化された
□ coordination 連携
□ democracy 民主主義国
□ like-minded 志を同じくする
□ tackle …に取り組む
□ contemporary 現代の
□ stand with ... …と協力する
□ development aid 開発援助
□ infrastructure 基盤、インフラ
□ 5G telecommunications systems 第5世代移動通信システム

15 □ vote of confidence in ... …に対する信任
□ emerge 脱する
□ build on ... …を基に前進する
□ put *one's* own mark on ... …に〜自身の足跡を残す
□ host 主催国として招く
□ the Quad 日米豪印戦略対話、クアッド
□ proof 証拠
□ attach priority to ... …を優先する、重視する
□ ambitious 野心的な
□ agenda 計画、課題
□ readiness 準備ができていること
□ objective 目標

Kishida's next moves will determine fate of Abe legacy

岸田首相の次の手立てが安倍元首相のレガシーの命運を決める

July 17, 2022　　　　　●Tracks 108-116 / 解説 p. 176、訳 p. 186

Track 108

1　Despite having left office two years ago, the death of former Prime Minister Shinzo Abe will have important and palpable consequences for Japan.

2　In many ways, he reset the course of contemporary Japan. Yet, for all that he accomplished during his record-setting tenure, a considerable part of his agenda remains undone and his death deprives those who continue to seek those objectives of their most passionate, committed and capable advocate.

Track 109

3　Any complete and honest reckoning of his legacy must also recognize that Abe was a divisive figure. His fervent belief demanded engagement and he was willing, unlike many other politicians in Japan, to let conviction guide him. If he was sometimes abrasive, then that was the price of his passion. It drove him and sometimes divided the nation.

4　Abe will be best known for being the country's longest-serving prime minister. That longevity restored stability to the Japanese government, ensuring not just consistency but genuine leadership. His tenure established him as a leading figure not just in Asia but throughout the world. It allowed him to forge relationships and friendships with his counterparts, a vital prerequisite to any pretension to real leadership. Ending the revolving door at the Prime Minister's Office may have been his most important legacy.

▼ **About This Editorial** ▼

安倍晋三元首相は総理として歴代最長の任期を務めたが、憲法改正やアベノミクスなど、実現に至らなかった課題や十分な成果の出なかった政策もある。安倍氏がもたらした安定性や継続性を、岸田首相は踏襲していくのか、それとも独自色を出すのかが注目される。

1
- □ despite …にもかかわらず
- □ leave office 辞任する
- □ palpable 目に見える、明白な
- □ consequence 影響

2
- □ for all ... …にもかかわらず
- □ accomplish 成し遂げる
- □ record-setting 記録的な
- □ tenure 在任
- □ agenda 課題
- □ undone 未完成の
- □ deprive A of B AからBを奪う
- □ committed 献身的な、熱心な
- □ capable 有能な
- □ advocate 擁護者、支持者

3
- □ reckoning 評価
- □ divisive 意見の分かれる、分断する
- □ fervent 熱意のある
- □ engagement 従事すること
- □ be willing to *do* ～することをいとわない
- □ conviction 確信
- □ abrasive 不快な
- □ price 代償
- □ drive 突き動かす
- □ divide 分断する

4
- □ be best known for ... …で最もよく知られる
- □ longest-serving 在位期間が最長の
- □ longevity 長さ、長寿
- □ restore 取り戻す
- □ stability 安定性
- □ ensure 確かにする
- □ consistency 一貫性、不変性
- □ forge 築く
- □ counterpart 同等の人→ここでは各国の首脳のこと
- □ prerequisite 必須条件
- □ pretension 自負
- □ revolving door 回転ドア→ここでは首相が次々と入れ替わることのたとえ
- □ Prime Minister's Office 首相官邸

163

Track 110

5 Stability meant policy continuity: the opportunity to lay out a vision and work to see it realized. Abenomics was his strategy to escape the malaise that gripped the Japanese economy. The official verdict was "Abenomics is working!" (as the official government website proclaimed) — outside assessments were not as charitable.

6 Abenomics was Japanese — or at least Liberal Democratic Party — orthodoxy: loose monetary policy, fiscal support and calls for structural reform. And, as was so often the case, the first two were pursued with vigor, the last one, not so much. Most observers credit Abenomics with consistency, coherency, the restoration of confidence while failing to trigger meaningful structural change. That shortcoming may well prove key to any final verdict.

Track 111

7 Central to economic policy is social reform, in particular, the empowerment of women to unleash their productive energies. Abe was no more successful with Womenomics. According to the most recent World Economic Forum analysis, Japan was 116th among 146 countries in gender gap rankings this year and last among Group of Seven industrialized nations. The failure to make progress was symptomatic of the tensions inherent in the Abe agenda — reforms needed for economic progress clashed with traditional beliefs about the appropriate social order. The latter prevailed.

5
- ☐ continuity 継続
- ☐ lay out ... …の計画を立てる
- ☐ see it realized それが実現されるのを見届ける
- ☐ malaise 低迷
- ☐ grip つかむ、がっちりとらえる
- ☐ verdict 判断、見解
- ☐ proclaim 宣言する
- ☐ charitable 寛大な

6
- ☐ Liberal Democratic Party 自由民主党
- ☐ orthodoxy 正道、正当な教義
- ☐ loose 緩和された
- ☐ monetary policy 金融政策
- ☐ fiscal support 財政支援
- ☐ call for ... …の要請
- ☐ structural reform 構造改革
- ☐ as is so often the case 非常によくある例の通り
- ☐ vigor 熱心さ
- ☐ credit A with B AをBで評価する
- ☐ coherency 一貫性
- ☐ restoration 回復
- ☐ shortcoming 欠点
- ☐ may well *do* おそらく〜だろう

7
- ☐ empowerment 権限を与えること
- ☐ unleash 解き放つ
- ☐ Womenomics ウーマノミクス→女性の活躍と牽引による経済の活性化。womenとeconomicsを合わせた造語
- ☐ World Economic Forum 世界経済フォーラム
- ☐ gender gap ジェンダーギャップ、男女の性差による格差
- ☐ Group of Seven industrialized nations 主要先進7カ国、G7
- ☐ be symptomatic of ... …を示している、象徴する
- ☐ tension 緊張状態
- ☐ inherent 内在する
- ☐ clash with ... …と対立する
- ☐ appropriate ふさわしい
- ☐ prevail 勝つ、優先する

8   Abe did restructure the national security bureaucracy. His activism demanded the consolidation of power in the Prime Minister's Office and a core component of his vision was strengthening of the national security apparatus. He empowered the National Security Secretariat, produced the first national security strategy and changed rules regarding the exercise of collective self-defense, among other key measures.

Track 112

9   He was unable to achieve his dream of rewriting the Constitution, however — one of his greatest frustrations. He did open the door to an invigorated debate about the charter's future. Whether Prime Minister Fumio Kishida takes up that task is one of the most important questions hanging over his administration.

10   Driving Abe was a belief that Japan was a great power and that it should act as one. As he said in a speech shortly after returning to office, "I am back and so shall Japan be." National security reform was a first step in that direction. But for Abe, assuming the appropriate international profile required constitutional reform that would lift the shackles off the country's ability to contribute to security, the real measure of global leadership.

Track 113

11   His can-do/must-do attitude appealed to many who feared a power vacuum in Asia. For some Asians, however, that attitude looked suspiciously like a readiness to overlook past misbehavior.

8
- [ ] restructure 構造改革する、作り直す
- [ ] bureaucracy 官僚組織
- [ ] activism 積極的な行動
- [ ] consolidation 統合
- [ ] core component 核心
- [ ] strengthening 強化
- [ ] apparatus 組織、機構
- [ ] empower …に権限を与える
- [ ] the National Security Secretariat 国家安全保障局
- [ ] regarding …に関する
- [ ] exercise 行使
- [ ] collective self-defense 集団的自衛権
- [ ] measures 対策

9
- [ ] the Constitution 憲法→一国の具体的な憲法を指す時はtheを付けて大文字で始める
- [ ] frustration 不満
- [ ] invigorated 活発な
- [ ] charter 憲章→ここでは日本国憲法のこと
- [ ] take up ... …に取り組む
- [ ] hang over ... …に差し迫る

10
- [ ] act as one それ（大国）としての役割を果たす
- [ ] return to office 任務に復帰する
- [ ] international profile 国際的な知名度
- [ ] require 必要とする
- [ ] constitutional reform 憲法改正
- [ ] life the shackles off ... …の足かせを外す
- [ ] contribute to ... …に貢献する
- [ ] measure 尺度、基準

11
- [ ] can-do やればできる
- [ ] must-do やらなければならない
- [ ] vacuum 空白
- [ ] suspiciously 不審なまでに
- [ ] readiness 用意ができていること
- [ ] overlook …に目をつぶる
- [ ] misbehavior 誤った行い

12 Abe should have been able to square that circle with strategic logic, reasoning that Japan needed good relations with like-minded neighbors and countries that shared its values to forge a coalition to sustain the status quo at a time of potential upheaval. Abe will be remembered for establishing the Indo-Pacific framework, a strategy that guides thinking today in many capitals. His failure to use that logic to build a more enduring and forward-looking relationship with South Korea — even though the fault was by no means his alone — will be the most obvious blot on that legacy.

> Track 114

13 And while Abe will be remembered for shifting baselines for relations with China, he was also a leader who worked assiduously to build better relations with Beijing and nurtured until the end of his tenure the hope of hosting Chinese leader Xi Jinping in Tokyo.

14 In the months to come, a key measure of Abe's legacy and influence will be how far Kishida goes to achieve those objectives. It is suspected that Kishida does not share all of Abe's ambitions and the former prime minister was continually nudging him from behind to go farther and do more. This week, Kishida promised to complete Abe's work but that will require political capital and the current prime minister has his own priorities.

> Track 115

15 As prime minister and as leader of his faction within the LDP, Abe never identified a successor, reasoning, perhaps rightly, that such a move would signal the end of his power. That meant that the party had to struggle to replace him when he stepped down two years ago.

12
- □ square the circle 不可能な（難しい）ことをやろうとする
- □ reason …と論じる
- □ like-minded 同じような考えを持つ
- □ neighbor 近隣の国
- □ coalition 連携
- □ sustain 維持する
- □ status quo 現状
- □ upheaval 大変動
- □ Indo-Pacific framework インド太平洋の枠組み
- □ capital 首都→ここではその首都がある国や政府の意味
- □ enduring 永続的な
- □ forward-looking 前向きな
- □ even though ... …だとしても
- □ be no means 決して…でない
- □ blot 汚点

13
- □ baseline 基準線
- □ assiduously 熱心に
- □ nurture 育む

14
- □ in the months to come 今後数カ月の間
- □ be suspected that ... …ではないかと考えられる
- □ ambition 野心
- □ continuously 絶えず
- □ nudge つつく、促す
- □ political capital 政治的資本→政治家がほかの政治家や有権者との関係、信頼などを通じて築く力
- □ priority 優先事項

15
- □ faction 派閥
- □ LDP 自民党→Liberal Democratic Party の略
- □ identify 特定する
- □ successor 後継者
- □ reason …と判断する
- □ struggle 苦労する
- □ step down 辞任する

16 Yoshihide Suga was no one's first choice for that job, which is why he may have only lasted a year as prime minister. Similarly, there is no person ready to galvanize and organize the forces that Abe headed within the LDP.

Track 116

17 Many of the most fervent advocates rode Abe's coattails to power. Without him, they lose a lot. The Cabinet shuffle expected later this summer will tell us a lot about Kishida's priorities, the power that Abe retains even after his passing and the immediate prospects for his legacy.

(977 words)

16
- [ ] be no one's first choice 誰の第一候補でもない
- [ ] similarly 同じように
- [ ] galvanize 活性化させる
- [ ] head 率いる

17
- [ ] ride *one's* coattails 〜の威光にあやかる
- [ ] Cabinet shuffle 内閣改造
- [ ] retain 持ち続ける
- [ ] passing 死去
- [ ] prospect 見通し

国内政治・外交 1 Japan needs a real economic security strategy

Economic security is key to Japan's national security but it is also an amorphous concept that is easily abused. The challenge for the Japanese government is crafting a strategy that truly advances the nation's security and isn't just a fig leaf for protectionism, mercantilism and the expansion of bureaucratic power. **(Paragraph 3)**

［語の成り立ちと由来］1つ目の下線部のamorphous「無定形の、定まった形のない」は語の成り立ちから学べることが多い。接頭辞のa- は「…なしの」を意味するギリシャ語の接頭辞で、atheism「無神論」やasymmetry「アシンメトリー、左右非対称」などのギリシャ語由来の語に見られるほか、asexual「無性の」やamoral「不道徳な」のようにラテン語由来の語との組み合わせもある。一方、morpheは「形」を意味し、metamorphosis「変形」やmorphology「形態学、形態論」といった語の一部になっている。2つ目の下線部のa fig leaf「イチジクの葉」は聖書由来の重要表現。旧約聖書の創世記において、アダムとイヴが知恵の樹から禁断の果実を食した後、イチジクの葉を用いて裸体の陰部を隠したという記述に由来するもので、転じて「不正や体裁の悪いものを不器用に隠すもの」の意味で使用される。

国内政治・外交 1 Japan needs a real economic security strategy

Long inchoate, this concern took concrete shape in 2010 when China cut off exports of rare earths to Japan during a confrontation over the Senkaku Islands. <u>Since then, the entire world has awakened to China's central position in global production chains and the power that bestows upon Beijing in international disputes.</u> **(Paragraph 6)**

［関係代名詞、それとも？］パラグラフ全体は、他国からの輸入に重要な物資を頼っていることで生じる懸念を中国との関係を例にして説明している。下線部の後半部分、the power that bestows upon Beijing の部分は注意が必要。that を主格の関係代名詞だと考えると他動詞である bestow の目的語が存在せず説明がつかないことになる。この that は直前の China's central position in global production chains「世界の生産網における中国の中心的な位置づけ」を受ける普通の代名詞で、the power と that の間に目的格の関係代名詞 that が省略されていると考えるのが正しい。the power (~~that~~) that bestows upon Beijing「それが北京に与える力」ということである。

国内政治・外交 2 Time for Japan to embrace realism in dealings with Russia

Abe had several motivations. As a conservative nationalist, he sought the return of territory he deemed an integral part of Japan; <u>success would have been a cornerstone of his legacy;</u> ... **(Paragraph 10、1〜3行目)**

［仮定法に注意］下線部で用いられている would have been という形がポイント。安倍元首相は北方領土の返還を求めてロシア外交を展開したが、ロシア側による平和条約締結交渉の停止表明により、実現には至らなかった。下線部の節の主語である success には「（実際にはうまくいかなかったが）もし成功していたら」という仮定のニュアンスが込められており、would have been ... はそれを受けた仮定法過去完了の形となっている。述語の動詞句に助動詞の過去形や「助動詞の過去形＋have＋過去分詞」の形を含む文は、何らかの仮定のもとに用いられていることが多いので注意が必要だ。

173

国内政治・外交 2 **Time for Japan to embrace realism in dealings with Russia**

> While Abe's successors <u>have not been as driven to solve the Russia problem</u>, they adopted his policies to win his support <u>and</u> because Japanese public opinion largely backed those positions. (**Paragraph 14、1〜3行目**)

[副詞の as] 1つ目の下線部 <u>have not been as driven to solve the Russia problem</u> の as は「同じくらい、同様に」を意味する副詞で、全体は「同じくらい必死にはロシアの問題を解決しようとはしていない」となる。何と「同じくらい」なのかについては、文脈から as Abe was「安倍元首相がそうだったのと」という内容を補って理解したい。2つ目の下線部の and は to win his support「彼の支援を得るために」という to 不定詞句と because Japanese public opinion largely backed those positions「日本の世論が概してそういう立場を支持したため」という because 節を結んでいる。

国内政治・外交 3 **Biden's visit takes the Japan-U.S. partnership to new heights**

> Prime Minister Fumio Kishida and Japan <u>could not have hoped for a better and more comforting visit</u> by U.S. President Joe Biden. (**Paragraph 1**)

[比較級を見落とすな] 比較級が用いられていることを無視して下線部分を「バイデン大統領のありがたい、励みになる訪問は望めなかった」のように解釈すると原文とはまったく異なる意味になってしまう。ここは実際にバイデン大統領が訪日したことを前提に「それ以上にありがたい、それ以上に励みになる訪問は（望んでも）望みようがなかったであろう」と言っているのであり、バイデン氏の訪日が岸田首相にとってこれ以上ないほどにありがたい、励みになるものであったというニュアンスである。

Biden's visit takes the Japan-U.S. partnership to new heights

The list of deliverables was long and meaty. <u>As important, though, was confirmation that Japan remains a priority for the United States, the alignment of the two men's visions for global order and the affirmation of Japan's critical role in the region and beyond.</u>
(Paragraph 2)

[CVSの倒置] 下線部冒頭のAs importantのasは1つ前の社説でも登場した副詞のasで「同じくらい、同様に」を意味し、この文全体が、As important (C) was (V) confirmation (S) というCVSの倒置構文となっている。直前の文で多くの重要な成果があったことが示唆されており、その「重要な」の部分を軸に、「同じくらい重要なのは…だ」と新情報であるSにつなげるためにこのような倒置が起きている。この種の倒置は原則として既出の情報を軸に新しい情報を話の中に導入するために起こるものなので、今回のAs importantのas「同じくらい」のようにCの部分に既出の内容との結び付きを示すような語句が含まれていることが多い。as以外にもmoreやlessの付いた形容詞句や、similarlyやequallyを含む形容詞句が文頭に来ている場合は注意したい。

IPEF is a good step although <u>much — if not virtually everything — depends on what the framework negotiations yield.</u> **(Paragraph 11、3〜5 行目)**

[if notの解釈] 下線部のmuch — if not virtually everythingをどう解釈するかがポイント。A if not Bは文字通りに解釈すれば「BまではいかなくともA」となるが、「A、いや、ひょっとしたらBかもしれない」といった意味を表すこともあり、両者はまったくニュアンスが異なるため注意が必要である。今回の場合、もしここが「Bまではいかなくとも」という否定的な意味なのであれば、あえてvirtually「ほとんど」を加えて細かく意味を規定する必要はないと思われる。よって、2つ目の意味で「多くのこと、いやひょっとしたらほとんどすべて」と解釈するほうが自然である。

Abenomics was Japanese — or at least Liberal Democratic Party — orthodoxy: loose monetary policy, fiscal support and calls for structural reform. And, as was so often the case, the first two were pursued with vigor, the last one, not so much. **(Paragraph 6、1〜4行目)**

[並列関係と省略] 最初の下線部では、Abenomics was Japanese「アベノミクスは日本的だ」まで読んでもどうも判然としない。後ろのダッシュ（ー）で囲まれた挿入部分を一度抜いて考えてみよう。そうすると、Japanese orthodoxy「日本の正道」というつながりが見える。挿入部分はその「日本の」という言葉をもう少し限定して「あるいは、少なくとも自民党の」と言い直したもの。当然、このLiberal Democratic Partyは単なる名詞句ではなく、「自民党の」という形容詞的な意味を持ち、orthodoxyを修飾している。もう1つの下線部では2つの節が接続詞を使用せずに並列された形になっているが、the last oneから始まる2つ目の節では共通要素の省略が起こっている点に注意が必要。the last one (was) not (pursued with) so much (vigor)と補って理解したい。

Driving Abe was a belief that Japan was a great power and that it should act as one. **(Paragraph 10、1〜2行目)**

[分詞句＋be＋Sの倒置] 下線部は「安倍元首相を駆り立てること」という動名詞句ではない。この文の主語はwasの後ろのa belief ...で「分詞句＋be＋S」という通常と異なる倒置形が使用されている。ここまでの段落でなされている安倍元首相の仕事の話を受けて、元首相その人から新情報である背景にあった思想に視点を移行させるためにこのような倒置形が用いられている。「ウクライナ侵攻」1本目の社説で見た例に似ているが、今回の英文はbe動詞がwasと単数の形であり、driving Abeを動名詞と解しても文法上あからさまな矛盾が生じないため、より注意が必要である。

日本には真の経済安全保障戦略が必要

1 岸田文雄首相率いる政府は、経済問題に焦点を当てた包括的な国の安全保障構想に尽力している。

2 首相就任後、岸田氏は経済安全保障が今年発表される見込みの国家安全保障戦略の最優先事項になると強調し、経済安全保障担当の大臣ポストを創設、政権として今年の通常国会に経済安全保障推進法案を提出すると公約した。

3 経済安全保障は日本の国家安全保障の鍵であるが、容易に乱用される漠然とした概念でもある。日本政府にとっての難題は、国の安全保障を本当の意味で推進し、保護貿易主義や重商主義、官僚の力の拡大のための単なる隠れみのではない戦略を策定することにある。

4 経済安全保障についての政府の考えは、岸田氏が自民党の政調会長として議長を務めた研究グループ、新国際秩序創造戦略本部の作業によって形作られてきた。同本部は、発展する国際秩序の中における日本の国力と地位は経済の活力と革新力にかかっていると結論づけた。

5 経済安全保障は、研究グループが結論を出したところによれば、戦略的自律性と戦略的不可欠性という2本の柱に基づく。1つ目は、日本に対して、国民の経済的な幸福と国の社会力および経済力を確保するための方法を持つよう求めるものだ。これは、主要な経済的投入物を他国に依存していることによって生じる脆弱性への不安を反映している。

6 長くくすぶっていたこの不安は、尖閣諸島をめぐる対立に際して中国が日本へのレアアースの輸出を停止した2010年に具体的な形となって現れた。それ以降、全世界が地球上の生産網における中国の中心的な役割と、そのことが国際的な紛争に際して中国政府に与える力に気づくことになった。

7 2本目の柱は、国際社会で重要と見なされる分野での産業力を日本が持つよう求める。言い換えれば日本は、世界のほかの国々が必要としている製品を作るべきで、そうすればこの国は欠くことのできないパートナーだと見なされる。このことは、半導体といった重要技術の自給自足を追求する、国の長年にわたる政策的選択とぴったり一致する。それが日本の政策立案者に対して、供給網のルートを日本経由に切り替えるよう企業に促す、さらなる弾みを与えてきた。

日本には真の経済安全保障戦略が必要

8　日本企業向けの2,000億円のファンドとともに、政府は台湾の半導体製造会社（TSMC）を誘致し熊本県で半導体工場を建設してもらうために十分な金額を提供した──その一方で新しい技術を開発し、既存の技術に新たな、あるいはより厳しい統制を課すための資金を確保していた。この最後の点に関しては、特に機密性の高い新技術を詮索の目から守るための秘密特許の制定が含まれることになる。

9　サプライチェーンの強靭性の推進と、新技術の開発および保護に加えて、新たな経済安全保障法は重要なインフラを保護することにもなる。各国政府は金融機関、通信ネットワーク、送電網といった社会的および経済的インフラの最重要要素への脅威を強く意識している。日本当局は、その安全と安心を確保するため、これらのサービスを運営する企業や機関と緊密に連携することになる。ここでもまた、中国製の部品がスパイ活動や（供給の）途絶に対して脆弱なのではないかとの不安がある。

10　真の経済安全保障戦略はそうした技術的な部分にとどまらず、日本がその経済力を国益推進のために用いる方法を見極めることになるだろう。たとえば、日本政府が経済支援や援助を利用して他国での影響力を最大化するにはどうすればよいか、議論があってしかるべきだ。透明性や自由経済主義などの、日本が優先する利益と価値を推進するために、国際貿易と投資制度を最新化する取り組みも行うべきである。規格を設定する機関、とりわけデジタルの技術や接続性を手がけるところにも力と注意を向けるべきだろう。

11　それらすべての努力において、日本は米国、オーストラリア、カナダ、欧州連合の加盟国など、同じ考えを持つ国々と密接に協力すべきだろう。事実、日本の経済安全保障重視の裏にある原動力の一つは、中国との戦略的競合において経済的な国策にますます依存している米国とのより緊密な連携だった。日本は米国との政策協調を円滑にするため、国家安全保障局内に経済安全保障担当班を創設した。

12　そうした多面的な協調の一例として、日本は経済的威圧への対抗措置となる幅広い連携を築く取り組みを主導するべきだろう。ある種の「保険」もしくはスワップ協定が検討されるべきだ。

13 行動が必要とされる一方で、慎重さも欠かせない。経済安全保障は融通の利く概念で、政府の一部には国の発展と経済活動を制御・管理したいとの願望がある。国の経済安全保障戦略が保護貿易論者と重商主義者の勢いを再び勢いづかせるのではないかとの懸念がある。その衝動は、外国為替及び外国貿易法の改正に際して、海外からの出資に関し、より厳格な精査の対象になるとして当初挙がっていた業種のリストからも明らかだ。そのリストには温泉運営会社、ペンの製造会社、野球場の管理会社が含まれる。そのため、中核となる経済的利益は狭く定義されることが不可欠である。

14 戦略の最後の要素は国の経済を活気づけるための目に見える取り組みだ。これは自明のことだが、容易に見落とされることもある。日本には国民が生活において幸せで安心していられることを保証する、着実な成長が必要だ。この論理からすると、「新しい資本主義」への岸田首相の取り組みは日本の経済安全保障の不可欠な一部だ。成長する経済は、その見返りがすべての日本人によって享受されない限り安定もせず、国民や国に安全保障を提供することもないだろう。

（訳・注　桑田）

日本はロシアとの対応で現実主義を受け入れるべき時だ

1 第二次世界大戦を終結させる正式な平和条約の交渉を中断するとのロシアの決定は、日本にとって好機に当たる。

2 なぜなら、その動きは日本政府に政策と戦略の再評価、ロシアの考え方に関する厳しい現実を認識すること、日本政府の意思決定を導いてきた不合理な期待との決別を強いるからだ。

3 第二次世界大戦の終結後、日本政府はモスクワの政府との平和条約の締結と、その戦争の最後数日間にソビエト軍によって奪われた国後島、択捉島、色丹島、歯舞群島——一括して北方領土として知られる——の返還の確保を求めてきた。

4 進捗は遅く不本意なもので、期待が進展をはるかに上回るものだった。1956年、両国は二国間の戦争状態を終わらせる共同宣言を発表し、ソ連政府は平和条約が締結された後に歯舞群島と色丹島を返還することで合意した。

5 1964年、両国は日本人の元島民による家族の墓参りを認めることに合意した。1992年には文化交流と関係育成のためにビザなしでの島への行き来が認められた。7年後、両国政府は四島の元島民に定期的な訪問を許可する、さらにもう1つの合意に達した。それに加えて、日ロ政府は島でのさまざまな共同経済活動にも合意した。

6 2018年、当時の安倍晋三首相とロシアのウラジーミル・プーチン大統領のシンガポール会談で、1956年の共同宣言に基づいて二国間の平和条約交渉を加速させることで両首脳が合意した後、期待が花開いた。領土の割譲を禁止する2020年のロシア憲法改正は、つかの間の楽観論に終止符を打った。

7 ウクライナへの侵攻を理由にロシアを罰する西側の制裁に日本が加わった今、ロシア政府は暗黙の意図を完全なまでに明らかにした。和平交渉を中断し、訪問プログラムを終了し、経済活動を停止したのだ。ロシアの外相は日本の「あからさまなまでに非友好的な立場とわが国の利害を損なおうという試み」を非難した。

8 岸田文雄首相は「この全体の状況はロシアのウクライナ侵攻によって作り出されたものだ」と正しく反応し、日本を非難しようとの試みを「極めて不当でまったく容認できない」と評した。そして首相は「日本は世界のほかの国々と協調して、ロシアへ

の制裁を断固として継続しなければならない」と付け加えた。

9 この強硬路線——日本政府は多数のロシアの個人、7つの銀行、そのほかの機関に制裁を課し、輸出禁止を実施したほか、同国の最恵国待遇を取り消す方針でいる——はロシア政府にとっては驚きに違いない。この10年間、日本はロシアとの関係改善を模索する中でほかのあらゆる違反に目をつぶってきた。2014年のクリミア半島併合後、日本は制裁を避け、安倍氏は進展につながるかもしれない個人的な関係を築こうとして何度となくプーチン氏と会談した。

10 安倍氏にはいくつかの動機があった。保守的な国家主義者として、安倍氏は自身が日本の不可欠な一部と見なした領土の返還を模索した。成功すれば彼の政治的遺産の基盤になっていただろう。それに日本は以前から常にロシア極東地域の膨大な資源、とりわけエネルギー供給に目をつけていて、安倍氏は良好な関係がそれらへのアクセスを保証してくれると期待していた。

11 同じように大きかったのが戦略的な考慮であった。領土の返還をもたらす関係が実現すれば、戦略的な環境の転換を示していただろう。ロシア政府との関係が十分に安全であれば軍事的な注意を北から移して、南方面をより重視できるようになっていただろう。

12 それは決して理論上の懸念ではない。2021年の最初の9カ月間で、日本はロシア軍機の存在を理由に199回のスクランブル発進をしていて、つい数週間前にもロシアのヘリコプターが日本の領空を侵犯した。今月にはロシア海軍の船舶数隻が本州と北海道を隔てる津軽海峡を通過した。2月にはロシアの船舶24隻がオホーツク海で中国海軍の船舶との共同演習に参加していて、これは昨年にロシアと中国の船舶10隻が日本列島の周囲を一緒に航行したことに続くものであった。

13 安倍氏はロシア政府と中国政府の間に距離を作ることを期待した。安倍氏がプーチン氏に接触したのは、ロシアの大統領に選択肢を与え、2つの隣国間で修正主義国の枢軸が統合されることを阻止するためだった。それは称賛に値する目標だ。中国とロシアはますます親密な関係になっていて、両国が先月発表した共同宣言は「無制限」の連携を示唆している。両国が拡大しつつある軍事協力という視点で見ると、そのことは気がかりだ。

日本はロシアとの対応で現実主義を受け入れるべき時だ

14　安倍氏の後継首相たちはロシア問題の解決にそこまで意欲的ではなかったものの、安倍氏の支持を獲得するために、また日本の世論がおおむねそうした立場を支持していたことから、彼の政策を採用した。侵攻後、その政策は維持できなくなった。

15　けれども、ロシアの不法行為への日本の容認姿勢にも限度がなければならない。主権国への侵攻はその限度をはるかに超えている。ロシアとの関係維持からくる進展の欠如を考慮すると、その再評価はよりいっそうやむを得ないものとなる。ロシアは日本をだまし続け、譲歩をせずに取れるものは何でも取ろうともくろんでいるように思われる。その一方で、ロシア政府は日米同盟が領土問題の解決の障害だと主張して、両国の仲を裂こうと躍起になっている。

16　現在見直し中の新たな国家安全保障戦略は、先の戦略で識別されていた「パートナー」とは対照的に、ロシアを「安全保障上の問題」と分類することになると報じられてきた――この変更は遅きに失したものだ。日本政府はロシアに対して、ウクライナ侵攻は容認できず、いつも通りのやり方は選択肢ではないと示さなければならない。人権と国際法のこの重大な侵害と闘う国々を分裂させる望みなどないとはっきり表明しなければならない。

17　日本にとって、今こそロシアとの関係をしっかりと見つめ、中身のない美辞麗句、戦術的なごまかし、弱い者いじめというロシア政府のありのままの振る舞いを認識するべき時だ。　　　　　　　　　　　　　　　　　　　　　（訳・注　桑田）

バイデン大統領訪日で日米パートナーシップはさらなる高みへ

1　ジョー・バイデン米大統領の訪日は岸田文雄首相と日本政府にとって、これ以上望みようがないほど素晴らしく、励みとなるものだった。

2　数多くの成果があり、その内容も充実していた。だが同じく重要なのは、米国にとって日本は今なお優先度の高い国だと確認されたこと、世界秩序に対する両首脳の展望が一致したこと、地域内外における日本の役割の重要性が確約されたことだ。

3　日本の唯一の同盟国として、米国は二国間同盟を「インド太平洋地域の平和と繁栄の礎」であるという長年の立場をあらためて表明したが、それは単なる外交辞令ではない。中国やロシアといった国々が武力の行使によってルールを書き換え国境を引き直そうとする中、バイデン氏が「米国は日本の防衛に全面的な関与を続ける」と発言したことは極めて意義深い。両国は「今日と未来の課題にともに取り組む」という大統領の公約は、今回の首脳会談に合わせて中ロ両軍の爆撃機が日本周辺の上空で共同演習を行ったという報道の後ではより大きな意味を持つ。

4　日米同盟の中核をなすのは、仮想敵国の間で米国は日本防衛のために核兵器を含むあらゆる能力を行使する、と目されていることだ。したがって首脳会談では常に抑止政策が優先され、今回もそのことに変わりはなかった。

5　岸田首相とバイデン大統領は両国が連携し、「同盟を絶えず現代化させ、二国間の役割および任務を進化させ、統合能力を強化させる、そのために日米はともに戦略をすり合わせ、目標の優先順位を明確にしていく」との決意を表明した。

6　連携は二国間だけにとどまらない。両首脳は沿岸警備隊を中心とした第三国の能力強化の推進と同時に、国家安全保障において重要度を増している宇宙およびサイバー領域で協力することに合意した。

7　米国は重大な役目を担っているが、それ以上に大切なのは日本の取り組みだ。この国の防衛は何よりもまず日本の責務である。同様に、日本の取り組みは政府の真剣さとパートナーとしての信頼性を米国に示す意味で重要だ。それゆえに岸田首相は、防衛力を抜本的に強化し、その裏付けとして防衛費の相当な増額を確保すると表明している。

バイデン大統領訪日で日米パートナーシップはさらなる高みへ

8 協力関係が拡大しているのは、経済問題の分野だ。かつては危険な摩擦の原因となっていたが、両国は今や地政学的競争の中心であるこの分野で連携している。バイデン大統領と岸田首相は基幹技術の保護と推進で協力し、サプライチェーンが強靱かつ安定した状態を保てるよう努めることを誓った。主な合意の一つは、日米商務・産業パートナーシップ（JUCIP）で採択された「半導体協力基本原則」に基づく、次世代半導体の開発を検討する合同タスクフォースの設立だ。

9 日米両国は新たに成立した経済安全保障推進法を遂行し、連携して経済安全保障を強化するための追加策をとるべきだ。この課題は、今夏に発足予定の経済政策協議委員会（経済版「2プラス2」）で取り上げられることが確実視されている。

10 バイデン大統領がインド太平洋経済枠組み（IPEF）を発表したことは、この地域に対する米国の関心と関与の表れとして歓迎されるものだ。その参加国リストは予想以上に長く、この地域における米国の同盟国すべてだけでなく、シンガポール、インドネシア、ベトナムといった東南アジアの主要な国々も含まれる。特に、地域的な包括的経済連携（RCEP）協定への参加を拒否しているインドが参加を決めたことは喜ばしい。

11 われわれは米国が環太平洋パートナーシップに関する包括的及び先進的な協定（CPTPP）への参加を再考することを望んでいるが、その見込みが薄いことは認識している。IPEFは幸先の良い一歩だが、多くのことが、いやひょっとしたらほぼすべてのことが枠組み交渉の結果次第だ。

12 バイデン大統領は日本と韓国を訪問した5日間で、インド太平洋地域への確固たる関与を表明した。米国は同盟関係を堅持しているだけでなく、同盟国やパートナー国とともに21世紀の規範を定めることを固く決意している。両首脳の共同声明で宣言されたように、両国は「新たな技術の出現であれ、気候変動の影響であれ、もしくは感染症等の国境をまたぐ脅威であれ、国際社会にとって最も顕著な課題に対処するうえで、積極的な役割を果たしていく」ことになる。

13 幸いなことに、これらの課題に対する日米の考えにはほとんど隔たりがない。長いリストではあるが、両政府が最重要項目としているのは、修正主義国家による脅威と、そうした危機に対処するために創造的に考え行動することの必要性だ。このことは、拡大するパートナーシップの非常に重要な前提条件であり基盤である。

14 バイデン氏は東京滞在中、日本に期待する役割も明らかにした。改革された国連安全保障理事会において日本が常任理事国になることへの支持を表明し、現代の課題に取り組むために民主主義国家および同志国間の連携を強化することの重要性を幾度となく繰り返した。日本は開発援助、地域インフラの構築、サイバーセキュリティの推進、安全・安心な5G通信システムの構築における米国との連携が期待されている。

15 これは日本と岸田首相に対する信任だ。岸田首相は安倍晋三元首相の影から抜け出し、日本の外交・安全保障政策に独自の足跡を残しながら、自身の成果を基に前進している。ホスト国として、バイデン大統領はじめ各国首脳を招き、日米豪印戦略対話（クアッド）やさまざまな二国間会議を主催したことは、首相が野心的な地域安全保障の計画を重視しているというだけでなく、彼らもその目標達成のために首相と協力する準備ができているという証しだ。　　　　（訳・注　宇都宮）

岸田首相の次の手立てが安倍元首相のレガシーの命運を決める

1　2年前に辞任していたものの、安倍晋三元首相の死は日本にとって重要かつ目に見える影響を及ぼすことだろう。

2　多くの意味で、安倍氏は現代日本の道筋をリセットした。しかし、過去最長となる在任期間中に成し遂げたことを考慮しても、氏の課題のかなりの部分は未完成のままで、彼の死はその目的を引き続き遂行する後継者たちから、最も情熱的かつ献身的で有能な擁護者を奪うことになった。

3　彼のレガシーの完全かつ率直ないかなる評価においても、安倍氏が意見の分かれる人物でもあったことを認めないわけにはいかない。彼の熱い信念は強い関わりを求め、多くのほかの日本の政治家とは違って、信じるところの導くままに行動することをいとわなかった。時に不快を与えることがあったとすれば、それはその情熱の代償だった。それが彼を突き動かし、時には国を二分した。

4　安倍氏はこの国で最も在任期間が長かった首相として何よりも知られることになるだろう。その長さが日本の政治に安定性を取り戻し、一貫性だけでなく真のリーダーシップを確かなものとした。安倍氏はその在任期間中にアジアだけにとどまらず、世界全体の中でも主要なリーダーとしての地位を確立した。そのおかげで各国首脳との関係および友情を築くことができたが、それは真のリーダーシップを自負するにはまさに必須条件であった。首相官邸の主が次々と入れ替わる状況に終止符を打ったことは、彼の最も重要な遺産かもしれない。

5　安定は政策の継続を意味し、つまり構想を立て、それが実現するのを見届けるまで取り組む機会が得られるということだ。アベノミクスは日本経済につきまとう低迷から脱するための彼の戦略であった。公式の見解は（政府の公式ウェブサイトで宣言していたように）「アベノミクスは成果を生んでいます！」だった──外部の評価はそれほど寛大ではなかった。

6　アベノミクスは日本の──もしくは、少なくとも自由民主党の──正道だった。緩和的な金融政策、財政支援、および構造改革の要請。そして非常によくある例の通り、最初の2つは熱心に推進されたものの、最後のものはそれほどでもなかった。ほとんどの専門家はアベノミクスを不変性、一貫性、信頼の回復では評価する一方、意味のある構造改革のきっかけにはならなかったと見る。その欠点が、いかなる最終的な判断においても鍵になるかもしれない。

7 経済政策の中心にあるのが社会改革で、なかでもその生産的エネルギーを解き放つための権限を女性に与えることだ。安倍氏はウーマノミクスにおいても成功したとは言えなかった。最新の世界経済フォーラムの分析によると、今年のジェンダーギャップ指数のランキングで日本は146カ国中116位、主要先進7カ国中では最下位だった。進展が見られずに終わったことは安倍氏の課題に内在する緊張状態を示すものであった――経済発展のために必要とされる改革が、ふさわしい社会秩序に関する伝統的な信念と対立したのだ。勝ったのは後者であった。

8 安倍氏は、国家安全保障関係の官僚組織の立て直しは実行した。彼の積極的な行動は首相官邸への権限の統合を求め、その構想の核心は国家安全保障機構を強化することだった。安倍氏は国家安全保障局への権限の付与、初めてとなる国家安全保障戦略の作成、集団的自衛権の行使に関するルールの変更などをはじめとする主要方針を実施した。

9 けれども、憲法を改正するという夢の実現はかなわなかった――安倍氏にとって最大の不満の一つだろう。憲法の将来についての活発な議論への扉を開いたことは確かだ。岸田文雄首相がその課題に取り組むかどうかが、彼の政権に持ち越しになっている最も重要な疑問の一つである。

10 安倍氏を突き動かしていたのは、日本は大国であり、大国としての役割を果たすべきだという信念であった。首相に復帰した直後の演説の中で、安倍氏は「私は復活しましたし、日本もそうならなくてはなりません」と述べた。国の安全保障の改革はその方向への第一歩だった。しかし安倍氏にとって、自身にふさわしい国際的な知名度を得るには、世界的なリーダーシップの真の基準となる安全保障に寄与できるよう、日本の能力の足かせを外す憲法改正が必要であった。

11 彼の「やればできる／やらなければならない」の姿勢は、アジアにおける権力の空白を恐れた多くの人々の心に訴えた。だが、一部のアジア人にとって、その姿勢は過去の誤った行いに目をつぶろうという積極的な態度と不審なまでに似通ったものに思えた。

12 大変動の可能性をはらむ時代において、現状を維持するための連携を築くには、日本は同じような考えを持つ近隣の国々や価値を共有する国々との良好な関係が必要だと論じることで、安倍氏はそのような新しい課題に戦略的なロジックで取り

岸田首相の次の手立てが安倍元首相のレガシーの命運を決める

組むことができたはずであった。安倍氏はインド太平洋の枠組みを確立したことで記憶されることだろう。この戦略は今日多くの国の政府における考えを導いている。そのロジックを韓国とのより永続的で前向きな関係を築くために使用できなかったことは――失敗は決して彼一人のせいではないとはいえ――そのレガシーにおける最も明白な汚点となるだろう。

13 そして安倍氏は中国との関係における基準線を動かしたことで記憶される一方で、中国政府とより良好な関係を構築しようと熱心に取り組み、その在任期間の終わりまで、中国の指導者である習近平氏を東京に招くという希望を抱いていたリーダーでもあった。

14 今後数カ月の間、安倍氏のレガシーと影響力の主な尺度は、岸田首相がそうした目標を実現させるためにどこまで踏み込むかになるだろう。岸田氏は安倍氏の野心のすべてを共有しているわけではないと考えられていて、元首相は、岸田氏がもっと踏み込んでもっと多くを行うように陰で絶えず促していた。今週、岸田首相は安倍氏の仕事を完成させると約束したが、それには政治的資本が必要だし、現首相には自らの優先事項がある。

15 首相かつ自民党内の派閥のリーダーとして、安倍氏が自身の後継者を指名したことは一度もない。そのような動きは自らの権力の終焉を表すものだとの考えからだろうし、おそらくその考えは正しかっただろう。そのため、安倍氏が2年前に辞任した時、党は彼の代わりを探すのに苦労しなければならなかった。

16 菅義偉氏は誰から見てもその職への第一候補ではなく、そのことが首相として1年しかもたなかった理由かもしれない。それと同じように、自民党内で安倍氏が率いていた勢力を活性化させて組織する準備ができている人物もいない。

17 最も熱心な支持者の多くは安倍氏の威光にあやかって権力を手にした。安倍氏がいなくなり、彼らは多くを失った。この夏の後半に予想される内閣改造は岸田首相の優先事項について、安倍氏が死後もなお持ち続ける力について、そして彼のレガシーの当座の見通しについて、私たちに多くを教えてくれるだろう。

（訳・注　桑田）

経済・財政

円ードル

151.80 – 15

高値　151.81 (21:18) 前日比

安値　150.04 (07:18) 前日比

日経平均

10月21日、円安・ドル高が進み、32年ぶりとなる1ドル151円台後半に

Tokyo Stock Exchange might not be ready for 'prime' time just yet

東証は「プライム」の機がまだ熟していないかもしれない

January 15, 2022 　　　　　　　　●Tracks 117-125 / 解説 p. 206、訳 p. 208

Track 117

1 Long disparaged for underperforming compared to U.S. and European competitors, the Tokyo Stock Exchange had a good 2021, with the Nikkei average having its highest year-end close in 32 years.

2 That performance is a good sign as the TSE prepares for a restructuring in early April that is intended to revitalize corporate governance and attract global investors.

Track 118

3 Early assessments have raised questions, however, about the ability of the proposed reforms to rejuvenate the market and win over skeptical investors. Much will depend on how firmly market regulators implement reform.

4 The TSE, which hosts 3,777 stocks, currently has four sections: first, second, Jasdaq and Mothers. The April reform will consolidate these divisions to three: prime, standard and growth. More important than the consolidation will be new requirements imposed on companies that seek to list on the prime section. Those new regulations will address market value, the number of outside directors on the board, the number of floating shares and other factors.

東証が４月から再編され、プライム、スタンダード、グロースの３つに分かれる。改革は海外投資家にとって魅力ある市場にするための第一歩にすぎず、情報開示やガバナンス、環境や持続可能性へのさまざまな取り組みを実行できるか、世界は注視している。

1
- □ [タイトル]Tokyo Stock Exchange 東京証券取引所
- □ disparaged 低く見られた、けなされた
- □ underperform 伸び悩む、出来が期待を下回る
- □ competitor 競合相手→ここでは欧米の株式市場を指す
- □ year-end 年末の
- □ close 終値

2
- □ TSE → Tokyo Stock Exchange の略
- □ restructuring 再編
- □ revitalize 再生する
- □ corporate governance コーポレートガバナンス、企業統治

3
- □ proposed reform 改革案
- □ rejuvenate 活性化させる
- □ win over ... …の心をつかむ
- □ skeptical 懐疑的な
- □ depend on how ... どれだけ…するかにかかっている
- □ regulators 規制当局
- □ implement 実行する

4
- □ currently 現在
- □ Jasdaq JASDAQ →Japan Association of Securities Dealers Automated Quotations の略。「ジャスダック」と読む
- □ consolidate 統合する
- □ consolidation 統合
- □ requirement 要件
- □ imposed on ... …に課される
- □ list 上場する
- □ regulation(s) 規制
- □ address 対象にする
- □ outside director on the board 社外取締役
- □ floating share 浮動株→市場に流通して売買される株式

Track 119

5   Most attention has focused on this prime section of the exchange, which is supposed to include the "best" companies in Japan. Currently, the TSE first section has 2,158 companies, or more than half those listed.

6   By all accounts, the current first section is bloated, with companies rarely removed once they gain admission, even if they have low liquidity and low market caps. It's hard to believe that there has been much winnowing when the new division will include 1,841 companies, 84% of the current occupants of the first section. Of the remaining companies, 1,477 (39% of all TSE-traded firms) will be in the standard section and 459 (12%) in growth.

Track 120

7   Those that make the cut to join the prime market will have a hard time competing with companies in leading sections of other exchanges. The median market capitalization of those Japanese companies is only $520 million, while it's about $2.8 billion in the NYSE and about $1.7 billion in the London and the Nasdaq Global Select markets. Just less than half of the prime members have price-to-book ratios of less than 1 — meaning they are valued at less than their net worth; in the United States and European markets, the number ranges from 10-20%.

8   Investors and analysts are skeptical that proposed reforms will close the gap. For example, the prime companies will be required to have tradable shares worth at least ¥10 billion. Global asset managers typically seek out investment targets that are worth 50 times that amount.

5
- focus on ... …に集まる
- be supposed to *do* 〜するはずである

6
- by all accounts どう考えても、誰の話でも
- bloated 肥大化した
- gain admission 加わることを許される
- liquidity 流動性
- market cap 時価総額→capはcapitalizationの略
- winnowing 選別
- current 現在の
- occupant 居住者→ここでは第1部上場企業のこと
- remaining 残りの

7
- make the cut 基準を満たす、枠内に入る
- compete with ... …と競合する
- median 中央値の
- NYSE ニューヨーク証券取引所→New York Stock Exchangeの略
- Nasdaq NASDAQ→National Association of Securities Dealers Automated Quotationsの略。「ナスダック」と読む
- price-to-book ratio 株価純資産倍率→株価を1株当たりの純資産で割った値
- net worth 純資産
- range from 10-20% 10%から20%までの間にある

8
- close the gap 差を縮める
- be required to *do* 〜することが要求される
- tradable 流通可能な
- asset manager アセットマネージャー→投資家の資産を運用する人・組織
- seek out ... …を探し求める
- be worth 50 times that amount その額の50倍の価値がある

Track 121

9   Moreover, many shares are not actually available for purchase. Instead, they are part of cross-shareholdings, arrangements that are designed to insulate management from any outside pressure. Those deals will not count as tradable shares, which is why the lower threshold is even less inviting.

10   A second problem is the flexibility given to companies to meet the new requirements. Fearful that too many may not qualify for the prime section, the authorities have decided that they will have an indefinite amount of time to transition as long as they submit a reform plan. It is believed that 296 companies will make use of this provision, which was reportedly included to mollify politicians who feared intense criticism if long-established members of the first section could not make the transition. It effectively strips the reforms of substance, however. There are reports that a deadline will be set. That is essential.

Track 122

11   There is a tension between the desire to use membership in the TSE first section to signal acceptance and status — and earn money on the initial listing — and the need for quality control to ensure that prime section companies merit international attention. Thus far, the status concerns have prevailed, which was long a problem with the old system.

12   TSE officials duly recognize these concerns. Their statements invariably note that the forthcoming changes are merely the beginning of a process. Hiromi Yamaji, president of the TSE, noted that "the announcement is the starting line of a long road toward sustainable growth and medium- to long-term enhancement of corporate value."

9
- □ moreover そのうえ
- □ be available for ... …が可能である
- □ cross-shareholding 株式持ち合い→複数の株式会社が相手企業の株式を所有すること
- □ arrangement 取り決め
- □ be designed to *do* ～することを意図する
- □ insulate 保護する
- □ count as ... …に含まれる
- □ threshold 入口、敷居
- □ inviting 魅力的な

10
- □ flexibility 柔軟性
- □ meet (要件を)満たす
- □ Fearful that ... …ということを恐れて →As the authorities are fearful that ... ということ
- □ qualify for ... …の資格を満たす
- □ authorities 当局
- □ indefinite 無期限の
- □ transition 移行する
- □ as long as ... …さえすれば
- □ make use of ... …を利用する
- □ provision 条項
- □ mollify なだめる
- □ long-established 長い伝統のある
- □ effectively 実質的に
- □ strip A of B AからBを取り去る、奪う
- □ substance 中身、本質

11
- □ signal …のしるしとなる
- □ acceptance 受け入れ
- □ status ステータス、地位
- □ initial listing (新規)上場
- □ quality control 品質管理
- □ ensure 保証する
- □ merit …に値する
- □ thus far これまでのところは
- □ prevail 勝る

12
- □ duly 十分に、しかるべく
- □ recognize 認識する
- □ invariably 一貫して
- □ forthcoming 来るべき
- □ starting line スタートライン→start lineとは言わない
- □ sustainable 持続可能な
- □ medium- to long-term 中長期的な
- □ enhancement 高まり
- □ corporate value 企業価値

Track 123

13 Central to that effort is a focus on changes that will make Japanese equities more inviting to foreign investors. The TSE aims to do that by increasing disclosure in English, increasing the number of independent nonexecutive board members to more than a third and requiring climate change-related disclosure in line with the Task Force on Climate-Related Financial Disclosures recommendations. These mandates can force change: The TSE requirement that first section members have more than two independent directors increased the share of companies with that representation from 21.5% in 2014 to 97% last year.

14 Those changes do not exist in a vacuum, however. Also important are changes to the Foreign Exchange and Foreign Trade Act as well as the Corporate Governance Code. The former's provisions are intended to limit investor opportunities to acquire intellectual property by dubious means, but they can be abused to undermine shareholder activism and governance reform.

Track 124

15 The latter was revised in June of last year to encourage a focus on sustainability as well as environmental, social and governance issues. Those changes have been applauded but here too much depends on rigorous implementation.

16 Japanese officials, politicians and businesses know that they need to change business practices to generate sustained attention, enthusiasm and investment from international investors.

Track 125

17 TSE reform, like other structural changes to the economy, is intended to do just that. But investors will not be mollified by cosmetic alterations. Real change is needed to win them over. They remain unconvinced. *(906 words)*

13
- ☐ central to ... …の中心となって
- ☐ equity 株式
- ☐ disclosure 情報開示
- ☐ independent nonexecutive board member 独立非業務執行取締役
- ☐ climate change-related 気候変動に関連した
- ☐ in line with ... …に沿った
- ☐ the Task Force on Climate-Related Financial Disclosures 気候関連財務情報開示タスクフォース
- ☐ recommendation 勧告
- ☐ mandate 命令
- ☐ force 強制する
- ☐ more than two 2よりも多い、3以上の
- ☐ representation 代表(する・されること)
  →ここでは上記の「3人以上の独立取締役がいる」役員構成のことを指す

14
- ☐ in a vacuum 孤立して→vacuumは「真空」の意味
- ☐ the Foreign Exchange and Foreign Trade Act 外国為替及び外国貿易法
- ☐ the Corporate Governance Code コーポレートガバナンス・コード
- ☐ the former 前者→外国為替及び外国貿易法を指す
- ☐ intellectual property 知的財産
- ☐ dubious 疑わしい
- ☐ abuse 乱用する
- ☐ undermine 弱体化させる
- ☐ activism 積極的な行動

15
- ☐ the latter 後者→コーポレートガバナンス・コードを指す
- ☐ revise 改正する
- ☐ sustainability 持続可能性
- ☐ environmental 環境的な
- ☐ applaud 称賛する
- ☐ rigorous 厳格な
- ☐ implementation 実行

16
- ☐ generate 生み出す
- ☐ sustained 持続的な
- ☐ enthusiasm 熱狂

17
- ☐ structural change 構造変化
- ☐ cosmetic うわべだけの
- ☐ alteration 修正
- ☐ unconvinced 納得していない

A weaker yen is no longer the asset of the past

円安はもはやかつてのような資産ではない

April 23, 2022　　　　　　●Tracks 126-132 / 解説 p. 207、訳 p. 211

Track 126

1　The Japanese yen has been in free fall this year, losing 10% of its value and hitting 20-year lows.

2　There are several causes for the plunge and it isn't clear that Japan's monetary authorities can do anything about it. Authorities have maintained their loose money policy, prompting questions about how eager they are to stop the decline. A weak yen has served Japan well; an unstable currency does not.

Track 127

3　The yen's deterioration has made it the worst-performing major currency this year in dollar terms. The Japanese currency surpassed ¥129 to the dollar this week before falling back to ¥128. A few weeks ago, there were fears that it would challenge the ¥130 mark; foreign exchange analysts now believe that ¥135 to the dollar could be breached in the near future.

4　There are a couple of explanations for the yen's fall. The first is rising commodity prices. When Japan spends more on the goods it needs to power its economy, it uses dollars to pay for those imports. When imports eclipse exports in value, the demand for dollars depresses the value of the yen. Japan has experienced monthly current account deficits before and the recent imbalances are thought to be the product of temporary phenomena: the pandemic and the war in Ukraine.

かつて日本が国内で製造した工業製品の輸出で繁栄していた時代には、円安は経済に大きな恩恵をもたらしていた。だが急激に円安が進み、海外から調達する原材料や輸入品の高騰が企業にも庶民にも打撃を与えている現在、円安への対処が喫緊の課題である。

1
- ☐ [タイトル]weaker yen 弱くなった円
  →円安の状態にある円（日本の通貨）
- ☐ in free fall 急降下して、急落して
- ☐ hit ... low(s) …来の安値に達する

2
- ☐ plunge 急落
- ☐ monetary 金融の
- ☐ authorities 当局
- ☐ loose（金融）緩和的な
- ☐ prompt 生じさせる
- ☐ eager 熱心な、やる気がある
- ☐ has served これまで役立ってきた
- ☐ unstable 不安定な
- ☐ currency 通貨

3
- ☐ deterioration 価値の低下
- ☐ worst-performing 最も相対価値［購買力］の低い
- ☐ in dollar terms 対ドル・ドル建てで
- ☐ fall back（数字を）戻す
- ☐ mark 大台
- ☐ foreign exchange 外国為替（取引）
- ☐ breach 突破する

4
- ☐ explanation 説明、原因、理由
- ☐ commodity 商品、物品→ここは主に工業原料も含めた輸入品を指す
- ☐ power …にエネルギーを与える、…を動かす
- ☐ eclipse ... in value …を金額においてしのぐ
- ☐ demand for ... …に対する需要
- ☐ depress 押し下げる
- ☐ current account deficit 経常（収支の）赤字→経常収支は貿易収支（物の取引の輸出－輸入。輸出が多ければ黒字）にサービス収支と2種の所得収支が加わる
- ☐ imbalance（貿易の）不均衡、アンバランス、輸出または輸入の超過状態
- ☐ product of ... …が生み出したもの
- ☐ phenomenon 現象→複数形は phenomena

Track 128

5   But those deficits have historically been of short duration; the last time the country had a deficit over the course of a year was in 1980. Most observers believe that the country is experiencing a structural change in its economy as a result of demographic change and the offshoring of production networks, and an annual deficit will become a regular occurrence. A steady and regular outflow of money is a drain on the economy and a sign of a fundamental problem.

6   A second explanation is the Bank of Japan's loose money policies, most evident in its ultralow interest rates. Japan has been trying to spur inflation for decades as flat prices depress spending, undermine innovation and lead to economic stagnation. Monetary authorities here have tried to get inflation to the 2% level to encourage a healthy level of spending and growth. Despite the adoption of unprecedented and unorthodox policies, inflation remains well below that target.

Track 129

7   Elsewhere, inflation is reaching generational highs, however. To fight that trend, monetary authorities in the United States, the European Union and England have increased interest rates. The U.S. Federal Reserve is widely expected to raise interest rates by 50 basis points next month, a move that will, when taken in conjunction with the decision to slow the acquisition of assets that it has been buying to support the economy during the pandemic, cause interest rates to spike. The widening gap makes dollar-, euro- and pound-backed assets more attractive to investors, prompting them to sell yen.

5
- [ ] historically 歴史的には、これまでは
- [ ] be of short duration 短期的である
- [ ] over the course of ... …にわたって
- [ ] observer 観測筋、専門家
- [ ] structural 構造的な、本質的な
- [ ] demographic 人口統計上の、人口の
- [ ] offshoring 海外に出すこと
- [ ] annual 年間を通しての
- [ ] regular occurrence 常に起きること
- [ ] outflow 流出
- [ ] drain on ... …から（金を）流出させる 排水溝、…を枯渇・弱体化させる要因
- [ ] sign 兆候
- [ ] fundamental 根本的な

6
- [ ] the Bank of Japan 日本銀行、日銀 →日本の中央銀行で政策金利やインフレ目標設定などを通じた金融政策も担う
- [ ] most evident in ... …に最も顕著に表れて
- [ ] interest rate 金利→interestは「利子」
- [ ] spur 促進する
- [ ] for decades 何十年かにわたって
- [ ] depress 抑圧する、抑える
- [ ] undermine 徐々に衰えさせる、じわじわとむしばむ
- [ ] stagnation 停滞
- [ ] adoption 採択、導入
- [ ] unprecedented 前例のない
- [ ] unorthodox 正攻法でない、異例の

7
- [ ] elsewhere 他国では
- [ ] generational 数十年来の
- [ ] the (U.S.) Federal Reserve (Board) （米国）連邦準備制度理事会、FRB →米国の中央銀行に当たる金融政策決定機関
- [ ] by （増減・差を表して）…分だけ
- [ ] basis point →金融等の用語で0.01%のこと。bpと略される
- [ ] take a move 実施する
- [ ] in conjunction with ... …と併せて
- [ ] slow 抑制する、鈍化させる
- [ ] assets （金融）資産→債券など
- [ ] spike 急騰する
- [ ] gap →日本と欧米の金融政策の差
- [ ] ...-backed …建ての
- [ ] prompt ... to *do* ～するよう…を促す

8   Normally, Japanese officials favor a weak yen because it helps Japanese companies earn higher profits. Their goods are more competitive in foreign markets and they still make more money when they remit those sales, which are invoiced in dollars. But Japanese businesses now rely increasingly on foreign production, which limits the value of a weaker yen to their bottom line.

Track 130

9   Worse, higher import prices hurt both producers and consumers. Inputs for domestic production are more expensive, cutting profits. The most obvious example is rising power bills: Tokyo Electric Power Co. has raised the electric bill for a typical household to ¥8,505 in May, while Tokyo Gas will raise rates to ¥5,784, 25% and 24% rises, respectively.

10   Japanese authorities are concerned. Finance Minister Shunichi Suzuki called the pace of the yen's decline "undesirable" and said his ministry is "monitoring the situation with a sense of urgency." Haruhiko Kuroda, governor of the Bank of Japan, has said that the sharp fall in the value of the yen will have a "negative effect." Prime Minister Fumio Kishida is probably most worried; the last thing he wants as he faces an election this summer is rising prices that hurt voters.

Track 131

11   In truth, however, signals are mixed. Financial officials want stability and flatter curves in exchange markets; but look closely at Suzuki's comments and the emphasis seems to be on the angle of the decline in the yen — the speed — rather than the direction. Meanwhile, Kuroda insists that a weak yen is good for Japan, believes that inflationary pressures are just temporary and refuses to move away from the low-interest rate policy. Market skepticism about Japanese policy is understandable, which reinforces current trends.

8
- □ weak yen 円安
- □ competitive 競争力の高い
- □ remit 送金する→ここでは日本で売上を回収すること
- □ invoice 請求する
- □ limit ... to *one's* bottom line …を最低限[微々たる値]まで減らす

9
- □ worse さらに悪いことには
- □ hurt …に被害を与える
- □ producer 生産者
- □ input 原材料、原料コスト
- □ cut 減少させる
- □ power bill 電気・ガス料金→powerは電力のみを指す場合が多いがここはガスも入れた「エネルギー」
- □ Co. = Company
- □ household 世帯
- □ respectively それぞれ

10
- □ concerned 懸念して
- □ Finance Minister 財務大臣
- □ call A B AをBと呼ぶ
- □ undesirable 望ましくない
- □ ministry 省→ここは財務省
- □ monitor 監視する、注視する
- □ sense of urgency 緊急事態だという意識、緊張感
- □ governor 総裁
- □ sharp fall in ... …の急落
- □ negative effect マイナスの影響
- □ the last thing (that) he wants 彼が一番望まない・したくないこと
- □ face …に直面する
- □ election this summer →参議院選挙
- □ voter 有権者

11
- □ signal 表れ、（メッセージで示す）意図
- □ mixed 一律ではない、多種混ざった
- □ financial official(s) 財務官僚、財務省
- □ flatter curve より平らなカーブ→円安への動きをできるだけ抑えたいということ
- □ emphasis 強調したい点
- □ direction 方向
- □ inflationary インフレの、インフレを誘発する
- □ move away from ... …を撤回する
- □ low-interest rate policy 低金利政策
- □ skepticism 懐疑的な見方、懐疑論
- □ reinforce さらに強める、後押しする
- □ current trend →円安傾向のこと

12   Given their size and volume, the only way that currency markets can be impacted is through coordinated intervention by the major economies. But economists believe that the gap in interest rates reflects differing conditions among major economies. Prices are going up here, but inflation in Japan is nothing like that in the U.S. or Europe. As an official at the International Monetary Fund noted, the yen's value is being determined by market fundamentals — different growth rates and price levels.

Track 132

13   The belief that the yen's value is a product of fundamentals means that there will be no concerted action by the Group of Seven. Even a joint statement by Japan and the U.S. would be insufficient to change the existing momentum.

14   Investors know that and discount talk of slowing the yen's decline. Politicians must hope that inflation will prove temporary and that its impact contained — at least until after the summer election. But structural change in the Japanese economy will continue — and the need to adapt will intensify. Old thinking will have to go, and the idea that a weak yen is the answer to Japan's economic ills will be a likely casualty.

(931 words)

12
- □ given …を考慮すると
- □ size and volume →ここでは為替市場の規模とその取引量のことを指す
- □ impact …に影響・効果を与える
- □ coordinated intervention 協調介入
- □ economy 経済体→経済活動の面から見たそれぞれの国や地域
- □ differing 異なる
- □ here = in Japan
- □ nothing like ... …とはまったくの別物
- □ that = inflation
- □ the International Monetary Fund 国際通貨基金、IMF →国連の専門機関の一つで世界の経済・金融・為替の安定・発展や円滑化・自由化などをはかる
- □ fundamentals 経済の基礎的諸条件

13
- □ the belief that A means that B A だと信じられているということは、B だということにほかならない
- □ concerted 協調した = coordinated
- □ the Group of Seven 主要先進7カ国、G7
- □ joint statement 共同声明
- □ momentum 弾み、(円安の)勢い

14
- □ discount 割り引いて考える、本気で信じようとは思わない
- □ talk 議論、意見
- □ slow …にブレーキをかける
- □ prove (結果的に)…だとわかる
- □ contain 抑え込む、封じ込める
- □ adapt 対応する
- □ intensify 強まる
- □ have to go なくなるべきだ
- □ answer to ... …の解決策
- □ ill 病巣、問題点
- □ likely おそらく
- □ casualty 犠牲者→ここでは「消え去るべき古い考え」であるということを示す

経済・財政 1 **Tokyo Stock Exchange might not be ready for 'prime' time just yet**

It is believed that 296 companies will make use of this provision, which was reportedly included to mollify politicians who feared <u>intense criticism if long-established members of the first section could not make the transition</u>. **(Paragraph 10、5〜8行目)**

[名詞句を修飾する副詞節] 下線部の後半のif節は「東証1部の老舗企業が移行できなければ」という意味の副詞節だが、動詞のfeared「恐れた」を修飾していると考えると意味が通らない。ここは、intense criticismにかけて考えるのが自然である。ifやwhenの副詞節にはこのケースのように名詞句を修飾していると考えるしかないものもある。その場合、名詞句に動詞的なニュアンスを読み込んで解釈するとわかりやすい。今回の下線部も、「東証1部の老舗企業が移行できなければ痛烈に批判される（ということ）」と理解してよいだろう。

．．

There is <u>a tension between the desire to use membership in the TSE first section to signal acceptance and status — and earn money on the initial listing — and the need for quality control to ensure that prime section companies merit international attention</u>. **(Paragraph 11、1〜4行目)**

[並列関係] 下線部は非常に長い名詞句となっている。a tension betweenと来た時点で「何と何の間か」と考えて、A and Bの構造を期待することが重要。the desire to ...がAに当たる要素であることは明らかなので、and Bを確認することになるが、この文には3つのandが出てくるため慎重に考えたい。1つ目のandは同じ無冠詞単数の形をしているacceptanceとstatusを結んでいると判断できる。また、2つ目のandはダッシュ（−）で囲まれた挿入句内であることに加え、earnという動詞が続くことから、the desire to ...という名詞句と並列になっているとは考えられない。ここから、between A and Bの形でthe desire to ...と並列されているのは、最後のandの後ろのthe need for ...の部分だと結論づけることができる。

経済・財政 2 **A weaker yen is no longer the asset of the past**

The U.S. Federal Reserve is widely expected to raise interest rates by 50 basis points next month, a move that will, when taken in conjunction with the decision to slow the acquisition of assets that it has been buying to support the economy during the pandemic, cause interest rates to spike. (**Paragraph 7、3～8行目**)

[同格語と長い挿入] 下線部はa moveを関係代名詞節が修飾して長い名詞句となっているが、このa move「措置」は直前で説明されている「アメリカのFRBが金利を上げようとしていること」を受けた同格語。「ウクライナ侵攻」4本目の社説でも言及したものと同じ表現方法である。moveを修飾している関係代名詞節の中では、コンマ(,)で挟まれた長いwhen節がwillとcauseの間に挿入されている。when節の中の名詞assetsにもかなり長い関係代名詞節 (that ... pandemic) が続いている点に気をつけたい。

Politicians must hope that inflation will prove temporary and that its impact contained — at least until after the summer election. (**Paragraph 14、2～3行目**)

[並列関係と省略] 下線部をits impact (S) contained (V)と読みそうになるかもしれないが、なぜここで突然過去形が出てくるのか、また、他動詞であるはずのcontainedの目的語はなぜないのか、という点に疑問を感じなければならない。that inflation will prove temporary and that its impact contained という2つの並列関係に目を向け、後半のthat節内では動詞が共通であるため省略されている、つまり、its impact will prove containedのwill proveの省略であるということに気づきたい。

東証は「プライム」の機がまだ熟していないかもしれない

1 米国やヨーロッパの競合相手と比べて伸び悩んでいるとして長い間低く見られていた東京証券取引所だったが、2021年は好調で、日経平均は年末の終値で32年ぶりの高値を付けた。

2 東証は、コーポレートガバナンスを再生し、世界の投資家を引き付けることを意図した再編を4月初めに控えているので、その実績は良い兆しである。

3 ところが、市場を活性化させて懐疑的な投資家の心をつかむための改革案に対して、早期の評価はその実効性に疑問を投げかけている。多くは市場の規制当局が改革をどれだけ毅然と実行するかにかかっている。

4 3,777社の株式が取引される東証には現在、第1部、第2部、JASDAQ、マザーズという4つの区分がある。4月の改革ではこれらの区分がプライム、スタンダード、グロースの3つに統合される。統合よりも重要なのは、プライムのセクションに上場しようとする企業に課される新たな要件だろう。その新しい規則は、市場価値、社外取締役の人数、浮動株の数、その他の要因が対象になる。

5 ほとんどの注目は取引所のこのプライムのセクションに集まっていて、そこは日本の「最良の」企業を含むことになるはずだ。現在、東証第1部には2,158社が所属していて、これは上場企業の半数以上に当たる。

6 現在の第1部はどう考えても肥大化していて、ひとたび企業の上場が承認されると、たとえ低い流動性や低い時価総額でも外されることはほとんどない。新しい区分は現在の所属企業の84%に当たる1,841社を含むことになり、かなりの選別がなされたとは信じがたい。残りの企業のうち、1,477社(東証上場企業の39%)はスタンダードに、459社(12%)はグロースに入ることになる。

7 プライム市場への加入を認められた企業は、ほかの証券取引所の主要セクションの企業との競合で苦労することだろう。そうした日本企業の時価総額の中央値はわずか5億2000万ドルなのに対して、ニューヨーク証券取引所では約28億ドル、ロンドン市場とナスダック・グローバル・セレクト・マーケットでは約17億ドルである。プライムに所属する企業の半数弱は株価純資産倍率が1未満で、これは純資産よりも株価が安いことを意味する。米国やヨーロッパの市場では、この数字は10%から20%の間にある。

8 投資家とアナリストは改革案がその差を縮めることに対して懐疑的だ。たとえば、プライムの企業には少なくとも100億円分の流通株式を持つことが要求される。世界のアセットマネージャーは通常、その額の50倍の価値がある投資目標を探し求める。

9 そのうえ、多くの株式は実際には購入することができない。代わりに株式持ち合いの一部になっていて、これは経営陣を一切の外部の圧力から保護することを意図する取り決めだ。そうした取引は流通株式にはカウントされず、そのことはプライム上場への低い敷居がさらに魅力に欠ける理由を説明している。

10 2番目の問題は新しい要件を満たすために企業に与えられた柔軟性だ。あまりに多くの企業がプライムセクションの資格を満たさないかもしれないことを恐れて、当局は企業が改革案を提出しさえすれば、無期限の移行期間を与えると決定した。296社がこの条項を利用すると考えられていて、伝えられるところによるとその条項が含められたのは、長い伝統のある一部上場企業が移行できなかった場合に強く批判されるのではと恐れた政治家をなだめるためだったという。けれども、それは実質的に改革を骨抜きにしている。期限が定められることになるとの報道がある。それは必要不可欠だ。

11 東証第1部の会員資格を受け入れとステータスのしるしとする——および上場に際して金を稼ぐ——ために利用したいという願望と、プライムセクションの企業が国際的な注目に確実に値するものにする、そうした質の管理の必要性との間に葛藤がある。これまでのところはステータスの懸念のほうが勝っていて、それは長きにわたって古い制度の問題であった。

12 東証の幹部もこれらの懸念を十分認識している。彼らの発言は一貫して、来るべき変化はプロセスの始まりにすぎないと指摘している。東証の山道裕己社長は、「発表は持続可能な成長と中長期的な企業価値の高まりに向けた長い道のりのスタートラインだ」と述べた。

13 その取り組みの中心となるのは、日本株を海外投資家にとってより魅力的にするような変化の重視だ。英語での情報開示を増やすこと、独立非業務執行取締役の数を3分の1よりも多くすること、および気候関連財務情報開示タスクフォースの勧告に沿った気候変動関連の情報開示を義務付けることによって、東証はそのような変化を実行しようとしている。これらの指令は変化を余儀なくさせられる可能性がある。第1部上場企業は社外取締役を3人以上持つものとする東証の要件により、それに該当する企業の割合は2014年の21.5％から昨年の97％に増えた。

東証は「プライム」の機がまだ熟していないかもしれない

14 けれども、それらの変化は孤立して存在しているのではない。外国為替及び外国貿易法とコーポレートガバナンス・コードの変更も重要だ。前者の条項は疑わしい方法で知的財産を獲得する投資家の機会の制限を目的とするものだが、株主アクティズム（行動主義）とガバナンス改革を弱体化させるために乱用される恐れがある。

15 後者は昨年6月、環境的、社会的、およびガバナンスの問題のほか、持続可能性の重視を推し進めるために改正された。そうした変更は称賛されてきたが、これに関してはあまりにも多くが厳格な実行ができるかどうかにかかっている。

16 日本の役人、政治家、企業は、世界の投資家からの持続的な注目、熱狂、投資を生み出すためにはビジネス慣習を変える必要があるとわかっている。

17 東証の改革は、経済のほかの構造変化と同様、まさにそれを行うことが目的だ。しかし、投資家はうわべだけの修正ではだまされない。彼らの心を勝ち取るためには真の変化が必要とされる。彼らはまだ納得していない。　　　　（訳・注　桑田）

円安はもはやかつてのような資産ではない

1 日本円は今年急落を続けており、その価値は10%下がって20年来の安値に達している。

2 急落の原因はいくつかあり、日本の金融当局がそれに対して打つ手があるかどうか定かではない。当局は金融緩和政策を維持しているが、われわれは彼らがこの下落を止める気がどれくらいあるのかという疑問を持たざるを得ない。円安は日本にとって十分役に立ってきたが、不安定な通貨はそうではない。

3 円の下落によって、円は対ドルで今年最も相対価値の低い主要通貨となった。その後128円まで戻したものの、今週、日本の通貨は1ドル129円を超えてしまった。また数週間前には130円の大台をうかがう恐れすらあった。今では外国為替取引のアナリストたちは近い将来1ドル135円を突破する可能性もあると考えている。

4 円の下落にはいくつかの理由がある。第一に、商品価格が上昇してきている点。日本が経済を動かすために必要な物品への支払いを増やしていく際、そうした輸入品への支払いにはドルが使用される。輸入額が輸出額を上回ると、ドルに対する需要が円の価値を押し下げる。日本はこれまでも月ベースで経常赤字が発生したことがあり、最近の貿易不均衡はパンデミックとウクライナ戦争という一時的な現象が原因だと考えられている。

5 しかし、歴史的に見るとこうした赤字は一時的なものだった。1年にわたって日本円が経常赤字の状態にあったのは1980年が最後である。多くの専門家は人口動勢が変化し生産ネットワークが海外に移転した結果、日本経済に構造変化が起きており、今後は年間を通じた赤字が当たり前に生じるようになると考えている。資金流出の常態化は経済を弱体化させる要因であり、これから根本的な問題が発生する兆しだと言える。

6 第二の原因は、超低金利政策に代表されるような、日銀の金融緩和政策だ。日本はこれまで数十年にわたってインフレを促進しようと努めてきた。物価の横ばいが消費を抑制し、技術革新をじわじわと阻害し、経済の停滞につながると考えられてきたからだ。日本の金融当局は、健全なレベルの消費と成長を促すために、インフレ率を2%台にしようと努めてきた。ところが前例のない、かつ異例の政策がとられてきたにもかかわらず、インフレ率はその目標値を大きく下回ったままだ。

円安はもはやかつてのような資産ではない

7 ところが、ほかの国々では、インフレ率は数十年来の高水準に達している。その傾向に対処するため、米国、欧州連合（EU）、英国の金融当局は金利を引き上げた。米国連邦準備制度理事会（FRB）は来月、0.5％の利上げを行うとの予想が広まっているが、パンデミック禍で経済を支援するためにFRBが続けてきた資産買入れのスピードを緩める決定と相まってこの動きがとられれば、金利の急騰を引き起こすことになるだろう。日本と他国の金融政策の違いが大きくなるにつれ、ドル、ユーロ、そしてポンド建ての資産は投資家にとってより魅力的になり、投資家による円売りがさらに進むことになる。

8 通常、日本の官僚は、日本企業の収益を押し上げる働きをすることから円安を好む傾向がある。海外市場で日本企業の製品の競争力が上がり、日本企業がドル建てで請求した売上を回収する際にも、円高の時より多くの利益を手にすることができる。しかし現在、日本企業はますます海外生産に依存するようになってきており、その結果、円安が企業収益に与えるメリットは抑えられてしまっている。

9 さらに悪いことに、輸入物価の上昇は生産者と消費者の双方に打撃を与える。国内生産のために買い付ける資材の値段は上がり、利益が減ってしまう。それが最も顕著に表れている例は、電気・ガス料金の上昇だ。東京電力はこの5月、標準的な世帯の電気料金を8,505円に値上げし、東京ガスはガス料金を標準世帯で5,784円に値上げする予定だ。これはそれぞれ25％、24％の値上げである。

10 日本当局も懸念を示している。鈴木俊一財務大臣は、円の下落のペースを「望ましくない」と表現し、財務省は「緊張感を持って状況を監視している」と述べた。日銀の黒田東彦総裁は、急激な円の価値の下落は「マイナスの影響」をもたらすと発言している。おそらく最も円安を懸念しているのは岸田文雄首相だろう。この夏に選挙を控えている彼が一番望まないものは、有権者に打撃を与える物価上昇だからだ。

11 ただ実際のところ、発言のニュアンスは一律ではない。金融当局者は為替市場において安定と変動の小ささを望んでいるが、鈴木氏のコメントをよく見ると、彼が重きを置いているのは円価がどちらに動くかということよりも円の下落の角度、すなわちスピードであるように思える。一方、黒田総裁は、円安は日本にとって良いことだという主張にこだわり、インフレ圧力はほんの一時的なものだと考え、低金利政策を撤回することを拒否している。これでは日本の政策に対して市場が懐疑的な見方をするのは当然で、それが現在の円安傾向にさらに拍車をかけている。

12 その規模と量を考えると、唯一通貨市場にインパクトを与えることができる方法は、主要経済国による協調介入である。しかし、経済の専門家たちは、主要経済国間の金利差には各国の状況の違いが反映されているのだと考えている。日本では物価は上がっているが、日本で起こっているインフレは米国や欧州のそれとは比べものにならない。国際通貨基金（IMF）の担当者が言及したように、現在の円価は市場のファンダメンタルズ（基礎的諸条件）、すなわち日本と諸外国の成長率や物価水準の違いによって決まってきている。

13 円価がファンダメンタルズの産物であるという考え方からすると、G7が協調して行動を起こすことはない。日米で共同声明が出されたとしても、現在の円安の勢いを変えるには不十分だろう。

14 投資家はそれをわかっているので、円安にブレーキをかけるといった話に本気で耳を傾けようとはしない。政治家たちは、インフレが結果的に一時的なものに終わり、その影響を何とか、少なくとも夏の選挙が終わるまで食い止められることを期待しているに違いない。しかし、日本経済の構造的な変化はこれからも続いていき、日本経済がそれに適応していく必要性はますます高まっていく。古い考え方は捨てていかなければならない。円安が日本経済の問題の解決策だという考えはおそらくその一つだ。

（訳・注　小川）

第4章 社会・文化

7月19日、会見でプロスケーターへの転向を表明する羽生結弦さん

Government clarity needed as Japan eyes border reopening for tourism

訪日観光再開に向けて政府は明確な意思疎通を

May 21, 2022 　　　　　　　●Tracks 133-141 / 解説 p. 250、訳 p. 254

Track 133

1　The Japanese government is planning to — gingerly — reopen the country to foreign tourists.

2　Successive administrations have opted for caution as they balanced the public health and safety impacts of reopening against the economic losses. Now, however, the government of Prime Minister Fumio Kishida seems ready to explore a more permissive policy to begin a return to normalcy and the economic rewards that follow. We encourage that evolution but urge the administration to remain sensitive to public concerns. Success in any COVID-19 control and containment policy requires public confidence and support.

Track 134

3　Japan closed its borders to foreign travelers shortly after the COVID-19 outbreak began two years ago, gradually widening the ban to include 159 countries and regions. It eased some of those restrictions — such as allowing foreign residents to return — but reopening proved to be a fitful process as new variants emerged and successive waves of infection battered the country.

▼ About This Editorial ▼

新型コロナウイルスの世界的流行で途絶えていた訪日観光客の往来を取り戻そうと、政府は段階的な受け入れ再開の準備を進めている。社会経済活動を活発にするためには必要なことだが、規制緩和に抵抗感を覚える国民との丁寧な意思疎通が不可欠だ。

1
- ☐ ［タイトル］clarity 明確さ
- ☐ ［タイトル］eye 視野に入れる、考慮する
- ☐ ［タイトル］border 国境
- ☐ gingerly 慎重に

2
- ☐ successive 連続する→安倍内閣、菅内閣のこと
- ☐ administration 政権、内閣
- ☐ opt for ... …を選択する
- ☐ caution 警戒、用心
- ☐ public health 国民の健康
- ☐ impact 影響
- ☐ explore 模索する
- ☐ permissive 寛容な
- ☐ normalcy 平常
- ☐ reward 報い、見返り
- ☐ evolution 展開
- ☐ urge 強く求める
- ☐ concern 懸念
- ☐ COVID-19 新型コロナウイルス感染症
- ☐ containment 封じ込め

3
- ☐ outbreak 大流行、感染爆発
- ☐ widen 拡大する
- ☐ ban 禁止
- ☐ ease 緩和する
- ☐ restriction 規制
- ☐ prove to be ... …であることがわかる、結果として…となる
- ☐ fitful 断続的な
- ☐ variant 変異型
- ☐ emerge 出現する
- ☐ infection 感染
- ☐ batter …に打撃を与える

4 While there has been a slowly growing trickle of business travelers and students since March — from 3,500 to 10,000 — tourists have not been allowed entry. That will now change. The government has proposed that it will from June allow small groups of fully-vaccinated visitors on package tours from four countries — the United States, Australia, Thailand and Singapore. This will be in addition to a reported doubling of the number of foreign visitors (to 20,000) allowed into the country.

Track 135

5 The policy change reflects a sense that Japan lags the global consensus on how to respond to the disease. Most countries have reopened their borders to visitors that are fully vaccinated or provide negative PCR test results. Kishida has repeatedly used international comparisons when discussing this issue and Japan's admission protocols are stricter than most.

6 Calls to readmit tourists have become louder and more urgent as the economy stumbles. COVID-19 and the Ukraine war have had a profound impact, slowing growth and pushing up prices. According to one estimate, the absence of foreign visitors cost Japan ¥10.96 trillion in lost revenues in 2020 alone, or more than ¥22 trillion since the pandemic began. Those losses contributed to the 1% decline in gross domestic product by a Cabinet Office estimation.

4
- ☐ trickle of ... ぽつりぽつりと訪れる…
- ☐ entry 入国
- ☐ propose 提案する
- ☐ fully-vaccinated 完全にワクチン接種をした→ここでは3回目の接種を完了したということ
- ☐ in addition to ... …に加えて
- ☐ reported 報じられている
- ☐ doubling 倍増

5
- ☐ reflect 反映する
- ☐ sense 意識
- ☐ lag …に後れをとる
- ☐ consensus ほぼ一致した意見
- ☐ comparison 比較
- ☐ issue 問題
- ☐ admission 受け入れ
- ☐ protocol プロトコル、規定

6
- ☐ call 要請
- ☐ urgent 切迫した
- ☐ stumble 低迷する
- ☐ profound 多大な
- ☐ estimate 推計
- ☐ absence 不在
- ☐ cost A B AにBの損失を与える
- ☐ trillion 兆
- ☐ revenue 歳入
- ☐ contribute to ... …の一因となる
- ☐ gross domestic product 国内総生産（GDP）
- ☐ Cabinet Office 内閣府
- ☐ estimation 概算

Track 136

7　In the absence of a change, those losses will grow. The number of foreign tourists had been climbing sharply since Japan made the promotion of tourism a priority. In 2019, 31.88 million tourists spent ¥4.81 trillion in Japan. Two years later, just 240,000 foreign visitors entered the country. And as the yen hits 20-year lows, Japan is an even more attractive tourist destination — if they can enter the country. And, it should be noted, many of those tourists were Chinese and they will not be able to visit even if Japan opens its doors.

8　The principal obstacle to those visitors is public reluctance. Japan has been successful at containing the spread and impact of COVID-19. According to the World Health Organization, Japan is one of the few countries that did not report excess mortality for 2020 and 2021. The U.S., by contrast, had nearly 1 million excess deaths; Germany had about 200,000.

Track 137

9　Japan's vaccination rate tops 81% and more than 57% have received a booster. This week, the country confirmed nearly 37,000 new COVID-19 cases, down more than 5,200 from the previous week, and a steady decline. There were 39 new COVID-19 deaths.

10　It is estimated that an infection rate of about 60% is the threshold for acceptance of a disease. In Japan, only 7% of the population is reported to have had the disease, and while that number is likely low — a considerable number of people with infections are asymptomatic or think they have the flu — it is nowhere near that level.

7
- [ ] climb 増える
- [ ] promotion 促進
- [ ] priority 優先事項
- [ ] hit ... low(s) …来の安値に達する
- [ ] destination 目的地
- [ ] note …に注目する

8
- [ ] principal 主な
- [ ] obstacle 障害
- [ ] reluctance 抵抗感
- [ ] the World Health Organization 世界保健機関
- [ ] excess mortality 超過死亡→ある時期に予測される死亡者数と比較してどれだけ増えたかを表す
- [ ] by contrast 対照的に

9
- [ ] vaccination rate ワクチン接種率
- [ ] top 上回る
- [ ] booster ブースター接種→3回目の接種のこと
- [ ] confirm 確認する
- [ ] case 患者
- [ ] previous 前の
- [ ] steady 着実な
- [ ] decline 減少

10
- [ ] threshold 閾値
- [ ] acceptance 受け入れ
- [ ] likely おそらく
- [ ] considerable 相当な
- [ ] asymptomatic 無症状の
- [ ] flu インフルエンザ
- [ ] nowhere near ... …には遠く及ばない

Track 138

11   That record has made the public suspicious of opening. In a December poll, 81% of respondents backed the ongoing ban on foreign nationals. Another survey, taken earlier this month revealed a slight shift. That number had fallen to 57%, while 32% wanted restrictions eased.

12   The prime minister is obliged to carefully move forward. With an Upper House election set for July, he cannot afford to be indifferent to public concerns. He will ensure that progress is slow and tentative. There will be careful messaging to maintain public support.

Track 139

13   Success depends on several factors, most — but not all — of which he can control. There must be surveillance of foreign visitors that is both effective and nonobtrusive. Especially important will be the security of the personal information generated by that process. Antigen tests must be made more widely available and inexpensive, preferably free.

14   There will need to be better preparation within the public health system. In particular, there is a need to be ready to treat foreigners with all the associated issues, such as payment and language. This will be more challenging if visitors venture away from major cities.

Track 140

15   There are two obvious problems. The first is the difficulty in extrapolating meaningful lessons from the pilot projects the government is launching. Reportedly, the initial groups will be in the tens of tourists. That seems to be too small a sample size to be very useful. It looks as though this is merely a confidence building exercise for the election.

11
- ☐ record 実績
- ☐ suspicious 懐疑的な
- ☐ poll 世論調査
- ☐ respondent 回答者
- ☐ back 支持する
- ☐ ongoing 継続中の
- ☐ national 国民
- ☐ survey 調査
- ☐ reveal 明らかにする
- ☐ slight わずかな

12
- ☐ be obliged to *do* ～せざるを得ない
- ☐ Upper House 参議院
- ☐ election 選挙
- ☐ set for ... …に予定されている
- ☐ afford to *do* ～する余裕がある
- ☐ be indifferent to ... …に無関心だ
- ☐ ensure 確実にする
- ☐ tentative 慎重な、試験的な
- ☐ maintain 維持する

13
- ☐ factor 要素
- ☐ surveillance 監視
- ☐ effective 効果的な
- ☐ nonobtrusive 邪魔にならない
- ☐ generate 生じる
- ☐ antigen 抗原
- ☐ available 利用できる
- ☐ preferably できれば

14
- ☐ preparation 準備
- ☐ in particular 特に
- ☐ treat 治療する、…に対応する
- ☐ associated 付随する
- ☐ payment 支払い
- ☐ challenging 難しい
- ☐ venture away from ... …からあえて離れる

15
- ☐ obvious 明白な
- ☐ extrapolate （既知の事柄から)推定する
- ☐ meaningful 有意義な
- ☐ lesson 教え、知恵
- ☐ pilot 試験的な
- ☐ launch …に着手する
- ☐ reportedly 伝えられるところによると
- ☐ in the tens of ... 数十の…
- ☐ look as though ... …のようだ
- ☐ merely 単なる

16 The second problem is the unpredictability of the virus itself. COVID-19 has proven resilient and adaptable. Variants keep appearing. While they seem to be weaker in virulence, that won't always be the case. As Japan reopens, the government must remain vigilant for the worst-case scenario.

Track 141

17 No matter what happens, however, the government needs to communicate with its citizens, clearly and effectively. There must be no doubt about what is being done and why. Public confidence is the foundation of any successful disease response.

(939 words)

16
- [ ] unpredictability 予測不可能であること
- [ ] virus ウイルス
- [ ] resilient 強靭な、回復力のある
- [ ] adaptable 適応性がある
- [ ] appear 出現する
- [ ] virulence 毒性
- [ ] won't always be the case いつもそうであるとは限らない
- [ ] vigilant 用心深い
- [ ] worst-case scenario 最悪の事態

17
- [ ] No matter what happens たとえ何が起こっても
- [ ] doubt 疑念
- [ ] foundation 基盤
- [ ] response 対応

社会・文化 **2**

Japan's disappointing ruling on same-sex marriage

大阪地裁、同性婚に関し残念な判決

June 25, 2022　　　　　　　●Tracks 142-148 / 解説 p. 251、訳 p. 257

Track 142

1　An Osaka court ruled last Monday that Japan's ban on same-sex marriage was not unconstitutional, a blow not only to the rights of gay couples but to human rights in general.

2　In keeping with the conservative tradition of Japan's judiciary, the Osaka District Court essentially deferred, arguing that the responsibility for such a change rests upon the shoulders of legislators. Parliamentarians must take action then. It is long past time for Japan's same-sex couples to enjoy all the rights afforded their heterosexual counterparts.

Track 143

3　In the Osaka case, three same-sex couples argued that they suffer "unjust discrimination" because the current legal system prevents them from getting married. In fact, discrimination goes well beyond the ability to get married. Individuals in same-sex relationships cannot inherit their partner's assets and have no parental rights over their partner's children. They are disadvantaged when paying taxes. They can be denied comfort and companionship in the most difficult personal struggles because their closest personal relationship is not recognized. The Osaka plaintiffs sought ¥1 million per person in damages, a paltry sum compared to the meaning and value of a ruling on their behalf.

▼ About This Editorial ▼

同性婚を認めない現状の民法や戸籍法の規定は憲法違反だと、3組の同性カップルが訴えた今回の裁判。昨年の札幌地裁の判決とは異なり、大阪地裁は同性婚を認めないことは合憲だと判断し国内外に衝撃を与えた。政府や司法は世界の潮流にもっと目を向けるべきだ。

1
- □ [タイトル]ruling 判決、司法裁定
- □ court 裁判所→ここでは大阪地裁のこと
- □ rule …と判決を下す
- □ ban on ... …の禁止
- □ unconstitutional 違憲の
- □ blow 打撃、ショッキングな出来事

2
- □ in keeping with ... …に倣って、一致して
- □ judiciary 司法（当局）
- □ defer 判断を回避・先延ばしにする
- □ rest upon the shoulders of ... …の肩に委ねられる、…に託される
- □ legislators 法律制定者たち→国会
- □ parliamentarian 国会議員
- □ it is long past time for ... to *do* もういいかげん…が〜してもいいころだ
- □ afford A B AにBを与える
- □ heterosexual 異性愛の
- □ counterpart 相当する人・物→ここでは「カップル」を指す

3
- □ case 訴訟、判例、争点
- □ unjust 不当な
- □ discrimination 差別
- □ legal system 法制度
- □ prevent ... from *doing* …が〜することを妨げる、…が〜できなくする
- □ go well beyond ... まったく…のみにとどまらない、…をはるかに超えて及ぶ
- □ inherit 相続する
- □ asset 資産
- □ parental right over ... …に対する親権→ここは相手の連れ子に言及
- □ disadvantage …に不利益を与える
- □ deny A B AにBを与えない
- □ comfort やすらぎ、心の安寧
- □ companionship 寄り添い、側にいてあげること→パートナーが危篤でも「親族」とは違いその病室に入れないなど
- □ recognize 認知する、法的に認める
- □ plaintiff 原告
- □ seek （裁判で）求める→soughtは過去形
- □ in damages 損害賠償として
- □ paltry わずかな、とるに足りない
- □ on *one's* behalf 〜のために（下されるべき）

4   Central to the case was the interpretation of Article 24 of the Constitution, which says that "Marriage shall be based only on the mutual consent of both sexes and it shall be maintained through mutual cooperation with the equal rights of husband and wife as a basis." The Japanese government argued that the Constitution does not mention same-sex marriage, so banning same-sex marriage should not be considered discriminatory.

Track 144

5   The court examined the purpose of marriage, asserting that the institution is designed by society to protect relationships between a man and a woman for giving birth and raising children. Given that rationale, the court concluded that the ban on same-sex marriage is constitutional.

6   The court took refuge in procedure, noting that "there have not been enough discussions among people in Japan" on how to best protect the interests of same-sex couples who choose to live together. It argued that it is not the court's job to create those protections; it is instead the job of the legislature. While noting that some jurisdictions have begun to provide "marriage-like" protections, the court added that a national approach should be realized through "establishment of systems based on unfettered discussions in the democratic process."

Track 145

7   That argument makes sense. Nevertheless, it is an abdication of the fundamental job of the judiciary — deciding the constitutionality of laws (or the absence of laws). Instead, the Osaka court opted to defer to public opinion. But a right is either constitutional or it isn't; popularity has little if anything to do with it. In fact, the most important role a court plays is when it makes a ruling that is not popular.

4
- □ central to ... …の中核をなして
- □ interpretation 解釈
- □ Article 24 第24条→婚姻の成立、両性の本質的平等や個人の尊厳をうたった条文で、本文に引用された部分の後に第2項として財産権、相続等に関し個人の尊厳と両性の本質的平等に立脚して法律を制定するよう示している
- □ the Constitution 日本国憲法
- □ be based on ... …に基づく
- □ mutual 互いの
- □ consent 合意
- □ both sexes 両性
- □ as a basis 拠り所として
- □ discriminatory 差別的な

5
- □ examine 精査する
- □ assert 主張する
- □ institution (結婚という)制度
- □ design (目的に合致するように工夫して)作り出す
- □ give birth 子供を産む・持つ
- □ raise 育てる
- □ given …を鑑みると、…を考慮して
- □ rationale 論理的根拠、根本的理由
- □ constitutional 合憲の

6
- □ take refuge in ... …(の不備)に逃げ込む、…を言い訳にする
- □ procedure (踏むべき)手続き、過程
- □ note コメントする、述べる
- □ how to best *do* 最もうまく〜するにはどうすればよいか
- □ interests 利益
- □ protection (法整備などの)守る制度[措置]、保護策
- □ instead そうではなくて
- □ jurisdiction 法定期権限を持つ組織
- □ marriage-like 婚姻相当の
- □ realize 実現する
- □ establishment 確立
- □ unfettered 制限のない、自由な

7
- □ make sense 一理ある
- □ nevertheless それでもやはり
- □ abdication 放棄
- □ constitutionality 合憲性
- □ absence まだないこと、欠如
- □ opt to *do* …することを選ぶ
- □ defer to ... …に判断を委ねる
- □ popularity 国民の意見に合うかどうか、世論への斟酌
- □ have (if anything) little to do with ... …とは(多少はあるかもしれないが)ほとんど無関係である
- □ make a ruling 裁定を下す

8   A more forward-leaning approach was taken by the Sapporo District Court, which in March 2021 backed the claim that not allowing same-sex marriage was unconstitutional. That court found that Japan's civil law and family registration law violate Article 14 of the Constitution, which states "all the people are equal under the law." This is the only other judgment on this question in Japan (although other cases are pending).

Track 146

9   As the Osaka court noted, Japan is making progress. But it is moving too slowly. Japan is the only Group of Seven nation that doesn't allow people of the same gender to marry. There are no legal protections for LGBTQ individuals against discrimination in housing or employment. As Amnesty International noted after the Osaka ruling, "Japan has failed to introduce national legislation to eliminate discrimination based on sexual orientation, gender identity, expression and sex characteristics."

10   Smaller jurisdictions have filled the gap. Shibuya Ward in Tokyo was first in April 2015 to offer "partnership certificates" to same-sex couples, which were not legally binding but offered political recognition. Setagaya Ward soon followed. In June 2017, Sapporo became the first city in Japan to officially recognize same-sex partnerships, and Ibaraki Prefecture was the first to offer prefectural support in July 2019. Osaka Prefecture followed suit in January 2020. In total, nearly 200 local governments now provide some sort of recognition for same-sex couples.

8
- [ ] forward-leaning 積極的な、つっこんだ
- [ ] take approach 判断・方針を取る
- [ ] back 支持する、受け入れる
- [ ] claim 主張
- [ ] not allowing ... …を認めないことは
- [ ] civil law 民法
- [ ] family registration law 戸籍法
- [ ] violate …に背く、違反する
- [ ] under the law 法の下で
- [ ] judgment 判断、判決
- [ ] question 問題
- [ ] pending 係争中の

9
- [ ] make progress 進歩する
- [ ] Group of Seven 主要先進7カ国、G7
- [ ] LGBTQ →lesbian, gay, bisexual, transgenderにquestioning（または queer「少数性志向者」）を加えた性マイノリティーを指す
- [ ] housing 住宅（確保）
- [ ] Amnesty International →人権保護活動を行う国際NGO組織
- [ ] introduce legislation 法案を提出する、法整備を進める
- [ ] sexual orientation 性的志向
- [ ] gender identity 性自認、自認性別

10
- [ ] smaller jurisdiction →前段落の「国単位の法整備が進んでいない」を受け「国」より小さい行政単位すなわち「（地方）自治体」を指す
- [ ] fill the gap 穴を埋める
- [ ] ward （都市の中の）「区」、行政区 →City（例：Sibuya City）とも呼称
- [ ] was first to *do* ほかに先駆けて～した→同段落後半のwas the first to *do* も同じ
- [ ] legally binding 法的拘束力[効力]を持つ、法的に有効な
- [ ] recognition 認めること、認知
- [ ] prefecture 県、府
- [ ] prefectural 県・府の
- [ ] follow suit それに続く、それに倣う

11   Some businesses have stepped up as well, offering benefits for and protections to LGBTQ employees. They have recognized that protecting those workers is the best way to attract talent and compete not only with domestic companies but international competition too. But companies can only go so far. Government action is required. If the Kishida administration is serious about rejuvenating the economy, it should recognize that extending equal protection to all employees will entice foreign firms to do business here.

12   That will require boldness from the government. The ruling Liberal Democratic Party is socially conservative and has been unwilling to adopt many policies that challenge conventional views of morality and propriety. In an October 2021 poll of those running in last fall's election, just 12% of LDP candidates favored same-sex marriage, while 38% were opposed.

13   Grim as those numbers are, there are grounds for hope. Some 50% of LDP candidates were undecided and support is growing. That October 2021 poll also showed that 61% of all candidates favored same-sex marriage, 15% were against and 25% were undecided. The public is even more supportive. An October 2018 poll by Dentsu showed that 78.4% of people aged between 20 and 59 "approve" or "somewhat approve" of same-sex marriage.

11
- [ ] business 企業
- [ ] step up 進み出る、本気で取り組む
- [ ] benefit 優遇措置、福利厚生
- [ ] talent 才能ある人々
- [ ] compete with ... …と競争して勝つ
- [ ] not only A but (also) B AのみならずBも
- [ ] domestic 国内の
- [ ] can only go so far できることはそれが限界だ
- [ ] administration 政権
- [ ] rejuvenate 再活性化する、再生する
- [ ] extend A to B AをBに広げる
- [ ] entice ... to *do* …が〜する気にさせる
- [ ] here →ここでは日本のこと

12
- [ ] boldness 大胆さ、あえての行動
- [ ] ruling 与党の
- [ ] Liberal Democratic Party 自由民主党
- [ ] socially 対（日本）社会の面からは
- [ ] be unwilling to *do* 〜したがらない
- [ ] conventional 従来からの、因習的な
- [ ] propriety （ある環境下での）妥当性、正しさ
- [ ] poll 意見調査
- [ ] those (who are) running 立候補者
- [ ] last fall's election →2021年10月の衆議院選挙を指す
- [ ] favor …に賛成する

13
- [ ] grim as ... are …は厳しい状況だが
- [ ] ground 根拠
- [ ] some （数字の前で）約…→50%は前段落最後の12%と38%を100%から引いた数字
- [ ] undecided 態度を決めていない
- [ ] all candidates →ここのデータは自民党以外の候補も含めての数字
- [ ] against 反対して
- [ ] the public 国民、一般の人々
- [ ] supportive 支持して
- [ ] Dentsu 電通→最大手の広告代理店。市場把握のために各種世論調査も行う
- [ ] approve of ... …を認める、…に賛成する

14   Yet according to that same Dentsu poll, 50.3% of people who identified as LGBTQ described themselves as "reticent" or "somewhat reticent" to come out to work colleagues. That is more evidence of the perniciousness of the current system. These citizens are denied the freedom to be themselves and denied the fulfillments heterosexual citizens enjoy. All of us are diminished as a result. The Japanese public knows this is wrong. We should demand that our legislators correct this injustice.

(970 words)

14
- □ identify as ... 自分を…だとする
- □ reticent 無口な、話したがらない
- □ come out 自分の本当の姿を話す、カミングアウトする
- □ work colleague 職場の同僚
- □ be evidence of ... …の証拠となる
- □ perniciousness 悪質性、不適切さ

- □ these citizens →LGBTQの人々
- □ be *oneself* 自分らしくいる
- □ fulfillment 希望がかなうこと、満足感
- □ diminish …の評判を落とす、…の民度を下げる
- □ injustice 不公平、権利の侵害

A despicable attack on Shinzo Abe — and a nation

安倍晋三氏、および国家に対する卑劣な攻撃

July 9, 2022

●Tracks 149-154 / 解説 p. 252、訳 p. 260

Track 149

1   The editorial commentary originally scheduled to fill this space was a cri de coeur to the United States, a plea for it to come to its senses and halt the devastating gun violence that has become a fact of daily life in that country. It is with extraordinary sadness and anger that we instead are forced to substitute this comment decrying the assassination of former Prime Minister Shinzo Abe.

2   As we write this, there is little that is known about the shooting. It would be irresponsible and reckless to speculate about the motives and reasoning behind the incident. Nevertheless, we can say two things with absolute certainty. First, we offer our deepest condolences to the former prime minister's family and loved ones. Second, this was an act of terrorism and there is no place for such behavior in Japan. We live in a democracy where disputes and differences are resolved by voting in elections, not with violence.

Track 150

3   Abe was attacked Friday morning in Nara on the first stop in a three-prefecture swing to campaign for Liberal Democratic Party candidates in Sunday's Upper House election. He was shot twice in the chest from behind allegedly by a Nara resident who was seized at the scene and taken into custody. Abe reportedly went into cardiac arrest while being airlifted to a local hospital, where he eventually succumbed to his injuries. We stand with Prime Minister Fumio Kishida who called the shooting "a heinous act … barbaric, malicious, and it cannot be tolerated."

▼ About This Editorial ▼

安倍晋三元首相が銃撃されて亡くなった事件は、銃犯罪がまれな日本で起きたという以上の衝撃を社会に与えた。私たちは政治的な姿勢や意見の違いを超えてこの忌まわしい犯罪を強く非難すると同時に、民主主義の意味とそのあり方を再確認しなければならない。

1
- [タイトル]despicable 卑劣な
- editorial commentary 社説
- scheduled to *do* ～する予定の
- cri de coeur 心の叫び
- come to *one's* senses 正気に返る
- devastating 衝撃的な、ひどい
- a fact of daily life 日常茶飯事
- extraordinary 大いなる
- be forced to *do* ～せざるを得ない
- substitute …に差し替える
- decry 非難する
- assassination 暗殺

2
- irresponsible 無責任な
- reckless 無謀な
- speculate about ... …について推測する
- motive 動機
- reasoning 論拠
- nevertheless それでもなお
- absolute certainty 絶対的な確信
- condolence 哀悼の意
- loved one 愛する人、大切な人→特に身近な家族を指す
- there is no place for ... …のための場所はない、…の入る余地はない
- dispute 論争、異議

3
- three-prefecture 3県の
- swing 周遊
- campaign 選挙運動をする
- candidate 候補者
- Upper House election 衆議院選挙
- allegedly …だとされている
- seize 捕まえる
- be taken into custody 身柄を拘束される
- cardiac arrest 心停止
- airlift 空輸する
- succumb to ... …で死ぬ、亡くなる
- stand with ... …と同じ考えである
- heinous 凶悪な
- barbaric 野蛮な
- malicious 悪意に基づいた
- tolerate 容認する

4 Thankfully, acts of political violence are rare in Japan. Aum Shinrikyo was the last major terror group to wage war against this country, releasing sarin gas on Tokyo subways in 1995, which killed 13 people, seriously injured 54 others and affected 5,800 more.

`Track 151`

5 The most prominent political assassination in contemporary Japan occurred in 1960 when a rightist attacked the socialist leader Inejiro Asanuma. In 1978, a man attempted to kill then Prime Minister Masayoshi Ohira, but he only mingled with reporters outside the Prime Minister's Office and never actually got close to Ohira. In the two latter cases, the weapons were a sword and a knife.

6 In 1992, Shin Kanemaru, an LDP heavyweight and the deputy prime minister was attacked by a man with a gun, but was not injured. Two years later, a gunman shot at Prime Minister Morihiro Hosokawa, but he too was unharmed. In 2007, Nagasaki mayor Itcho Ito died after a gunman shot him.

`Track 152`

7 Mercifully, guns remain a rarity in Japan. In fact, this country has one of the lowest rates of gun violence in the world. According to a police white paper, there were 21 arrests for the use of firearms in 2020, and 12 of them were gang related. World Health Organization figures show that Japan had just nine firearm-related deaths in 2018, down from 23 the year before. The rate of firearm deaths per 100,000 people is 0.01; for comparison, the U.S. number exceeds four per 100,000.

4
- □ terror group テロ集団
- □ wage war against ... …に戦いを挑む
- □ sarin gas サリンガス
- □ affect …に影響を与える

5
- □ prominent 有名な
- □ contemporary 現代の
- □ rightist 右翼の人
- □ then 当時の
- □ mingle with ... …と混ざり合う
- □ Prime Minister's Office 首相官邸

6
- □ LDP 自由民主党→Liberal Democratic Party の略
- □ heavyweight 重鎮
- □ deputy prime minister 副首相、副総理
- □ shoot at ... …を狙って撃つ→銃弾が当たったという意味までは含まれない
- □ unharmed 無傷の

7
- □ mercifully 幸いにも
- □ rarity 珍しい存在
- □ white paper 白書
- □ firearm 銃器
- □ gang related 暴力団関係の
- □ World Health Organization 世界保健機関
- □ figures（公式発表の）数値、データ
- □ per …当たりの
- □ for comparison 比較用の、ちなみに
- □ exceed 上回る

8 Much of the credit goes to strict gun control laws, which were, ironically, written by the U.S. Occupation authorities. Those laws have been loosened a little but the culture here remains fundamentally hostile to gun possession. There are reports that the person who attacked Abe may have built his own weapon, which indicates that while existing gun controls work as intended, they may have to be updated to account for new dangers.

Track 153

9 There is a more fundamental issue at hand: respect for democracy and the absolute imperative to resolve political differences through the ballot box exclusively. Half a world away, another political leader has been removed from power through the political process as he lost the confidence of his party. That is how political change is done.

10 There is no place for violence in this process. The attempt by any individual or group of individuals to impose their will on the country through violent means is terrorism, pure and simple. That is unacceptable and must be condemned by all — whatever the political stripe or inclination.

Track 154

11 Japan is a democracy and it is currently engaged in the purest expression of the democratic pageant and process. The attack on former Prime Minister Abe in Nara on Friday is attack on us all.

12 As Chief Cabinet Secretary Hirokazu Matsuno said, "Such violence cannot be permitted." We must join together to condemn this violence, show that it has no place in our lives or our country and reaffirm our commitment to Japanese democracy and the peaceful resolution of political differences.

(750 words)

8
- ☐ Much of the credit goes to ... …によるところが大きい→creditは「称賛、功績」の意味
- ☐ strict 厳しい
- ☐ gun control laws 銃規制法
- ☐ ironically 皮肉なことに
- ☐ Occupation authorities 占領軍
- ☐ loosen 緩やかになる・する
- ☐ fundamentally 根本的に
- ☐ hostile to ... …に反感を抱いて、…に厳しい
- ☐ possession 所持
- ☐ existing 既存の
- ☐ work as intended 意図されたように機能する
- ☐ update 更新する
- ☐ account for ... …を考慮する

9
- ☐ at hand 目の前の
- ☐ imperative 原則
- ☐ ballot box 投票箱
- ☐ exclusively もっぱら…だけ
- ☐ half a world away 世界を半周したところで
- ☐ be removed from power 権力の座から降ろされる→英国のボリス・ジョンソン首相の辞任を指す
- ☐ confidence 信頼
- ☐ political change 政変

10
- ☐ impose A on B AをBに押しつける
- ☐ will 意思
- ☐ means 方法、手段
- ☐ pure and simple 紛れもない
- ☐ unacceptable 許されない
- ☐ condemn 非難する
- ☐ whatever …が何であろうと
- ☐ political stripe 政治的な姿勢→stripeは「しま模様」の意味
- ☐ inclination 傾向、意向

11
- ☐ be engaged in ... …を実践する、…に従事している
- ☐ currently 現在
- ☐ pageant 誇示、野外劇

12
- ☐ Chief Cabinet Secretary 官房長官
- ☐ reaffirm 再確認する
- ☐ commitment 強い関与、約束、身を捧げること

An ice skating superstar steps down

フィギュアスケート界のスーパースター、競技会引退

July 23, 2022　　　　　　　　●Tracks 155-160 / 解説 p. 253、訳 p. 262

Track 155

1　The quadruple axel — a 4½ rotation jump — has never been completed in competitive figure skating.

2　It's a demanding feat, requiring strength, poise, stamina and confidence. It is one of the very few remaining challenges for Japanese figure skater Yuzuru Hanyu, who retired from competitive skating this week after an extraordinary career. He is considered one of the greatest figure skaters ever, and his departure leaves a gaping hole in the sport. It will be filled eventually, but he will be missed.

Track 156

3　Born in Sendai in 1994, Hanyu began skating at the age of 4, and he made his junior international debut nine years later at the age of 13. A victory in Japan's Junior Championships in 2008 allowed him to compete the following year in the World Junior Championships. He made his senior international debut two years after that and won the bronze medal in his first world championship appearance in March 2012.

▼ About This Editorial ▼

オリンピックなど数々の大会を制してきた羽生結弦選手は、その華麗な演技はもちろん、フィギュアスケートに全身全霊で挑む姿でも世界中のファンを魅了した。競技生活からは引退するものの、新たな表現の場で活躍する姿を見せてくれることだろう。

1
- □ ［タイトル］step down 引退する
- □ quadruple axel 4回転アクセル
- □ rotation 回転
- □ competitive 競技の

2
- □ demanding 高い技術が求められる
- □ feat 偉業、離れ業
- □ require 必要とする
- □ poise 冷静さ
- □ confidence 自信
- □ remaining 残っている
- □ extraordinary 並外れた
- □ departure 立ち去ること、引退、出発
- □ gaping ぽっかり開いた
- □ eventually いずれは

3
- □ Junior Championships ジュニア選手権
- □ compete in ... …に出場する
- □ appearance 出場

4   Many more awards would follow. He was world champion in 2014 and in 2017. He collected two Olympic gold medals, in Sochi in 2014 and at the next Winter Games in Pyeongchang in 2018. His win in 2014 was the first Olympic gold for an Asian male singles skater and the back-to-back golds were the first in over half a century. He was a four-time Grand Prix Final Champion (from 2013-2016) and in 2020 won the Four Continents Championships. Hanyu is also the first man to achieve a "Super Slam," meaning he won all major international competitions, including the Olympics and World Figure Skating Championships, at junior and senior levels. He is one of only two male single skaters to win seven world championship medals in the postwar era.

Track 157

5   His performances redefined the sport. Hanyu set 19 world records, the most among singles skaters since the introduction of the modern judging system. He is the first man to receive over 100 points in the men's short program, over 200 points in the men's free skate and over 300 total points in competition.

6   That record is the product of commitments to both athleticism and aestheticism. For Hanyu, success in ice skating demanded not just physical skills and strength but style as well. He is credited with crafting performances for particular events and audiences. He not only entertained, but told a story as he skated. Observers credit his use of popular culture in his performances, giving audiences something they could relate to.

4
- ☐ the Winter (Olympic) Games 冬季オリンピック
- ☐ male 男性の
- ☐ back-to-back 連続の
- ☐ four-time 4回の
- ☐ Grand Prix Final グランプリファイナル→世界6カ所で開催されるグランプリシリーズの上位6名が出場する大会
- ☐ the Four Continents Championships 四大陸選手権→ヨーロッパ以外の国と地域の選手で競われる大会
- ☐ the World Figure Skating Championships 世界フィギュアスケート選手権

5
- ☐ redefine 再定義する
- ☐ introduction 導入
- ☐ judging system 採点方式
- ☐ short program →規定の必須要素で構成されたプログラムを2分40秒(±10秒)で滑走する
- ☐ free skate →プログラムに含むことのできる要素を組み合わせて4分(±10秒)で滑走する

6
- ☐ commitment to ... …への献身
- ☐ athleticism 運動能力
- ☐ aestheticism 美意識
- ☐ be credited with ... …で評価される
- ☐ craft 精巧に作り上げる
- ☐ audience 観客
- ☐ entertain 楽しませる
- ☐ relate to ... …に共感する

Track 158

7   His effervescent personality and good looks helped as well. Most important was his passion. He skated because he had to give expression to something inside him. This, more than the grace or the power, is what appealed to millions of fans worldwide who cheered his every success. The passion of the "Fanyus," who showered the ice after each performance with Winnie the Pooh stuffed animals — Hanyu's favorite — matched his own.

8   Less well known — at the time — and yet more proof of his power and commitment were his performances despite agonizing injuries. He competed at the Pyeongchang Winter Olympics nursing an injury to his right ankle that had prevented him from participating in the 2017 Grand Prix final as well as Japan's domestic championships. He resumed training only a month before the Games, but was still able to defend his gold medal, the first male skater to do so since 1952.

Track 159

9   An ankle injury also thwarted his quest for a third Olympic gold at this year's Beijing Winter Games. He tried the quad axel in his performance, coming tantalizingly close — completing the four and a half rotations but falling to the ice during the landing — and finishing out of the medal count. Only after the competition did he acknowledge that his ankle was bothering him and that he had had an injection of painkillers before taking the ice for the final performance.

7
- ☐ effervescent はつらつとした
- ☐ personality 性格
- ☐ give expression to ... …を表現する
- ☐ appeal to ... …の心に訴える
- ☐ Fanyus →fanとHanyuを組み合わせた造語 Fanyuの複数形で、「羽生選手のファンたち」の意味
- ☐ shower …に（称賛などを）注ぐ、浴びせる
- ☐ Winnie the Pooh くまのプーさん
- ☐ stuffed animal ぬいぐるみの動物 →stuffedは「詰め物をした」「剝製にした」の意味

8
- ☐ agonizing ひどい、つらい
- ☐ nurse 治療する、かばう
- ☐ prevent ... from *doing* …が～するのを妨げる
- ☐ participate in ... …に参加する
- ☐ domestic 国内の
- ☐ resume 再開する
- ☐ defend （王座を）守る、防衛する

9
- ☐ thwart 妨げる
- ☐ quad axel 4回転アクセル→quadはquadrupleの略
- ☐ tantalizingly close あともう少しのところで、惜しいところで
- ☐ finish out of the medal count メダル獲得に届かずに終わる
- ☐ acknowledge 認める
- ☐ bother 悩ませる
- ☐ painkiller 鎮痛剤
- ☐ take the ice リンクに立つ

10 Hanyu isn't hanging up his skates. At his farewell news conference, he promised to "pursue my ideal figure skating outside of competitions." That means, he explained, "skating in a way that is more in tune with the current times. I want to put on shows that fans and people who have never seen skating before would want to see and to create places and performances that will satisfy the people who support me."

Track 160

11 While he gave it all that he could in Beijing, he has not given up on the quad axel. He continues to work on the jump even as the next generation of skaters takes up that challenge. A young American, 17-year-old Ilia Malinin, landed one during a warmup in May.

12 Hanyu may not get the credit for being the first to pull off the move in a competition, but he should not be envious. He should be secure in knowing that he pushed the boundaries of the sport and his enthusiasm has shaped a generation of skaters who follow him. We are grateful for all that he has done and wish him every success in his next endeavors.

(825 words)

10 ☐ hang up *one's* skates スケート靴を脱ぐ、スケートから引退する→野球選手やサッカー選手の引退の場合はhang up *one's* spikes(スパイクを脱ぐ)のように言う

☐ farewell お別れの
☐ in tune with ... …に合わせて
☐ put on shows ショーを開く
☐ satisfy 満足させる

11 ☐ give it all that ... can 全力を尽くす
☐ give up on ... …をあきらめる
☐ take up that challenge その難題に挑む

☐ Ilia Malinin →その後、9月14日のUSインターナショナルクラシックでも成功させた
☐ warmup ウォーミングアップ = warm-up →英語ではwarming-upよりもこのほうが普通

12 ☐ get the credit for ... …の功績を認められる
☐ pull off ... …を成功させる
☐ be envious うらやむ
☐ be secure in knowing that ... …だと知って安心する

☐ push the boundaries of ... …の限界を押し広げる
☐ enthusiasm 熱意
☐ be grateful for ... …に感謝する
☐ endeavor 挑戦

社会・文化 1 **Government clarity needed as Japan eyes border reopening for tourism**

... Prime Minister Fumio Kishida seems ready to explore a more permissive policy to begin a return to normalcy and the economic rewards that follow. **(Paragraph 2、3〜5行目)**

［頻出フレーズ］下線部のa return to normalcy「正常への復帰」は時事英文では頻出のフレーズ。1920年のアメリカ大統領選において、第一次世界大戦とスペインかぜの蔓延によって混乱した世界を正常に戻そうという趣旨で、立候補者だったハーディングが用いたスローガンに由来する。その後、広く「正常に戻すこと、通常の状態に戻ること」という意味で用いられるようになった。

┈┈┈

It is estimated that an infection rate of about 60% is the threshold for acceptance of a disease. In Japan, only 7% of the population is reported to have had the disease, and while that number is likely low — a considerable number of people with infections are asymptomatic or think they have the flu — it is nowhere near that level.
(Paragraph 10)

［語の成り立ちと由来／指示語］最初の下線部のasymptomatic「無症状の」のa-は「国内政治・外交」1本目の社説で確認したamorphousのa-、つまり、ギリシャ語由来の「…なしの」を意味する接頭辞である。また、2つ目の下線部のthat levelが何を指すのかはこのパラグラフ全体に目を向けて理解したいところ。直前で感染を経験した人が日本では7％しかいないとされていること、また、無症状の人や自覚のない人もいるため、実際には7％よりも多いだろうということが指摘されているが、しかし、それでも、it is nowhere near that level「そのレベルにはまったく届かない」と言っている。とすれば、このthat levelは1行目の「60％」を指していると理解するのが最も自然だろう。

社会・文化 2 Japan's disappointing ruling on same-sex marriage

It is <u>long past time</u> for Japan's same-sex couples to enjoy all the rights afforded their heterosexual counterparts. **(Paragraph 2、4〜6行)**

[前置詞の用法] 下線部の単語の意味をくっつけて「長い過去の時間」などと解釈すると混乱のもと。ここで用いられているpastは前置詞で「…を過ぎて」という意味であり、long past ...で「…を過ぎて長くたっている→とっくに…を過ぎている」となる。したがって、この文の直訳は「日本の同性婚カップルが異性婚カップルに認められているあらゆる権利を享受できるようになるべき時はとっくに過ぎている」であるが、もちろんこれは「とっくに過ぎているので早急にそうなるべきだ」というニュアンスである。

<u>Grim as those numbers are</u>, there are grounds for hope. **(Paragraph 13、1行目)**

[C as SVの形] as節で動詞の補語となるべき語句が前に出て、C as SVという語順となっている場合、まずは「SはCであるが」という逆接の意味で考えてみるとよい。今回もシンプルに逆接で解釈して問題ない。ただし、まれにこの形で理由を表現している場合もあるので、文脈と矛盾するような場合は、「SはCであるので」という解釈も検討してみよう。Cの前にさらにasを加えて、as C as SVとなることも。また、類例として(as) much as SV「SはVするけれども」という逆接表現も合わせて理解しておきたい。

A despicable attack on Shinzo Abe — and a nation

The editorial commentary originally scheduled to fill this space was <u>a cri de coeur</u> to the United States, a plea for it to come to its senses and halt the devastating gun violence that has become a fact of daily life in that country. **(Paragraph 1、1〜4行目)**

[頻出のフランス語表現] 下線部の a cri de coeur はフランス語に由来する語で「心からの叫び、嘆願」という意味。英語の語彙にはフランス語に由来する単語が多いことが知られているが、英語化せずにフランス語のまま借用されている語句も相当数あり、時事英文や硬い評論文などではよく用いられる。特に政治や経済などに関連するものとして、carte blanche「白紙委任、全権委任」やcoup d'état「クーデター」、fait accompli「既成事実」、laissez-faire「(政府の) 無干渉主義の」などがある。

There is no place for violence in this process. <u>The attempt by any individual or group of individuals to impose their will on the country through violent means is terrorism, pure and simple.</u> **(Paragraph 10、1〜3行目)**

[名詞句の解析] attempt「試み」のような行動を示唆する名詞から文が始まったら、誰による、どうしようという「試み」なのか、と考えながら読むことが大切。そうすれば、直後のby any ... individualsが「誰による」の部分に対応し、そして、その後ろのto impose ... violent meansの部分が「どうしようという」の部分に対応していることが読み取れ、「誰であれ個人や個人の集団が暴力的な手段を使って国に自らの意志を押しつけようとすること」という主語名詞句の意味がスムーズに読み取れる。最後のpure and simpleは直前の名詞であるterrorismを修飾し、「まったくの、純然たる」という意味を表す。

社会・文化 4 An ice skating superstar steps down

Less well known — at the time — and yet more proof of his power and commitment were his performances despite agonizing injuries. **(Paragraph 8、1〜3行目)**

[CVSの倒置] Less well known ... and yet more proof of his power and commitment (C) were (V) his performances (S)というCVSの語順になっていることに注意。直前で羽生選手のわかりやすい、誰もが知る長所が語られていることを受け、そこからあまり知られていない魅力という新たな情報へと話をシフトするためにこのような倒置が使用されている。「国内政治・外交」の3本目でも確認したように、Cに含まれているlessやmoreといった比較級は前の文とのつながりを示唆するもの。なお、ここのyetはmoreを強めるものではなく、and yetという形で逆接の意味を表現していることにも注意したい。

Only after the competition did he acknowledge that his ankle was bothering him and that he had had an injection of painkillers before taking the ice for the final performance. **(Paragraph 9、5〜8行目)**

[否定語句等が文頭に出た場合の語順] 英語では否定語句やonlyを含む副詞要素、また、「so＋形容詞／副詞」などが文頭に出ると、SVの部分が疑問文と同じ形になる。たとえば、be動詞や助動詞を用いた文では主語とそれらの位置が入れ替わり、助動詞のない一般動詞の文ではdo (does, did)を前に置く。今回のケースは過去形の一般動詞の文なので、通常はhe acknowledged ...となるところが、did he acknowledge ...となっている。このタイプの構造では副詞句が文頭に出ているパターンが多いが、否定語を含む名詞句が文頭に来た場合でも、Not a single book did he read last year.「昨年彼は一冊たりとも本を読まなかった」のように同様の現象が起きる。

253

訪日観光再開に向けて政府は明確な意思疎通を

1 日本政府は、外国人観光客の受け入れ再開を用心深く検討している。

2 これまでの内閣は、受け入れ再開がもたらす国民の健康・安全への影響と経済的損失とを比較して、警戒する方針を継続してきた。しかし今や、岸田文雄政権は日常を取り戻してそれに伴う経済的見返りを得るために、より寛容な政策を模索する準備ができているようだ。われわれはその展開を支持するが、政府には国民の懸念への配慮を怠らないよう強く求める。新型コロナウイルス感染症の対策・封じ込め政策を成功させるには、国民の信頼と支持が不可欠だ。

3 2年前に新型コロナウイルス感染症が大流行した直後から、日本は外国人旅行者の入国を禁じ、徐々に禁止の対象を広げて159の国と地域とした。外国人居住者の日本への帰国を認めるなど制限の一部を緩和したものの、新たな変異型の発生とそれらに続く感染の波が相次いで国に打撃を与えたため、受け入れ再開のプロセスは断続的なものとなった。

4 3月以降、ビジネス客や学生の入国は3,500人から徐々に1万人まで増えたが、観光客は入国を許されていない。今後、それが変わることになる。政府は6月から、3回のワクチン接種を終えた旅行者を、添乗員同行の少人数ツアーで米国、オーストラリア、タイ、シンガポールの4カ国から受け入れる提案をした。訪日外国人の入国許可は2万人へと倍増されると報じられているが、この制限緩和はそれに追加されるものだ。

5 今回の方針転換は、日本がこの感染症への対応に関して世界的な共通認識に後れを取っているという意識を反映している。ほとんどの国では、ワクチン接種を完了した、あるいはPCR検査の陰性証明を提出した人々の入国を再開している。岸田首相はこの件について国際比較を繰り返し取り上げて、日本の受け入れ規定は大半の国よりも厳格だと説明している。

6 経済が低迷する中、観光客の受け入れ再開を求める声はより大きく切実になっている。新型コロナウイルス感染症とウクライナ戦争は多大な影響を及ぼしており、経済成長を鈍化させ物価を押し上げている。ある試算によると、外国人観光客の不在による日本の減収額は2020年だけで10兆9,600億円、新型コロナウイルスが蔓延し始めてからの通算で22兆円超に上った。内閣府の試算では、その損失は国内総生産を1%減少させた。

7　変化がないままでは損失は拡大していく。日本が観光振興に力を入れ始めて以来、外国人観光客の数は急上昇していた。2019年には3,188万人の訪日客が日本で4兆8,100億円を使った。その2年後、訪日外国人の数はわずか24万人となった。円相場が20年ぶりの安値を更新した今、日本はさらに魅力的な観光地となっているが、それは入国できれば、の話だ。なお、注目すべきは当時の観光客の多くが中国人だったことだ。日本が門戸を開いたとしても彼らは入国できないだろう。

8　そういった観光客を阻む最大の要因は、国民の抵抗感だ。日本は新型コロナウイルス感染症の広がりと影響をうまく抑制してきた。世界保健機関（WHO）によると、日本は2020年と2021年に超過死亡が報告されなかった数少ない国の一つだ。対して米国は超過死亡数が100万人近く、ドイツは約20万人だった。

9　日本のワクチン接種率は81％を超え、57％超が追加接種を受けている。今週、日本では新たに約37,000人の新型コロナウイルス感染者が確認されたが、前週と比べて5,200人以上少なく、着実に減ってきている。新型コロナウイルスによる新たな死亡者は39人だった。

10　病気として定着したと認められる閾値は、感染率約60％だと推定されている。日本では人口の7％しか発症が報告されていない。この数値は（実際より）低いと思われるが──感染者の相当数が無症状、あるいはインフルエンザだと見なしている──閾値のレベルにはほど遠い。

11　このような実績が、往来の訪日再開について国民を懐疑的にさせてきた。12月の世論調査では、回答者の81％が現在も続く外国人の入国禁止を支持した。今月行われた別の調査では、若干の変化が見られた。支持の数が57％に下がり、32％が入国制限の緩和を望んでいる。

12　首相は慎重に事を進めなければならない。参議院選挙を7月に控え、国民の懸念に無関心でいるわけにはいかない。岸田氏はゆっくりと慎重に一歩一歩進めていくことになるだろう。国民の支持を維持するために丁寧な説明が求められる。

13　うまくいくかどうかはいくつかの要因に左右されるが、すべてではないにしろその大半は岸田氏がコントロールできるものだ。外国人観光客に対しては、効果的かつ邪魔にならない程度の監視が必要だ。特に重要なのは、その過程で生まれる個人情報の保護である。抗原検査はもっと多くの場所で受けられるように、また安価に、できれば無料にすべきだ。

訪日観光再開に向けて政府は明確な意思疎通を

14 保健医療体制についてはより周到な準備が必要だ。特に支払いや言語など、外国人の治療に付随する問題に対処できるよう備えなければならない。観光客が主要都市から離れた場合、対応はより難しくなる。

15 明らかな問題が２つある。第一は、政府が始めようとしている実証事業から有意義な知恵を導き出すことの難しさだ。伝えられるところによると、当初の観光客グループの人数は数十人単位だという。これではサンプル数が少なすぎてあまり意味がないように思われる。選挙を控え自信をつけるための単なる実習のように見える。

16 第二の問題は、ウイルスそのものが予測不可能なことだ。新型コロナウイルスは強靭かつ適応性があることが証明されている。次々と変異型が現れる。弱毒化しているようだが、常にそうとは限らない。日本が受け入れを再開するに当たり、政府は最悪の事態を想定して警戒を続けなければならない。

17 一方で、政府はたとえ何が起きても国民に明確に効率よく伝える必要がある。何が行われていて、それはなぜなのか、疑念があってはならない。国民の信頼は、疾病対策を成功させるための基盤だ。　　　　　　　　　　　　　　（訳・注　宇都宮）

大阪地裁、同性婚に関し残念な判決

1　今週月曜日（6月20日）、大阪地裁は日本が同性同士の結婚を認めていないことは違憲ではないという判決を下した。これは同性愛者カップルの権利にとってのみならず、人権全般にとってもショッキングな裁定だった。

2　日本の司法の前例主義的な伝統に合わせるかのように、大阪地方裁判所は同性婚を認める方向への法改正は立法府の領分であると主張し、基本的に判断を回避した形だ。それならば、国会が行動を起こすべきだ。もういい加減に日本の同性カップルたちが異性同士の夫婦に与えられているすべての権利を享受できるようになっていいころだ。

3　今回の大阪地裁の訴訟では、現在の法制度が自分たちの結婚を妨げていることを理由に、自分たちが「不当な差別」を被っていると3組の同性カップルが主張した。実際のところ、差別は結婚を許されるかどうかだけではない。同性同士の関係にある人々は相手の資産を相続することができず、相手の子供に対して親権がない。税金を支払う際も彼らは不利な扱いを受ける。また彼らが個人として最もつらい状況に遭遇した場合でも、自分にとって最も親密な個人間の関係が法的に認められないばかりに、やすらぎや寄り添いを拒否される可能性もある。大阪での裁判の原告たちは損害賠償として一人当たり100万円を求めたが、これは彼らが起こした訴訟に対する判決の意味合いや価値に比べればささいな金額にすぎない。

4　今回の判例で核心となったのは憲法第24条の解釈だ。この条項は、「婚姻は両性の合意のみに基づいて成立し、夫婦が同等の権利を有することを基本として、相互の協力により、維持されなければならない」とうたっている。日本政府は憲法が同性婚について言及していないことを理由に、同性婚を認めないことが差別だとは考えられないだろう、という立場を取っている。

5　大阪地裁は結婚の目的を精査し、結婚という制度は子供を産んで育てる男女間の関係を守るために社会が作り出したものであると主張している。そうした論理的根拠に基づき、同地裁は同性婚を認めないことは合憲であると結論づけた。

6　同地裁は、一緒に生活することを選ぶ同性のカップルの利益をどうすれば最善の形で守れるかに関して「日本国民の間ではまだ十分な議論がなされていない」と述べ、手続き論に逃げ込んだ。そうした人々への保護策を作り出すのは裁判所の仕事ではなく、立法府の仕事であるとも主張している。「婚姻相当」の保護を打ち出

大阪地裁、同性婚に関し残念な判決

し始めた自治体が現れたことにも言及しつつ、同地裁は「民主主義的過程の中での自由な議論に基づいた諸制度の確立」を通じて国レベルの保護手段が実現されるべきであると付け加えた。

7 その議論にも一理ある。とはいえ、大阪地裁の判断は司法が持つ基本的な職務——法律の合憲性（あるいは法律の欠如）について判断するという職務——を放棄するものだ。その代わりに、大阪地裁は議論を世論に委ねる選択をした。ただ、権利というものは、合憲か違憲かのどちらかである。世論を斟酌するかどうかがそこに入り込む余地は多少はあったとしても、ほとんどない。実際、裁判所が果たす最も重要な役割は、世間一般の考え方とは違う判決を下すことである。

8 過去には、よりつっこんだ判断が札幌地方裁判所によってなされている。同地裁は、2021年3月に同性婚を認めないことは違憲である、という主張を支持した判決を出した。同地裁は、日本の民法や戸籍法が、「すべて国民は法の下に平等である」と規定している憲法第14条に違反していると判断した。日本ではこの問題に関して大阪地裁のもの以外ではこれが唯一の判決である（ただし、ほかの事案はまだ係争中だ）。

9 大阪地裁の判決にもあったように、日本は、進歩はしている。だが、その進歩の速度はあまりにも緩慢である。日本はG7参加国の中で唯一同性同士が結婚することを認めていない国だ。家探しや雇用における差別に対してLGBTQの人々を守る法的保護が日本には存在しない。大阪地裁の判決後にアムネスティ・インターナショナルがコメントしたように、「日本は性的志向や性自認、性表現、性的特徴に基づく差別を排除する国内法が整備できていない」のだ。

10 自治体などでは、こうした（法と実社会との）隙間を埋める動きがある。東京都渋谷区は2015年4月に、同性のカップルに対して法的効力はないが行政体としての認知を提供する「パートナーシップ証明」の発行を日本で初めて開始した。ほどなくして世田谷区もそれに続いた。2017年6月には、札幌市が日本で初めて公的に同性のパートナー関係を認知する都市となり、2019年7月には茨城県が都道府県レベルで初めてそうした支援を提供した。大阪府も2020年1月に後に続いた。今では日本全国で200近くの地方自治体が同性のカップルに対して何らかの認知を提供している。

11 企業の中にもLGBTQの従業員に福利厚生や保護制度を提供して支援を充実させるところが出てきた。それら企業は、そうした職員を守ることが才能ある人材を引き付け、対国内企業のみならず国際的な競争にも打ち勝つための最善策なのだと認識するようになってきている。だが、企業にできることはそこまでである。政府の行動が必要だ。もし岸田政権が経済を本気で再生しようとしているのであれば、すべての被雇用者に平等な保護を広げることが海外企業の日本誘致につながると認識すべきである。

12 それには、日本政府に思い切った行動が必要だ。与党自民党は社会的保守派で、道徳感や人としてあるべき振る舞いに関して旧来の考え方を打破するような多くの政策を採用することにかねてより消極的である。昨秋の衆議院選挙に出馬した候補者に対して2021年10月に行われた調査によると、自民党候補者のうちたった12%が同性婚に賛成だった一方、38%が同性婚に反対だった。

13 これらは非常に厳しい数字だが、希望の持てる根拠もいくつかある。自民党の候補者のうち約50%は態度を表明しておらず、支持は増えている。前述の2021年10月に行われた調査はまた、出馬した全候補者のうち61%が同性婚に賛成し、15%が反対で25%は態度保留という結果だった。一般の国民の間ではさらに同性婚に賛成の割合が増える。2018年10月に電通によって実施された調査では、20歳から59歳の年齢層の78.4%が同性婚に対して「賛成」または「どちらかというと賛成」という結果が出ている。

14 一方で、電通の同じ調査によると、LGBTQであると自認した人々の50.3%が職場の同僚にカミングアウトすることに「ためらいがある」あるいは「幾分ためらいがある」と自身について回答している。その事実は現在の法制度の不備を示す何よりの証拠だ。LGBTQの国民は、そうありたい自分になる自由を奪われ、異性愛者の国民が享受するさまざまな充足感を奪われているのだ。その結果、日本人全員の可能性が狭められることになる。日本の国民はこれが間違っていると知っている。われわれは国会議員たちにこの不当性を是正するよう求めるべきだ。

（訳・注　小川）

安倍晋三氏、および国家に対する卑劣な攻撃

1 当初、このスペースを埋める予定だった社説はアメリカ合衆国に向けた心からの叫びで、どうか正気に返って、あの国では日常茶飯事になった衝撃的な銃による暴力を止めてほしいという訴えだった。それに代わって安倍晋三元首相の暗殺を非難するこの論評に差し替えざるを得なくなったのは、大いなる悲しみと怒りを伴うことである。

2 これを書いている時点で、銃撃に関してわかっていることはほとんどない。事件の背景にある動機や論拠を憶測することは無責任かつ無謀なことだろう。それでもなお、絶対的な確信を持って言えることが2つある。まず、元首相の親族と愛する家族に対して心からの哀悼の意を伝えたい。次に、これはテロ行為であり、日本にはそうした行動の存在する余地はない。私たちは議論や意見の相違が暴力ではなく選挙での投票によって解決される民主主義の国で暮らしている。

3 安倍氏は金曜日（7月8日）の午前中、日曜日に行われる衆議院選挙での自民党候補者の選挙運動のため、3県を回る遊説の1カ所目となった奈良県で襲撃された。安倍氏は奈良県在住とされる人物によって背後から胸を2発撃たれ、犯人はその場で捕まって身柄を拘束された。伝えられるところによると、安倍氏はヘリコプターで搬送中に心停止に陥り、その後、搬送先の地元の病院で負傷により亡くなった。私たちは銃撃を「凶悪な行為……野蛮で、悪意に基づいていて、決して容認できない」と評した岸田文雄首相と同じ考えである。

4 ありがたいことに、政治的な暴力行為は日本ではまれである。オウム真理教がこの国に対して戦いを挑んだ最後の大きなテロ集団で、1995年に東京の地下鉄でサリンガスを散布、13人が亡くなり、54人が重傷を負ったほか、5,800人以上に影響が及んだ。

5 現代の日本で最も知られている政治的暗殺事件は、右翼の男が社会党の浅沼稲次郎委員長を襲った1960年に発生した。1978年には男が当時の大平正芳首相の殺害を試みたが、首相官邸の外の記者に紛れ込んだだけで、大平氏には近づけずに終わった。この2つの事例では、武器は刀とナイフだった。

6 1992年には自民党の重鎮で副総理だった金丸信氏が銃を持った男に襲われたが、けがはなかった。2年後、銃を持った男が細川護熙首相を狙って撃ったが、細川氏も無傷だった。2007年には長崎市の伊藤一長市長が男に銃で撃たれた後に亡

くなった。

7 幸いにも、日本では今なお銃は珍しい存在だ。実際のところ、この国は銃による暴力事件の発生率が世界で最も低い国の一つである。警察白書によると、2020年の銃器の使用での逮捕は21件で、そのうちの12件が暴力団がらみだった。世界保健機関の数字では、2018年の日本の銃器関連の死者はわずか9人で、前年の23人から下がっている。人口10万人当たりの銃器による死者数は0.01人。ちなみに、米国での人口10万人当たりの数字は4人を上回っている。

8 これは厳しい銃規制法によるところが大きく、皮肉な話だがこの法律は米国の占領軍によって書かれたものだ。これらの法律は少し緩やかになってきたが、この国の文化は依然として銃の所持に対して根本的に厳しい。安倍氏を襲撃した人物は武器を自作したかもしれないとの報道があり、そのことは既存の銃規制法が意図されたように機能している一方で、新たな危険を考慮に入れたものへと改正される必要があるかもしれないことを示している。

9 目の前にはより根本的な問題がある。民主主義の尊重と、政治的な相違は選挙を通じてのみ解決するという絶対的な原則である。世界を半周したところでは、別の政治指導者が自身の党の信頼を失ったため、政治的なプロセスを通じて権力の座から下ろされた。それこそまさに、政変が行われるやり方である。

10 このプロセスに暴力が入り込む余地はない。いかなる個人または個人の集団であろうとも、暴力的な手段を通じて自分たちの意志を国に押しつけようとする試みは、紛れもないテロ行為である。それは許されないし、すべての人によって非難されなければならない――政治的な姿勢あるいは傾向が何であろうとも。

11 日本は民主主義の国で、現在は民主主義の誇示とプロセスの最も純粋な形での表現を実践している。金曜日の奈良県での安倍元首相への攻撃は、私たち全員に対する攻撃でもある。

12 松野博一官房長官が述べたように、「あのような暴挙は許すことができない」。私たちは今回の暴挙を非難するために1つになり、私たちの生活や私たちの国にその余地がないことを示し、日本の民主主義への強い関わりと、政治的な差異の平和的な解決を再確認しなければならない。　　　　　　　　（訳・注　桑田）

フィギュアスケート界のスーパースター、競技会引退

1　4回転アクセル——4回転半のジャンプ——はこれまで、フィギュアスケートの競技大会で成功されたことが一度もない。

2　それは高い技術が要求される偉業で、強さ、冷静さ、スタミナ、そして自信を必要とする。並外れた現役生活を経て、今週、競技としてのフィギュアスケートから引退した日本のフィギュアスケーターの羽生結弦選手にとって、それは残された数少ない課題の一つである。彼は史上最も偉大なフィギュアスケーターの一人と見なされていて、彼の引退はそのスポーツにぽっかりと大きな穴を残す。その穴はいずれは埋まるとしても、彼の引退は惜しまれることだろう。

3　1994年に仙台で生まれた羽生選手は4歳でスケートを始め、9年後の13歳の時にジュニアの国際大会デビューを果たした。2008年の全日本ジュニア選手権優勝により、翌年の世界ジュニア選手権に出場。その2年後にシニアの国際大会にデビューし、2012年3月には初めて出場した世界選手権で銅メダルを獲得した。

4　その後も多くの賞が続くことになる。2014年と2017年には世界選手権で優勝した。オリンピックで獲得した2個の金メダルは、2014年のソチと、次の2018年の平昌冬季オリンピックでのものだ。2014年の優勝は男子シングルでアジア人初となるオリンピックの金メダルで、2大会連続の金メダルは半世紀以上ぶりのことだった。グランプリファイナルのチャンピオンになること4回（2013年から2016年まで）、2020年には四大陸選手権で優勝した。羽生選手はまた、オリンピックと世界フィギュアスケート選手権を含めた、ジュニアとシニアの主要な国際大会のすべてを制覇する「スーパースラム」を達成した初めての男子選手でもある。戦後に世界選手権でメダル7個を獲得した男子シングルの選手は二人だけで、彼はそのうちの一人だ。

5　彼の演技はフィギュアスケートを再定義した。羽生選手は19個の世界記録を出していて、これは現在の採点方式が導入されて以降、シングルの選手では最多となる。男子のショートプログラムで100点以上、男子のフリースケーティングで200点以上、総合得点で300点以上を記録した最初の男子選手である。

6　その記録は運動能力と美意識の両方への献身のたまものである。羽生選手にとって、フィギュアスケートでの成功には身体的スキルや体力だけでなく、様式美も必要だった。彼は特定のイベントや聴衆に向けた演技を作り上げたとして高く評価さ

れている。彼は見る人を楽しませただけでなく、滑りながら物語を伝えた。関係者たちは演技でのポピュラーカルチャーの使用が、観客に共感できる要素を与えていると評価する。

7　彼のはつらつとした性格とルックスの良さも貢献した。何よりも重要なのは彼の情熱だった。羽生選手は自分の内面にある何かを表現しなければならないという理由でスケートをした。このことは、優雅さや力強さ以上に、彼のすべての成功に声援を送った世界中の何百万人というファンの心に訴えた。演技が終わるたびにくまのプーさんのぬいぐるみ——羽生選手のお気に入り——を次々とリンクに投げ入れた「Fanyus」の情熱は、本人のそれと匹敵するものだった。

8　その当時はあまり知られていなかったが、それでも彼の力と責任感のさらなる証拠となるのが、ひどい負傷を押しての彼の演技だった。羽生選手は日本の国内選手権や2017年のグランプリファイナルへの出場を断念させることになった右足首の負傷を抱えながら、平昌での冬季オリンピックに参戦した。練習を再開したのは大会のわずか1カ月前だったが、それでも男子のスケート選手としては1952年以来初めてとなる2大会連続での金メダルを獲得することができた。

9　足首の負傷は今年の北京冬季オリンピックでの3個目となる五輪の金メダルへの挑戦も妨げることになった。羽生選手は演技中に4回転アクセルを試み、あともう少しというところで成功には至らず——4回転半は回り切ったものの、着氷時に転倒した——メダル圏外に終わった。競技終了後に初めて、羽生選手は足首の痛みに悩まされており、最終演技のためリンクに立つ前に鎮痛剤を打っていたことを認めた。

10　羽生選手はスケート界を去るわけではない。引退発表の記者会見で、「競技会の外で理想のフィギュアスケートを追求する」ことを約束した。本人の説明によると、それは「もっと今の時代に合った形でのスケートをすることです。ファンの方々や、これまでスケートを見たことのない方々が見たいと思うようなショーを開いたり、私を応援してくださる方々が満足できるような場所や演技を創造したいと思います」ということだ。

11　北京では持てる力のすべてを出し切った一方で、羽生選手はまだ4回転アクセルをあきらめていない。次の世代のスケート選手たちがその難題に挑む中でも、彼はジャンプに取り組み続ける。5月には17歳のイリア・マリニンという若いアメリカ人選手が練習中に着氷に成功した。

フィギュアスケート界のスーパースター、競技会引退

12 羽生選手は競技会でそのジャンプを成功させた第一号としての功績は認められないかもしれないが、うらやむべきではない。競技の限界を押し広げ、その熱意が後に続くスケート選手の世代を形作ってきたことを知り、安心するべきである。私たちは彼が成し遂げてきたことすべてに感謝するとともに、次の挑戦での活躍を願っている。 　　　　　　　　　　　　　　　　　　　　　　（訳・注　桑田）

ジャパンタイムズ社説集 2022

2023年1月5日　初版発行

編　者　ジャパンタイムズ出版 英語出版編集部
　　　　© The Japan Times Publishing, Ltd., 2023
監　修　北爪 隆
解　説　北村 一真
発行者　伊藤 秀樹
発行所　株式会社 ジャパンタイムズ出版
　　　　〒102-0082 東京都千代田区一番町2-2 一番町第二TGビル2F
　　　　ウェブサイト　https://jtpublishing.co.jp/
印刷所　日経印刷株式会社

本書の内容に関するお問い合わせは、上記ウェブサイトまたは郵便でお受けいたします。

定価はカバーに表示してあります。

万一、乱丁落丁のある場合は送料当社負担でお取り替えいたします。
(株)ジャパンタイムズ出版・出版営業部宛てにお送りください。

ISBN978-4-7890-1856-2
Printed in Japan

本書のご感想をお寄せください。
https://jtpublishing.co.jp/contact/comment/

読者アンケートのご案内
〜ご感想・ご意見をお待ちしております〜

ジャパンタイムズ出版のコーポレートサイトが新しくなりました。
本書のご感想・ご意見をぜひお寄せください。

アンケートURL

https://jtpublishing.co.jp/contact/comment/

ウェブサイトや Twitter 公式アカウントなどで読者の声を紹介いたします。
掲載された方には**ギフト券**または**オリジナルグッズ**プレゼント！

ジャパンタイムズ発行の英字紙